THE SOCIAL NETWORKS
OF OLDER PEOPLE

THE SOCIAL NETWORKS OF OLDER PEOPLE

A Cross-National Analysis

Edited by
Howard Litwin

PRAEGER

Westport, Connecticut
London

Library of Congress Cataloging-in-Publication Data

The social networks of older people : a cross-national analysis /
   edited by Howard Litwin.
     p. cm.
   Includes bibliographical references and index.
   ISBN 0–275–95327–0 (alk. paper)
    1. Aged—Social networks—Cross-cultural studies.   I. Litwin,
Howard.
   HQ1061.S6482   1996
   305.26—dc20   96–16265

British Library Cataloguing in Publication Data is available.

Library of Congress Catalog Card Number: 96–16265
ISBN: 0–275–95327–0

First published in 1996

Praeger Publishers, 88 Post Road West, Westport, CT 06881
An imprint of Greenwood Publishing Group, Inc.

Printed in the United States of America

The paper used in this book complies with the
Permanent Paper Standard issued by the National
Information Standards Organization (Z39.48–1984).

10 9 8 7 6 5 4 3 2 1

Dedicated to the memory of

Zeev Ben-Sira,

mentor and colleague

Contents

Figure and Tables

Figure

Tables

Acknowledgments

The idea for a cross-national analysis of the social networks of older people was nurtured during a sabbatical stay at the University of Toronto in late 1994. I would like to express my warm appreciation to the people who made that visit possible and, as such, laid the foundation for the production of this book: Victor Marshall, the Director of the Centre for Aging Studies, Marion Bogo, Acting Dean of the Faculty of Social Work, and Ben-Zion Shapiro, Associate Dean. I also value the advice of Canadian colleagues who served as stimuli in the development of this work: Barry Wellman, who put me in touch with Leroy Stone from Statistics Canada, Ernie Lightman, who was supportive both during and after my stay, and Judy Globerman and Lynn McDonald.

This is essentially a collaborative work. I owe a great deal to the contributing authors who willingly accepted the challenge posed by my invitation to participate in this endeavor, and who worked together with me in a truly cooperative and friendly spirit. As such, I thank Lars and Gerdt, Claudine and Alain, François and Viki, Leroy and Carolyn, Tuula and Marja, Clare, Jim and Melanie, Marjolein and Theo, and Gail. I am also incredibly indebted to the advances of technology, which, through the invention of electronic mail, facilitated immediate and continuous contact with each of the authors, despite the great distances between us.

Consultations on preparation of the book also took place face to face in several important meetings in Toronto, Ottawa, Atlanta, Bangor (Wales), Paris, and Amsterdam. I am grateful to the people and organizations who made these travels possible, particularly my home institution, the Hebrew University of Jerusalem, through its faculty travel grants, Statistics Canada, the British Council, and the European Association of Gerontology. I would also like to thank Kees Knipscheer for facilitating the participation of the Dutch team.

The interest and encouragement of the editorial staff of the Greenwood Publishing Group deserve special mention. I would like to note particularly Mildred Vasan, whose initial support was instrumental in getting the book off the ground, Lynn Flynt who provided important guidance in the early stages of the project, and Liz Murphy, Education, Anthropology, and Health editor, who saw the project through to fruition.

Philippa Bacal produced several of the camera-ready tables, and I thank her for her careful work.

Finally, and most importantly, I thank my own primary social network, Malca and Shira, whose love and support provided all the benefits that social networks are known to provide, and without which nothing can be done in quite the same way, nor in as satisfying a manner.

THE SOCIAL NETWORKS
OF OLDER PEOPLE

1

Introduction

Howard Litwin

The sociological construct of *social network* is increasingly being invoked around the world in the policy debate on the social care of elderly people (Abrams, 1980; Litwin and Auslander, 1992; Schilling, 1987; Steinbach, 1992; Wellman and Hall, 1986; Wenger, 1994a; Yoder, Leaper, and Jonker, 1985; Zarit, Pearlin, and Schaie, 1993). A social network constitutes the collection of interpersonal ties that individuals maintain and that provide them with several possible benefits, such as the augmentation of self-concept, the fostering of feelings of belonging, and the provision of both cognitive guidance and tangible assistance in fulfilling the tasks of daily living (Cohen and Syme, 1985; Ell, 1984; Litwin, 1995a). The term frequently implies family and friendship ties, but may also encompass other forms of interpersonal contact, such as relationships with neighbors, work associates, and service personnel (Chappell, 1991b; Gottlieb, 1981; Kendig, 1986; Litwak, 1985). Given the potential for informal support that may be forthcoming from one's social network, the relevance of the network phenomenon for the elderly and for frail elements of society has been underscored in a variety of settings (Hooyman, 1983; Sauer and Coward, 1985; Shuval, Fleishman, and Shmueli, 1982).

Accordingly, the network phenomenon has become the object of social research over the past few decades. This emerging field of inquiry includes a variety of approaches and a range of methodologies. Some researchers, for example, employ a comprehensive interpretation of the network notion. In studies that address a range of populations, they call for the measuring of the broad range of possible social ties in a respondent's immediate social milieu (Cochran, Larner, Riley, Gunnarsson, and Henderson, 1990; Fischer, 1982; McCallister and Fischer, 1978; Norbeck, Lindsey, and Carrieri, 1981; Wellman, 1979). Several recent studies of the social networks of elderly people echo this orientation, seeing the elder's network as the locus of a wide variety of social ties (Auslander and Litwin, 1990; Gallo, 1984; Litwak, 1985; Lubben, 1988; Sauer and Coward, 1985; Taylor and Chatters, 1986).

However, some utilizations of the social network concept tend to adopt a more partial or specialized view of the phenomenon. These may range from focused consideration of specific support network configurations (Adams, 1986; Campbell and Lee, 1992; Dykstra, 1993), to analysis of paths of familial exchange (Coward and Dwyer, 1990; Stoller, Forster, and Duniho, 1992), and examination of other informal caregiver groupings in the locality (Felton and Berry, 1992; MacRae, 1992). Indeed, the term "social network" may variously reflect the structure or content of social relationships (House and Kahn, 1985), the actual or perceived availability of social support (Wethington and Kessler, 1986), or any of a range of dynamics that comprise social interrelationships, to name but a few of the construct's recent manifestations.

The presumed widespread existence of informal social support networks is currently cited as justification for the delimiting or the refocusing of governmental intervention on behalf of needy sectors of the population (Baldwin, 1993; Gordon and Donald, 1993; Langan, 1990; Walker, 1982). This is particularly the case in regard to the long-term care of older adults in the community. As the debate on the relationship between social networks and social policy intensifies, however, it seems that the frames of reference concerning the social construct in question are becoming ever more elusive.

It is not at all clear, for example, whether the notion of social network used to support social policy development in different national settings is being applied in similar ways. Nor is it evident whether the means for measuring the phenomenon are methodologically compatible. Nonetheless, policymakers from several countries are looking to each other for guidance in this burgeoning area of social provision. It is timely and important, therefore, to consider the social network construct in a comparative international perspective, and to examine its application critically in relation to evolving policies of social care.

This book thus constitutes an attempt to address critically the state of the art of gerontologically focused network analysis, and to clarify the emerging interrelationship between informal support networks and social policies for the elderly. It presents a unique collection of social network studies that focus upon elderly populations in nine different countries. The country reports presented in this book were solicited especially for inclusion in this comparative analysis. Most of them draw upon contemporary empirical research in their respective countries. All of them, nevertheless, offer their findings in a new light, as follows from the guidelines for preparation of the chapters for the cross-national comparison.

The countries selected to be included in the analysis are: the United States, Canada, the United Kingdom, France, Spain, the Netherlands, Sweden, Finland, and Israel. These specific countries reflect national settings, particularly in Europe, in which populations have aged most dramatically (U.S. Bureau of the Census, 1992) and where governments are actively seeking ways to constrain the growth of social welfare expenditures. Moreover, outstanding researchers in each of these settings are involved in the analysis of aged cohorts, providing a first-hand opportunity to examine the potential and the means for inclusion of social network factors in the formulation of social policy for the elderly in the respective countries.

The book begins here with an introductory presentation of the organizational framework that guides the inquiry, including a selective review of the factors that led to formulation of the analytic framework. Nine chapters, each devoted to a network study carried out in a separate country, follow. The work concludes with a summary chapter which applies a meta-analysis to the data presented in the country reports, critically comparing the state of knowledge of social networks of elderly people in each setting, and drawing conclusions as to the future interchange between social network research and social policy development on behalf of the eldest cohorts of society.

THE ANALYTIC FRAMEWORK

The county reports were prepared in relation to a series of guiding questions which reflect nine areas of inquiry: (1) study methodology, (2) the study sample, (3) structural analysis of the social network, (4) structural network variations by sociodemographic characteristics, (5) measures of social support, (6) classification of network types, (7) the interface between informal networks and formal care services, (8) implications of the findings for social policy, and (9) directions for future research. Chapter authors were encouraged to relate to as many of these topics as their data allow in order to permit the execution of the concluding cross-national analysis. The result is an impressive array of network data providing both up-to-date within-country accounts as well as a base for cross-country comparison.

The specific areas of inquiry upon which this analysis focuses reflect the particular aspects of social network analysis that are most relevant to the consideration of the role of networks in the care of elderly people. They are spelled out in the following sections, with attention to the central issues that emerged in each area and that contributed to the formulation of the preparation guidelines. The actual questions posed to chapter authors are included in each corresponding subsection.

Study Methodology

The perceived essence of the phenomenon known as social network may vary according to the method by which its measurement is operationalized. One major difference in this regard pertains to whether the nature of the network is conceptualized prior to data collection and hence shapes the construction of the survey instrument, or whether it is derived as a result of the trends found in the data themselves. The former case may be characterized as an "inferred network" approach; the latter might be termed a "derived network" methodology.

An example of the inferred approach is a French study in which the elderly respondent's potential network is measured in terms of predetermined network variables—in this case, household composition, marital status, number of living children, and frequency of visits from family, friends, and neighbors (Curtis, Bucquet, and Colvez, 1992). Wenger (1995a) refers to such predetermined network markers as proxy measures and cautions that they may not provide an accurate reflection of the actual social network in question. The derived network methodology, on the other hand, is exemplified by a study in New York State in which survey data are used to establish the composition of care networks, and in which a pattern of network expansion is subsequently identified (Stoller and Pugliesi, 1988).

The connection between the theoretical conceptualization of social networks and their measurement has been more fully spelled out by van der Poel (1993), who cites four different approaches to network measurement: (1) the "interaction approach," which focuses upon the contacts between network members, (2) the "role relation approach," which sees the type of role relationships as the primary determinant of one's network, (3) the "affective approach," which is based upon subjective evaluation by respondents of the people most important to them, and (4) the "exchange approach," which views specific rewarding behaviors as the foundation for determining the composition and the scope of one's network. Each approach entails differing perceptions as to the nature of the network phenomenon, and differing means by which to capture its essence.

Yet another manner of conceptualizing the social network, with implications for measurement, is the ego-centered approach. In this mode, the network is generated by each respondent in response to a particular probe, such as requesting respondents to name the people with whom they interact the most and with whom they have close personal ties (Dykstra, 1990a). The ego-centered generated network methodology thus attempts to combine both qualitative and quantitative aspects of social network measurement and, as such, is considered to be the most comprehensive of the various approaches. Given the depth and the scope of the approach, however, and the time required for data collection, it usually produces studies of limited sample size.

Perhaps in response to the logistic difficulties inherent in the generated network approach, another means of network measurement has recently been attempted. This method may be termed a "deductive network approach" and is reflected in the work of Lubben (1988) and Wenger (1994e). Both of these researchers have constructed abbreviated network inventories stemming from previous extensive empirical work. In the former case, Lubben created a network scale for the elderly based upon relevant network variables drawn from the oft-cited longitudinal analyses of Berkman and Syme (1979). This scale has been subsequently validated and applied in new comparative network research. Wenger's short network form, on the other hand, is derived from her own previous qualitative and quantitative work and has been used continuously since (Wenger, 1984, 1986, 1989).

In light of the potential differences in interpretation of network data due to the differing methodologies at work in this field, chapter authors in this collection were asked to specify the approach employed in their respective studies. The instructions given to them in this regard were as follows:

Methodology/approach: How was network studied, which instruments were employed, which assumptions were there behind the methodological approach, and how does the approach relate to theories of social network.

Study Sample

While the size and nature of the sample of empirical studies of social networks of elderly people are important factors in determining the generalizability of their findings, there is actually a wide range of sample types evident in this field of inquiry. A review of close to 100 articles on the topic published in *Sociological Abstracts* over the past decade revealed that about two-thirds of them provide specific data on the study sample. Of these, the majority category (40 percent) reflect studies based upon small samples of 200 respondents or fewer. Only one-fifth of the studies, on the other hand, utilize large data bases of 1,000 respondents or more.

Differences are also evident in the nature of the respective samples. The larger samples tend to be drawn from regional or national surveys utilizing probability sampling (Angel and Angel, 1992; Baldassare, Rosenfield, and Rook, 1984; Levitt, Antonucci, Clark, Rotton, and Finley, 1985–86; Olsen, Olsen, Gunner-Svensson, and Waldstrom, 1991; Starrett, Todd, Decker, and Walters, 1989). The smaller samples are more frequently purposive aggregates reflecting a particular characteristic of interest to the researcher, as, for example, bereaved spouses (Lund, Caserta, van Pelt, and Gass, 1990), new residents of residential care facilities (Bear, 1993), and relocated urban dwellers (Eckert, 1983).

An additional frequent source of study sample is the framework of social services to which respondents may belong. Such samples range from the relatively small, as in the case of 200 random day-hospital and senior center attendees (Chappell, Segall, and Lewis, 1990), to the very large, as in a study of 3,559 participants in California's Multipurpose Senior Services Project (Mor-Barak and Miller, 1991). Still other samples focus upon ethnicity or national origin as the inclusion principle. Among these, for example, may be cited studies of Maltese-born elderly people in Australia (Cauchi, 1990), African–American elders in Ohio (Petchers and Milligan, 1987), and a comparative analysis of elderly Swedes and Turks (Imamoulu, Küller, Imamoulu, and Küller, 1993).

Finally, the representativeness of study samples is yet another matter of concern. While probability sampling is the principal means in a great many of the reported studies reviewed here, a few others clearly focus upon convenience samples. In one case, a snowball approach is noted as the method of sample construction (Johnson and Barer, 1992). In another, focus group interviews serve as the basis for data collection (Morgan and March, 1992). Given the range of styles and foci in existing network study samples, therefore, chapter authors in this book were asked to specify the following information in their country reports:

> Description of the setting and study sample, its degree of representativeness of the country's elderly population, where and how it differs from selected groups of elderly people in the country, and other relevant sample characteristics.

Structural Analysis

Underlying a great many network studies in the literature is a descriptive analysis of the structural components of the social entity in question (Seeman and Berkman, 1988). This may include both morphological and interactional aspects of the phenomenon (Mitchell, 1969). Examples of the former are size, density, and range of the network. Expressions of the latter may be found in frequency of contact, relationship intensity, and reciprocity of exchange among network members.

While a great many of the network studies incorporate structural characteristics of the social network in their analysis, however, the specific structural variables chosen for inclusion tend to vary from study to study. Kaufman (1990), for example, cites the use of network size, composition, and dispersion as the morphological variables of interest, and relational dynamics, intensity, orientation, and content as the interactional aspects under consideration in his study of functionally impaired older persons. In their study of elderly African–Americans, on the other hand, Bryant and Rakowski (1992) choose to focus on contacts with family members, contacts with friends, and social involvement outside the home as the primary network structure variables under consideration.

It is important to specify the included structural variables in network studies, for two reasons: (1) the need to clarify the structural means by which a social network is defined; (2) the benefit that can be gained from comparisons of network structure across studies. For example, if network size is a variable that is addressed in most studies of the social networks of elderly people, a normative network size can potentially be determined to serve as a basis for future comparative analyses. The same may be said for other structural network variables of interest.

Authors contributing chapters to this book were requested, therefore, to specify the structural aspects of the network addressed in their respective studies. Specifically, they were asked to provide the following information:

Description of the structural characteristics of the networks under study: size, composition, interactional aspects such as frequency and mutuality of interaction, duration of ties, degree of residential proximity, degree of interpersonal closeness (intimacy), and so on.

Structural Variation

The structural components of network analysis provide an additional source of important information—that is, they allow comparative analysis of subgroupings of interest, in order to discern systematic differences in network behavior and network influence among different groups. Such intergroup comparisons are frequently executed on relevant sociodemographic variables within the framework of cross-sectional study designs.

A wide range of such comparisons regarding the social networks of elderly people may be found in the literature. Thus, for example, elders' social networks have been differentially analyzed on the basis of ethnicity and social class (Thornton, White-Means, and Choi, 1993), race (Biegel, Magaziner, and Baum, 1991), and nationality (Imamoulu et al., 1993). Another common base for intergroup comparison is the gender of both elderly respondents and their caregivers, although the findings are not always consistent in this regard (Chappell et al., 1990; Cohen, Sokolovsky, Teresi, and Holmes, 1988; Krause and Kieth, 1989). Personal status variables such as age (Morgan, 1988; Palinkas, Wingard, and Barret-Connor, 1990), health and functional status (Chappell, 1989), and marital status (Strain, 1992) constitute additional differentiating characteristics in social network studies of older people. Finally, residential patterns are occasional targets of comparative inquiry of the networks of elderly cohorts. This includes the type of residence (Stacey-Konnert and Pynoos, 1992), the structure of the community in which one resides (Wenger and St. Leger, 1992), and rural–urban differences in general (Lee and Whitebeck, 1987; Wenger, 1995b).

In order to learn about intergroup variations within the different national samples reviewed in this collection, the attention of authors was directed to the issue of sociodemographic factors. Thus, the country reports should include:

Analysis of characteristically differing network structures according to relevant sociodemographic characteristics of the sample, such as age (young–old, old–

old, etc.), gender, marital status, rural/urban dwellings; and according to functional capacity of the elderly anchor (center) of the networks under consideration.

Social Support

Social networks are frequently believed to function as support networks, even though many of them tend to behave in a way that may be most unhelpful (Litwin, 1995a). The terms "social network" and "support network" are, in fact, often used interchangeably in the literature, with insufficient attention paid to the conceptual differences between them and to the measurement implications of these differences (Chappell, 1991b; Wenger, 1995a). When considering the social networks of elderly cohorts, therefore, it is important to distinguish social support behaviors from the structural aspects of the network. This is particularly the case insofar as older adults' social networks are most frequently invoked by policymakers in their capacity as informal sources of ongoing care and support.

Although there are several variations on the social support theme, the phenomenon is generally divided into two major categories of assistance: emotional support and instrumental support. The emphasis in empirical studies may be placed on one of the two types of support, or on both of them equally (Curtis, Bucquet, and Colvez, 1992; Dykstra, 1993). Antonucci and Akiyama (1987b) further distinguish the support function according to its means of measurement, differentiating quantitative measures of social support from qualitative ones. The support phenomenon, thus, is a complex one. While many researchers agree that social support promotes both emotional and physical well-being, however, the precise measurement of support remains problematic (Jacobson, 1987).

There is also lack of agreement as to how social support networks actually contribute to well-being among the elderly. Occasional reports cite the absence of support as the explanation for respondents' lack of welfare. LaGory and Fitzpatrick (1992), for example, found depression related to limited social supports. Kaye and Monk (1991) similarly found gaps in their respondents' social support networks to be closely associated with decrements in personal contentment.

Baldassare and colleagues (1984), on the other hand, adopt a more direct approach, citing the existence of social relations as important predictors of happiness, even after controlling for the effects of sociodemographic and health factors. However, other studies raise doubts as to the possibility of finding a singularly convincing relationship between support and well-being among the aged.

In her study of very elderly people living in a deprived section of London, for example, Bowling (1990) found that physical health status was a stronger predictor of life-satisfaction than were social network characteristics. In a similar vein, Mullins and Mushel (1992) found that social network measures, and particularly the variable of emotional closeness, had little impact on the experience of loneliness among older persons. They conclude that only partial support for a social support model may be granted.

Given the importance of the support function of the social network and the problematics identified in its measurement, special attention is given here to examples of social support in the country reports, where available. Authors were, thus, requested to specify:

> Measures of social support utilized to consider the degree of support available to the elderly, underlying trends found regarding the distribution of supports, and consideration of the contribution of social support availability (or absence) to the well-being of older persons.

Network Types

A recent and still relatively rare development in the study of social networks is the classification of network types within populations of interest. Rather than correlating specific structural or support measures with a particular outcome variable, the goal of typology construction is to discover systematic covariance among groupings of network characteristics. Such typologies may, in turn, provide a new means for tracing the development of social networks, for mapping the shifts that occur as people move from one type of network to another, and for predicting differential service needs on the basis of network type.

In certain instances, the classification of network types is carried out as a secondary part of network analysis. The findings in such studies are largely preliminary and exploratory. Adams (1986), for example, categorized the social networks of unmarried elderly women in Illinois as either (1) small and intimate, or (2) local, new, and dense, on the basis of a primary or secondary friendship orientation. Lieberg and Pederson (1983) distinguish between "loose" networks and "tight" networks in a comparative study of residential areas in a Swedish city. Auslander and Litwin (1990) identified "close" and "distant" networks among the elderly in Jerusalem by means of factor analysis of the role relationship categories in respondents' personal networks.

However, studies giving more focused and systematic attention to the task of typology construction are emerging in the literature. Mugford and Kendig (1986), for example, conceptualize network types of the elderly in Australia on the basis of two variables: network size and multiplexity of ties—that is, singularly focused versus multifaceted relationships. The network types they posit range from "intense" (small and multiplex) to "diffuse" (large and uniplex), with three variations between these two extremes: "complex," "balanced," and "attenuated" networks.

Wenger's extensive work in social network classification stems from both a quantitative survey approach and intensive qualitative study of elderly persons in

Wales (Wenger, 1984, 1989, 1990). She has identified five distinct network types on the basis of three primary factors: (1) the availability of close kin in the locality, (2) the level of involvement of family, friends, and neighbors, and (3) degree of interaction with community and voluntary groups. Subsequent use of computer algorithm has produced an assessment instrument that makes it possible to classify one's network type as: (1) local-family-dependent, (2) locally integrated, (3) local self-contained, (4) wider-community-focused, or (5) private restricted.

Finally, Litwin (1995b) has made use of computerized analysis in the identification of network types among elderly Soviet immigrants to Israel. Cluster analysis based on six discriminating criterion variables—network size, composition, percentage of intimates, frequency of contact, duration of ties and proximity—has produced four identifiable network types, termed (1) the kin network, (2) the family-intensive network, (3) the friend-focused network, and (4) the diffuse-tie network, which have proven in subsequent analyses to predict different levels of social support among respondents.

The classification of network types is, thus, a growing endeavor, with particular relevance for the development of social policy. If prior knowledge of different network types can, indeed, help predict formal service needs of elderly people, it would seem that typology construction can contribute much to the policy debate. It is interesting and useful, therefore, to clarify the degree to which network classification is on the research agenda of different countries. Toward this end, chapter authors were requested to respond to the following questions:

> Did the study uncover characteristic variations in network structure and function such that differing network types may be identified? How was this done, and what were the results? What is the relationship of network types to measures of well-being, functional need or disability, service utilization, etc.?

The Interface between Informal Networks and the Formal Sector

A question of particular importance in addressing the role of social networks vis-à-vis social policy for the elderly is what occurs in practice when the informal components of social care (the social network) encounter the agents of social policy, usually in the form of formal care services. Do the two systems proceed to function in a complimentary manner, or does a new situation arise, in which one of the care systems overcomes the other? Does one's initial contact with one of the systems preclude or otherwise influence subsequent contact with the alternative system? In short, what are the dynamics of the interface between older adults' informal networks and the formal service sector that is designed to serve them? (See Bass and Noelker, 1987; Bulmer, 1987; Hoch and Hemmens, 1987; Litwin and Auslander, 1988; Twigg, 1989; Whittaker, 1986.)

There is, as yet, only limited data available offering the opportunity to respond to these questions, even though the answers to these probes would seem to be critical for the development of a policy of social care. The trends revealed in the data, moreover, are not unequivocal. A selected review of recent studies on this topic demonstrates the state of knowledge at hand.

A Swiss study examined, for example, whether the establishment of a formal neighborhood aid agency served to supplement or to replace informal support among elderly residents (Meyer-Fehr and Suter, 1992). The data indicate that three years following entry of the formal agency into the neighborhood, respondents reported receiving less assistance from friends, relations, and neighbors, and providing less to them in return. An increase was reported, on the other hand, in the amount of informal aid received from family members. The investigators characterize the result of their study as reflecting a partial replacement effect.

An Israeli analysis similarly finds evidence for a substitution effect when informal social networks encounter formal social services (Litwin and Auslander, 1993). However, a study in London found network variables to have little predictive value regarding elders' contact with physicians (Bowling, Farquhar, and Browne, 1991), and a Dutch study found no significant network influence on the use of home health-care services (Kempen and Suurmeijer, 1991). The informal network did, on the other hand, constitute the primary source of referral of elderly relatives to residential care facilities in Florida, even though one-third of the elders who relocated felt the move to be unnecessary (Bear, 1989).

The interface between informal components of the social network and formal service representatives is, thus, a topic that requires further investigation. However, few studies relate directly to this area in data collection efforts. Discussion of the issue, at least in part, stems frequently from inference. Accordingly, chapter authors in this collection were asked to specify, in any way they could, the relationship between informal support networks and formal social care services in their respective countries. This includes:

> Identification of the types of members of the social network from the formal care system, discussion of the relations between informal networks and formal care services, and characterization of these relations as primarily reflective of mutual cooperation and exchange (interweaving), reinforcement of the informal network by the formal care system, or substitution of the informal network's caregiving by the formal care system.

Implications for Policy and Practice

Following from the previous topic, it is clearly efficacious to tie research findings on social networks to planning and development decisions in the sphere of social policy. Few sources in the literature, however, actually spell out the implications of their findings for policy and practice. Outstanding in this regard are a few selected works that detail the practice suggestions (Kaufman, 1990; Mor-Barak, Miller, and Syme, 1991) or the policy ramifications of study outcomes (Curtis et al., 1992; Schreck, 1991; Wenger, 1993). The planning recommendations raised thus far in such discussions are variously aimed at clarifying service needs (Ezell and Gibson, 1989), targeting high risk groups (Levitt et al., 1985–86), or augmenting the social network for preventative reasons (Kaye and Monk, 1991).

In order to address this significant but relatively untapped topic, participating researchers in this book were requested to include, if possible:

> Discussion of selected findings and their implications for maintenance of current social policy arrangements, or for change. What is the prognosis for implementing a social policy based upon community-based care in which the informal network plays a significant and ongoing role in caregiving?

Needed Future Research

Finally, and necessarily, an inquiry of this nature is bound to uncover unanswered questions and to underscore unresolved dilemmas in the area under investigation. As such, authors of the country reports were each asked to indicate:

> Areas for needed future research and conclusions.

PLAN OF THE BOOK

Network analyses from nine different countries are arranged in two general groupings for the purpose of presentation. First are those that reflect an essentially inferred network approach—that is, they explore relevant network characteristics but do not relate to the social network as a holistic entity that is defined a priori by the respondent. Within this grouping there is a further division in that some of the reports view the network features individually, whereas others consider selected variables in combination in order to derive comparative network formations.

Thus, Andersson and Sundström begin the inquiry with a secondary analysis of network-related data on the Swedish elderly, which emanates from various sources of survey data. Attias-Donfut and Rozenkier carefully consider the exchanges that take place within multigenerational family systems among the elderly French population. Béland and Zunzunegui go one step further in their exploration of the social networks of elderly Spaniards. Their data set is, indeed, a collection of individual network features, but they view these variables collectively in a multivariate analysis.

The remaining two chapters in the first grouping reflect an approach that may be considered a derived network methodology. Both studies apply cluster analytic techniques to selected network characteristics drawn from national social surveys. Stone and Rosenthal address social network types among elderly people in Canada, and Melkas and Jylhä consider the different network constellations of the elderly in Finland.

The second major group of studies similarly combines two somewhat different approaches to network investigation within a more general theme. The four country reports in this grouping all relate to the social network as a predefined social entity. However, two of the studies utilize prevalidated network inventories to consider the social networks of the elderly in their respective countries. Wenger applies her Practitioner Assessment of Network Type (PANT) questionnaire to a sample of British older persons. Lubben utilizes the network scale (LSNS) he developed as a means to address the networks of a sample of elderly people in Los Angeles, California.

The final two country reports, on the other hand, reflect a direct ego-centered approach to network delineation in which respondents identify the people whom they personally consider to comprise their social networks. Broese van Groenou and van Tilburg present findings from their analysis of the social networks of the Dutch elderly. Auslander reports the results of a network analysis of elderly Jewish residents of Jerusalem in Israel.

The concluding chapter, which follows the country reports, considers the data from each country in a comparative analysis. Thus, similarities are cited and significant divergences are pointed out. The implications of both common trends and exceptions to the rule are addressed in this summary discussion in relation to the social care of older people.

2

The Social Networks
of Elderly People in Sweden

Lars Andersson and Gerdt Sundström

Social networks are chiefly conditioned by three factors: (1) the circumstances into which an individual is born, or the demographic situation that prevails in a given context, (2) the circumstances that follow from one's life situation, such as career pattern, position in the life cycle, and so on, or what may be called personal life style, and (3) the opportunities that exist to select partners, friends, and acquaintances, or what might be called personal choices. When elderly people are asked to describe their social networks, their answers generally reflect a mixture of these factors.

In discussing the social networks of older adults in Sweden, our intention is not to try to disentangle these determining elements or to uncover causal connections between them. Instead, these network determinants will serve as interrelated bases from which to view the phenomenon in question. Thus, demography and manifestations of personal life style (whether actively chosen or not) are described from official Swedish statistics. Descriptions of contacts and experiences with network members, on the other hand, are drawn from self-reports by elderly Swedes as obtained in social surveys.

As no comprehensive studies of total networks among the elderly have been done in Sweden, several sources are used here to illustrate and discuss the social networks in question. With regard to partial or purposive networks, there are, indeed, some examples of surveys of care networks, and two of them are detailed later on. In addition, owing to a reliable history of population records in our country, we are able to describe the changes that have occurred in several aspects of social networks among elderly people in Sweden. As may be understood from this introduction, therefore, a major part of our presentation is based on secondary analysis of data emanating from various sources.

The first major study upon which we call is a recent national representative study, mainly built on the "Eurobarometer" conducted in the Spring of 1992 in the then 12 countries of the European Community (Commission of the European Communities, 1993). The fieldwork with interviews for the Swedish version of the Eurobarometer was performed from April to June 1993. In total, 1,022 interviews were gathered from a simple random sample of noninstitutionalized Swedes 60 years and older. The response rate was 75.3 percent.

It is worth noting that representative Swedish samples can easily be drawn because the entire population is recorded in registers with a personal code. A 10-digit identity code is assigned to each and every person and shows, among other things, the year, month, and date of their birth. Interviews in the Swedish phase of Eurobarometer were conducted in respondents' homes. Analyses revealed no systematic attrition with regard to age, sex, and socioeconomic status. Thus, the results obtained in the Swedish Eurobarometer may be said to be generalizable to the total population of individuals in Sweden aged 60 and above.

As the results show, males made up 47 percent of the sample. Six out of ten were married or cohabiting, 18 percent single, 4 percent divorced, and 17 percent widows/widowers. Close to four out of ten lived in single households, and about 60 percent belonged to two-person households. Only 3 percent were members of a household of more than two persons. On the average, the respondents had 2.3 children, but 16 percent had no children at all.

As most parts of the questionnaire are a direct translation of the European original, a unique opportunity is available to compare the life situation of elderly Swedes with those in the same age group in the European Union (Andersson, 1993, 1994). In 1995, Sweden also became a member of the European Union (formerly known as the European Community), but it will be referred to in this chapter in accordance with its status as an autonomous nation at the time of the study. Correspondingly, the term "European Union" refers here to the 12 member states at the time of the study.

The interviews for the second major study to which we refer—the Ädel–ULF study—were conducted during the spring of 1994 at the initiative of the National Board of Health and Welfare. This endeavor placed primary emphasis on describing the living situation of the oldest old, their health and function, and their use of care services. The material consists of a stratified sample of 1,379 noninstitutionalized elderly Swedes. Persons living in service apartments, group dwellings, or institutions were excluded from the sample. Approximately 200 men and 200 women in each of the age groups 75–79, 80–84, and 85+ were interviewed (Sundström, 1994a). The response rate in this inquiry was 72.8 percent. Analyses revealed that here, too, no systematic attrition was evident with regard to age, sex, and socioeconomic status. The results from the Ädel–ULF can thus also be generalized to the total population in Sweden, in each of the six age/gender subgroups.

Finally, an early survey from 1954 is used as background and as a basis for comparison. It is a nationally representative study, which covered 1,064 persons aged 67 and above, living in their own homes. Interestingly, the response rate in this initial survey was remarkably high—more than 99 percent.

DEMOGRAPHY AND SOCIAL NETWORKS

In January 1994, Sweden had a population of approximately 8.75 million people. About 17.6 percent were over 65 years old, and most of them were pensioners. There has been a steady increase in the proportion of elderly during the last century. However, there were quite a few elderly in preindustrial times as well. The high mortality rates in that period affected chiefly infants and youth. For the sake of comparison, in 1750, 6 percent of the population were 65 and older, and 3 percent were 70 and older.

As we move toward the year 2000, the proportion of persons aged 65 and over in Sweden is estimated to decrease slightly, to 17 percent of the total population. But within the elderly population there will be a shift upwards, resulting in an increase of those aged 80 and above from 4.4 to 5.0 percent—in round figures, 70,000 persons. The entire elderly cohort is expected to increase once again after the turn of the century, and by the year 2025 will comprise approximately 20 percent of the total population. Thus, Sweden remains demographically "ahead" of most countries in terms of population aging. The average life span in 1993 was 75.5 years for men and 80.8 years for women.

Fundamental aspects of demography such as mortality, matrimony, and fertility, have decisive influences on social networks. As a spouse stands at the center of most networks, it is essential to note how much Swedish matrimony has changed over time.

In 1749 (the first year of readily available statistics), 7 percent of persons aged 50 and above had never been married (single); 100 years later, the proportion of the never-married had risen to 9 percent. The singles phenomenon among young couples culminated in the 1910s and 1920s, resulting in a 17 percent never-married rate among those aged 65 and older in the 1950s. In 1994, the singles figure was once again down to 9 percent. Surveys show, in fact, that even the oldest old (85+ and 90+) increasingly have a spouse. A comparison of 1987 with 1994 shows, for example, that the proportion of singles decreased from 16 percent to 12.7 percent among persons aged 85 and above, and from 17 percent to 15 percent among people 90 years old or older. On the other hand, the proportion of people who are divorced has increased slightly during the same period, from 3.4 percent to 4.3 percent among those aged 85 and above and from 3.1 percent to 3.6 percent among those aged 90 and above.

The delayed effect of earlier matrimony and fertility has led to a trend in which the number of elderly people with offspring continues to increase in Sweden. It can be estimated that about 33 percent were childless in 1930–35. This figure decreased to 27 percent in 1954 and to 19 percent in 1994. It is expected to continue to drop, moreover, to 15–16 percent.

Not only is the rate of marriage among elderly people increasing, but marriages last ever longer. Traditionally, the marital union was expected to be life-long, but life expectancy varies. In the eighteenth century, for example, marriage for a farmer's wife lasted only about 15 years. In previous generations, moreover, many children had never met their grandparents, because the grandparents were already dead by the time the children were born.

Today, a typical marriage in Sweden can last for 40 to 50 years. A dramatic increase in golden wedding anniversaries is an outward sign of the fact that ever larger proportions of marital cohorts remain intact. This increase can be credited to both lowered mortality and greater age equality between spouses. Augmented by a compressed span of childbearing among women, four and even five-genera-tion families are becoming more visible today. In general, the dominant trend is one of close kin networks, which are becoming ever more extended, despite a rise in countervailing influences, such as divorce.

PERSONAL LIFE STYLE

To clarify the issues of demography, it is not enough to describe the potential availability of close kin. We also need to know their whereabouts—that is, the physical distance between them. With regard to the spouse, this is usually self-evident. For consideration of other kin, however, we make use of survey data that partly illuminate the issue.

One fundamental aspect of physical closeness is whether or not people live alone. In the Nordic countries, and particularly in Denmark and Sweden, there are now two main options for living arrangements in later life: co-residency with a spouse and living alone. Both life styles have become more common in the recent decades.

Moreover, households are becoming smaller for all age groups among the elderly cohort—a process that started in the Nordic countries some time after the Second World War. From a "traditional" level of about 10 percent who lived alone, the rate increased to 27 percent in 1954 (men 19 percent, women 34 per-cent), to 34 percent in 1975 (men 19 percent, women 47 percent), and to 39 per-cent in 1988–89 (men 24 percent, women 50 percent). Thus, living alone has become much more common for elderly women, but much less so for men.

Living alone rises with age in Sweden. Among persons aged 80 and above in 1994, 59 percent live alone. These figures do not take into account residents of institutions (6 percent of the 65+, 23 percent of the 80+). Other living arrangements, such as co-residency with offspring, siblings, or others or residing in institutions, have largely vanished or shrunk considerably. This is not a development unique to the Nordic countries, however, as can be witnessed in international comparisons with the OECD countries (Sundström, 1994b).

In Sweden, the number of solitary households does not seem likely to increase any further. The remaining elderly are either married (51 percent), institutionalized, or—rarely—live with offspring (2–3 percent). Yet, averages such as these do not fully describe the prospects of aging. When we talk about living alone in old age, what we really should think about is the risk rather than the average prevalence.

The risk of eventually living alone and of dying in that situation is, of course, much higher than suggested by the average rate, as both parties in a couple usually do not die simultaneously. On the other hand, the time spent living without a spouse may actually have decreased as an effect of a larger increase in life expectancy among males in recent years. Swedish longitudinal data indicate that some 70 percent of aged women will live alone during the last years of their life, as compared to 30 percent of the men (Lundin and Sundström, 1994).

The other aspect of this increase in single households is the declining co-residency with offspring. It is relatively rare for adults to live with their parents. In 1954, 27 percent of the elderly in Sweden lived with one or more offspring, in 1975 it was 9 percent, and it has since decreased to 2 percent. There are hardly any grandchildren present in contemporary elderly households, and they were never very frequent (Sundström, 1987); adults living with their parents were, and still are, mostly sons who never married. In fact, adult two-generation households are often families in which the elder party provides housing and other services for the younger one, rather than the converse. It seems that the older generation shelters those of their offspring who have the least capacity for independence (Sundström, 1987).

We have strong reasons to believe that these changes are, to some extent, the outcome of conscious choices made by elderly or elderly-to-be, and, of course, by their offspring and other kin. Studies clearly indicate a preference for solitary living (but preferably with a spouse). Access to rather inexpensive public services and modern housing has also enabled the elderly to maintain a lifestyle independent of kin.

Nevertheless, the offspring that "moved out" did not go very far. The majority of elderly (63 percent) have a child living within 15 kilometers, which is a proportion near to that reported from other countries. The exception are elderly from the upper social strata, who tend to have offspring at a somewhat greater distance (but who do not see them less often than do the others). For proximity to other kin, information is more sparse. In the 1970s, 87 percent of persons aged 65–74 had a sibling, and 51 percent of them had their closest sibling(s) within a 15-kilometer distance (Statistics Sweden, 1980). Norwegian data, which seem to hold for Sweden as well, indicate that of those who have kin, 84 percent have them within their own municipality (Gulbrandsen and Ås, 1986).

The notion that the population was more stable in former days and, thus, that there were more kin close by is not supported by data. Gaunt (1983) studied mobility in two parishes around 1880, one in central Sweden and one in southern Sweden. He found that, according to population records, fewer than half of those 60 years and above had been born in the parish.

Gaunt also chose to study the situation for 50-year-old women, in particular with regard to caregiving responsibilities. In the two parishes, only 37 percent still had children left in the parish. As many as 83 percent had no father or mother in the vicinity, and only 5 percent had both their parents in the parish. Migration, in particular, made it increasingly difficult to retain social networks among the elderly. In addition, only about half of those 60 years and older had a spouse who was still alive, and relatively few had kin close by. However, about 75 percent did have children who were still alive.

In summary, it seems that it is becoming less common for elderly people to have no kin at all. Moreover, a decreasing proportion of the elderly—about 1 percent only—may be said to be truly isolated in the sociological sense of the term.

Family

Before proceeding with the description of social networks, it is essential to elaborate on the concept of family in relation to network. One fundamental problem, of course, is the definition of family, both in itself and with regard to household. A convenient standpoint is that family is what individuals themselves define as family. However, in order to analyze the extent of networks, it is necessary to identify whether, for example, elderly parents are included in what the individual regards as family.

Trost (1993) conducted a study in 1989, in which a simple random sample of Swedes aged 20 to 59 were asked to describe what they regard as their family. The answers showed a very varied picture. Those who were married mentioned their spouse, and those who had children in the household included them. However, children who had moved away from home were mentioned by only some of the respondents, as were parents.

Mentioned by some were also brothers and sisters, grandchildren, stepchildren, step-parents, brothers-in-law, sisters-in-law, ex-spouses, the spouse's kin, friends, dogs, cats, and horses. Trost notes, moreover, that many of those living alone cited family members, which means that in their view family is not limited to the household. About 15 percent mentioned ten or more members of their family. What is clear from the answers is that in defining family, individuals do not necessarily restrict themselves to household, ties of kinship, or marriage/cohabitation.

Respondents were also asked to identify what they considered to be a family in response to specific examples. While all considered a married couple with children to be a family, only 75 percent considered a married couple without children to constitute a family, and 60 percent, a cohabiting couple without children. Only one-third considered a parent and a child a family if they were not a sharing household. In sum, only the constellation of mother, father, child/children who share household is considered by all to be a family. Apart from that, definitions are disparate (Trost, 1993).

An additional complicating factor when making historical comparisons is that up to the end of the eighteenth century, the term "family" also included farmhands and maids (Gaunt, 1983). Etymologically, the term itself is of obscure origin. In summarizing his results, Trost identifies three psychological factors that determine whether someone will be included in the individual's family—emotional closeness, fairness, and caregiving responsibility.

What implications does this have for the interpretation of the answers to the network questions in the Eurobarometer, in which respondents were asked about their family contacts and about their contacts with friends? A fairly reliable conclusion is that one group—distant kin—falls in-between. To most respondents in Sweden, kin are not close enough to be regarded as family, yet they are not the same as friends. Although the contacts may be sparse, they can certainly add to a network, in particular brothers and sisters, as helpers to the elderly.

Household

In many instances, "household" is a more convenient concept with which to work than "family". The household, defined as the group of people who eat and sleep together, was about the same size from the end of the sixteenth century to the end of the 1880s. It was made up of four to five persons. In 1890, for example, average household size in Sweden was 4.6. The size of the average household in Sweden today, on the other hand, is only about 2.2 persons. The increase in the number of one-person households explains much of the decrease in household size over the last century. Understandably, household size is larger in the countryside than in the cities. For example, in inner-city Stockholm, two-thirds of all households consist of single persons (Andersson, 1992).

PERSONAL CHOICES

To reiterate, the average household size is small in Sweden. Among people aged 65 and over, about 50 percent live with a spouse, 40 percent reside alone and 6 percent are in institutions; 4 percent share a household with an adult child or with a sibling. With these conditions in mind, what is the rate and the nature of contacts between elderly persons and family, friends, and others in the social network?

Social Contacts: International Comparisons

According to the Eurobarometer, 32 percent of the elderly in Sweden meet their family every day and almost 70 percent at least once a week ("How often do you see your family these days?"). These figures are considerably lower, however, than those reported in some Mediterranean countries. In Italy, for example, 71 percent report daily contact with the family, in Greece 65 percent, and in Spain 61 percent (Andersson, 1993; Commission of the European Communities, 1993).

One pertinent question is why the figures for daily contacts with family are so low in many countries (Denmark: 14 percent; the Netherlands: 19 percent; United Kingdom: 22 percent; Sweden: 32 percent), even though 55 percent of people 60 years and older are married? The answer certainly lies in the obscure conception of family. While some people consider the spouse as a sufficient representative of "family," others will not answer in the affirmative unless they have had contact with offspring (and in a few cases additional kin). The latter seem to consider family as an awkward term for spouse, and assume that it must include others over and above the spouse.

A similar question concerning contacts with friends shows the same pattern as does the one concerning the family. In Sweden, 17 percent see their friends every day and 69 percent at least once a week. Once again, the figures for everyday contact are high in countries such as Portugal (66 percent), Spain (61 percent), and Greece (52 percent), whereas they are low in the Netherlands (9 percent), Germany (10 percent), and Denmark (13 percent). Interestingly, the contact figures for Swedish elderly are low at both extremities of the scale. There are only 1.6 percent who report either that they have no friends or that they never see them—the lowest rate of all 13 nations. In comparison, in the Netherlands (10 percent), Luxemburg (7.5 percent), France, and Italy (6.3 percent), there are substantially more people who either have no friends or never see them.

Among elderly Swedes, singles meet friends every day to a significantly higher degree than do married people or cohabitees (23 vs. 13 percent). On the other hand, the elderly in the highest income quartile meet friends every day to a significantly lesser degree than do elderly in the three lower quartiles. This is in contrast to family contacts, in which case the frequencies are reversed. One part of the explanation for this phenomenon may be that there are more males in the highest income group who are still alive.

Another fundamental question becomes obvious when the figures for contacts with family and friends are compared with the figures for a similar question in the same study, in which the respondent is asked to rate how often he or she has performed various activities "in the past week." Two of the activities concern social contacts: "Seen a member of your family" and "Met a friend." A comparison with the previous two questions reveals an interesting pattern.

One could expect that the percentage for "having seen a member of your family during the past week" would be about the same as the sum of the three response alternatives (every day, two or more times a week, once a week) in answer to the general question, "How often do you see your family these days?" However, this is only true for a few countries situated in north-western Europe: Sweden, the United Kingdom, and the Netherlands. In other countries—especially in Portugal, Belgium, Luxembourg, Italy, Spain, and Greece—the figures for the actual contact (". . . the past week") are much lower than the figures for the generalized contact (". . . these days"). The latter notion may be interpreted as being interwoven with the cultural norm that individuals have internalized—a norm that implies that the elderly in southern Europe are expected to be part of a closely knit network.

The difference between the questions is of the same magnitude when it comes to contacts with friends. Again, the figures are fairly similar for Sweden, the Netherlands, and France, while they differ substantially for Portugal, Spain, Belgium, Germany, Luxembourg, and Greece.

Social Contacts and Loneliness

One conspicuous observation is that in the countries where the discrepancies are the greatest between the "ideal" and the "real" frequency of contacts with family and with friends, reported feelings of loneliness are at their highest levels, and vice versa ($rs = 0.68, p < .01; rs = 0.52, p < .05$, respectively). This is not the first study to show that loneliness is more frequent in the traditionally family-oriented cultures of southern Europe than in the more individualistic cultures of northern Europe. We have found ample support that the percentage of elderly who experience loneliness increases as one moves south through Europe (e.g., Imamoulu et al., 1993; Jylhä and Jokela, 1990; WHO, 1983).

Is it possible that contact discrepancy has something to do with this? As a matter of fact, one assumption is that loneliness originates from an experienced discrepancy between "ideal" and "real" level of social interaction. Johnson and Mullins (1987) write that "for any particular level of opportunity for social contacts, a person's evaluation of its adequacy or deficiency is based on a subjective comparison (not necessarily conscious) of that level with the level of social interaction that is expected, needed, or desired." The present results support such an assumption.

Another question concerns the causes of contact discrepancies. One possibility is that such discrepancy can be understood as an effect of modernization and due to a cultural lag in which ideal and real contact patterns become dissociated through the differential rate of change. Alternatively, contact discrepancy may be related to one's position in the life-cycle. If entering old age means marginalization within a closely knit social (family) network, contact discrepancy can be an expression of a subjective comparison between now and then from an individual point of view. This explanation does not necessarily presume modernization.

Finally, the frames of reference can be expanded. From a general resource perspective, the interpersonal realm makes up just one level of analysis. There are also personal and structural levels to take into consideration. It has been demonstrated that there is a north–south differentiation with respect to several factors on the structural level (economy, power, status, etc.), which could add to an understanding of differences in loneliness (Andersson, 1993; Commission of the European Communities, 1993).

Social Contacts: Age Comparisons

When the Eurobarometer material is divided into the same three age groups as the Ädel–ULF study (75–79, 80–84, 85+), a somewhat varied pattern appears. Among men, 67, 57, and 67 percent, respectively, report that they see their family at least once a week. Among women, the corresponding figures are 64, 71, and 67 percent. Clearly, the 80–84 age group has the lowest contact frequency among men, whereas the situation is the opposite for women, although the fluctuations are not statistically significant. Thus, there is no obvious decrease (or increase) in family contacts with age, and, apart from the 80–84 age group, the figures are fairly similar for men and women.

It is worthy of note that this variation in the contact patterns is also evident in the data from the Ädel–ULF study in relation to frequency of contact with children. The frequencies of at least weekly contact with children for men in the three respective age groups are 64, 57, and 65 percent. The corresponding figures for women are 60, 73, and 60 percent. Due to lack of statistical significance and of obvious explanations for the variations, however, these differences should not be overemphasized. With respect to contacts over the telephone, on the other hand, the figures for at least weekly contact do not differ between the subgroups: they are all between 90 and 94 percent.

Another observation from the Eurobarometer material is with regard to contacts with friends at least once a week. The figures for males in the three age groups are 64, 54, and 44 percent, respectively, the corresponding figures for females are 73, 61, and 63 percent. Thus, in contrast to family contacts, contacts with friends are more frequent among women than among men in all three age groups. The male contact frequency rates also show a steady decline, whereas the trend is not so marked among females.

Family Contacts and Loneliness

It is also noteworthy that, for both men and women in the three age groups, frequency of contact with family covaries with loneliness. In the 80–84 age group, for example, where men had the lowest frequency of weekly contact with family, the figures for loneliness are the lowest (8.7 percent often feel lonely). Among women in the same age group who had the highest frequency of weekly contact with family, the loneliness figures are the highest (11.1 percent often feel lonely). The reasons for this relationship between frequency of contact with family and loneliness can only be speculated about. One possible explanation is that the loneliness of an elderly person prompts an increased number of visits by family members. Nevertheless, the greater frequency of visits does not necessarily alleviate feelings of loneliness on the part of the elder.

CAREGIVING NETWORKS

Numerous Swedish studies on caregiving networks dating as far back as 1954 supply information on help needs and help providers. The notable trend is that the elderly live more independently, regardless of their help needs. Social security programs provide the means for this independence via economic assistance, provision of public home help, and other social services.

In Sweden, it is the legal responsibility of society to ensure that care is provided for the elderly. Since 1956, children have had no legal responsibilities toward their aged parents. Providing social service programs is the task of the municipalities, which bear the ultimate legal responsibility for ensuring that people living in their region receive the support and the help they need. As such, elderly people are guaranteed proper housing as well as competent help and support in their homes. Municipalities are also expected to supply appropriate housing alternatives for elderly people with special needs.

The role of the public sector in Sweden differs from that of most other countries insofar as it functions as a major provider of services. For the most part, those who are involved in caregiving—either as caregivers or as recipients—tend to favor public-sector care more than do those who have no contact with informal caregiving. The establishment of public home help was a carefully designed policy, which was, and is, preferred by the public. Surveys of elderly persons confirm this (Andersson, 1993, 1994). For older persons living alone, moreover, public home help is essential for daily life, and for many it is of vital importance.

However, public services have suffered cutbacks since the late 1980s. In 1975, for example, 38 percent of those aged 80 and above benefited from public home help, compared to only 21 percent in 1994. Despite the cutbacks, however, local studies have not found any elderly who live in misery or with insufficient help and support. The answer to this apparent contradiction may lie in additional results from the Ädel–ULF study, which indicate that the health and functional capacity of elderly Swedes has improved greatly—a tendency that was noticeable already in the 1970s and 1980s. This improvement appears to have balanced the cutbacks in services.

How much care is provided for the elderly in Sweden, and how does it compare with the care provided to the elderly in other countries? The Eurobarometer included a question which covered various sources of informal and formal care in the respondent's home: "Does anyone give you regular help or assistance, with personal care or household tasks, because you find it difficult to do these by yourself?" (If Yes) "Who gives you regular help or assistance?"

Among those who reported a care need (12 percent—by far the lowest proportion among all 13 countries), public home care and care by the immediate family (spouse and children) were about equal in level (50.8 and 53.9 percent, respectively). It should be noted, however, that the question measures only contact and not the number of hours of care provided. The percentages for the remaining source-of-care categories are: kin (7.1 percent), private help (7.0 percent), friends (3.1 percent), neighbors (0.8 percent), and voluntary organizations (0 percent).

With respect to informal care, the percentage of people receiving help from a spouse is the same in Sweden as the average in the European Union—32 percent. The comparable figures for help from adult children in separate households is 19 percent in Sweden, and 21 percent in the EU countries. The major difference between the countries is found in the percentage of help received from adult children who share a household with a frail elderly person. As noted earlier, co-residency with offspring is next to nonexistent in Sweden and consequently help from co-resident children is rare. The same applies to Denmark and the Netherlands (2–4 percent), whereas such help is quite frequent in countries such as Germany (20 percent), Portugal (26 percent), Spain (30 percent), Italy (34 percent), and Greece (39 percent) (Andersson, 1993).

There is, of course, an overlap between formal and informal care. It is often claimed that those who receive formal help also receive substantial help from kin, friends, and neighbors. However, this has not been supported by results from major studies (Andersson, 1993; Sundström, 1994a); as shown earlier, the help from kin, friends, and neighbors is minimal—at most, 20 percent of those who receive public care also receive care from other sources. Considering that the majority of public care recipients live alone, this is hardly surprising.

What does this mean for the relationship between formal and informal supports? Some scholars maintain that once public care has been received, the individual tends to forget about additional care. However, there is also the possibility that the irregularity of informal help often makes it more difficult to elicit in standardized questionnaires.

In general, the overlap of care sectors—formal and informal—is more common among people with simpler care needs, whereas those with more severe needs tend to receive care almost exclusively from the family or from public sources. Longitudinally and slightly simplified, the caregiving process can be described as beginning with the family, supplemented perhaps by other sources. As infirmity progresses, however, either public care takes over, or the family (spouse, and possibly children) continues alone (Sundström, 1994a).

On the whole, a greater proportion of the elderly in Sweden receive formal home care, in contrast to the greater share of elderly in the European Union receiving private help and help from co-resident children. In addition, a larger percentage of the elderly in the European Union receives help from distant family members and from neighbors than do elderly Swedes.

A comparison of the frail elderly in Sweden and Israel shows great differences between these countries in lifestyles and living arrangements. For the few frail elderly Israelis who live alone, the differences are somewhat smaller. Older Israelis tend to use the available public home help or private help, whereas the Swedish elderly are more likely to be institutionalized or to use public home help when frailty besets them (Habib, Sundström, and Windmiller, 1993).

Gender Differences in Informal Care

Data from the Ädel–ULF study can be used for an analysis of the gender distribution of spousal help. Among four types of household chores, it is about three times as common for the wife to help her husband with shopping than the other way around. The corresponding figures for cleaning, laundry, and cooking are 4.5, 9, and 20 times, respectively. With respect to four types of physical care needs, which of course are more infrequent, the figures for help with showers, help getting up from bed, help with dressing, and help with toileting, are 3.5, 4, 5, and 13 times respectively.

Thus, it seems that the unevenness of the distribution of help between spouses is somewhat greater for household chores than for physical care needs. This may simply be an expression of a greater impact of traditional gender roles on carrying out instrumental activities of daily living.

The gender differences for help from children are not as pronounced as those between spouses. It is 1.5, 3.5, 3.5, and 4 times as common for daughters to help with shopping, cleaning, cooking, and laundry, respectively, than it is for sons; and 2, 3, 6.5, and 9 times as common for daughters to help with dressing, toileting, showers, and getting up from bed. Help from daughters-in-law and sons-in-law are negligible at this level of analysis.

EXTENDED NETWORKS

To get an impression of the elderly person's relationship with extended networks, a few more questions from the Eurobarometer study are presented. For example, how does contact with the younger generation appear? One of the questions in the Eurobarometer read: "How much contact do you have with young people, say younger than 25, including any members of your family?" The results show that there is generally quite a lot of contact between young and old. Perhaps surprisingly, the proportion claiming to have "a lot" of contact with young people is the highest in Sweden (53 percent), followed by Ireland and Denmark (46 percent).

The respondents were also asked whether they thought they were treated with more or less respect after reaching old age. Most elderly Swedes reported that they were treated as usual (78 percent)—that is, neither better nor worse. Moreover, the proportion who thought they were treated with more respect (12 percent) is about the same as the proportion who thought they were treated with less respect (10 percent). There is a somewhat higher proportion among males, who perceive themselves as being treated with more respect (15 percent), than among females (9 percent).

Comparatively speaking, the Swedish elderly comprise the lowest proportion of those who believe that they are treated with less respect. It is also true that in Sweden we find the lowest proportion of those who say they are treated with more respect, but that, of course, is the effect of having such a large proportion who experienced no change. Apparently the elderly in Sweden experience relatively little change in attitude as an effect of aging. Irrespective of what "being treated as usual" means, aging for them does not seem to be particularly dramatic.

The respondents also rated how they were treated by a wide range of public and commercial agencies, professionals, and so on. There were only a strikingly few elderly Swedes who thought they were "treated as if they were second-class citizens or not able to think for themselves," by "public social security/pension agencies," "local authorities," "banks/financial institutions," "post offices," "shop keepers," "transport staff," "solicitors or lawyers" or "their own family," in all cases 4 percent or less. The only figures that differ slightly are those for "politicians" (6 percent) and "doctors/the health service" and "media" (7 percent)—which is, perhaps, not surprising, considering the divergent views that are debated both in politics and the media.

These results contrast with the evidence from the European Union. In fact, the Swedish elderly obtained the lowest percentages across 9 of the 11 agencies and individuals. For doctors/health service the percentage is the second-lowest after Denmark, and for the media the percentage is the third-lowest after Luxembourg and Denmark. Since Denmark's figures stand out as low in comparison with the other EU countries (Commission of the European Communities, 1993), there is apparently a consistent difference between the situation in the Scandinavian countries as compared to the other countries in the study.

CONCLUSIONS

It is evident from this review of network-relevant data that there is a need for in-depth exploration guided by theoretical considerations of social networks among the elderly in Sweden. Large-scale surveys alone cannot capture the essentials of the complex pattern of social contacts. Moreover, large-scale surveys need to be combined with studies in which the concept of family, for example, is elucidated. Pertinent questions in this regard would include whether there is a varying definition of family over time. For most adults in Sweden children may have to be part of the household in order to be considered part of the family, whereas the elderly in other settings may include children outside the household. The increasing number of international comparisons highlights the need to use comparable concepts.

Notwithstanding the weaknesses of the data presented in this chapter, a fairly solid picture of the informal networks of elderly Swedes stands out. After a fairly fast change over recent decades, the number of single households has stabilized at approximately 40 percent of the total. While living alone is often portrayed as being tantamount to isolation and loneliness, however, the data suggest just the opposite. In spite of the large proportion of those living alone, the elderly in Sweden come out near the top in all network-relevant measures in the 13-country comparison (the Eurobarometer). They have the third-highest figure (after Denmark and Ireland) for contacts with family during "the last week" (73.4 percent), and the second-highest figure (after Ireland) for contacts with friends (70.1 percent). Elderly Swedes come out first in contacts with young people, and their perceptions of the extended network are the most positive in 9 out of 11 cases. In addition, the percentage who often feel lonely (6 percent), is the second-lowest (after Denmark).

In view of the fact that the two Scandinavian countries, Denmark and Sweden, consistently demonstrate the highest social contact figures, the obvious next step is to continue the analysis by asking to what extent the figures reflect a Scandinavian model. In addition to factors like adequate material assets, economic independence, availability of transport, a high quality of life, and so on, there are also macrovalues underlying the Scandinavian model, such as those of solidarity and egalitarianism (Daatland, 1992; Listhaug, 1990).

The contact patterns between the generations have remained fairly stable since at least 1954—the date of the earliest large-scale study—despite the fact that the total economy and the social services have increased tremendously. It seems, therefore, that studies of the value system underlying society would contribute to yet a better understanding of the social networks of the elderly.

3

The Lineage-Structured Social Networks of Older People in France

Claudine Attias-Donfut and Alain Rozenkier

The curtain lifts in a Parisian theater. On stage, a mother and daughter engage in conversation. The daughter—only a child—begs her mother not to leave her home alone. The mother—a young divorcee—wants to go out and meet men. In the next scene the same characters are on stage, but 25 years have passed, and the roles are reversed. An old woman asks her daughter to keep her company and not to leave her on her own, while the young woman is called to be with her husband and children.

This play, cited by Cohen (1994) as an illustration of the generation dilemma, leads us straight to the heart of our discussion. The social networks of older people revolve primarily around the unique axis of intergenerational relations. In order to discuss this topic in depth, one must first consider the evolution of these relationships over the course of time. Most relationships experienced by older people are long-standing ones formed at an earlier stage in their lives. They are charged with numerous memories and complex feelings, such as gratitude or resentment, obligation or need, as well as with explicit and implicit expectations, fulfilled or otherwise.

This linear view is certainly valid in examining familial structures and relations. However, a different approach may also be adopted to assess the influence of time: the simultaneous interviewing of all generations of a given family in order to examine their relationships, interactions, and histories. This latter approach is the one we follow in the research that forms the basis of this chapter—a study implemented among three generations of selected families.

We also relate to an earlier inquiry that focused on people aged 75 and over. Both studies were undertaken in France, separated by an interval of a few years, but they relate to very distinct samples and provide complementary information. We shall relate to both studies concurrently, after first presenting the sampling methods and research methodology employed.

STUDY SAMPLES

The tri-generational study (Attias-Donfut, 1995) mainly examines the nature, form, and dynamics of familial relations. In order to construct a sample of families comprising three generations of adults, the theoretical design focused on the intermediate generation and thereafter moved on to their parents and adult children. The first step was, therefore, to select a birth cohort appropriate for the middle generation. Demographic tables suggested that the age range of 49 to 53 offered the best chance of meeting our double requirement, having at least one surviving parent and at least one adult child.

Close to 8,000 people from this cohort were chosen at random from data drawn from the French census of 1990. These individuals were contacted by telephone to ascertain the presence of surviving parents and adult children. A random sample of about 2,000 people was then constructed from among respondents meeting the conditions of the survey. During face-to-face interviews, by means of questionnaires, respondents were asked to supply the address of one parent and one adult child. Among the parent generation, 1,217 interviews were completed, for a response rate of 74 percent. Among the children, 1,493 interviews were carried out, for a corresponding response rate of approximately 80 percent. The final sample totaled 4,668 respondents belonging to 1,958 tri-generational families.

Limited to multigenerational family systems, the sample is representative of the 60 percent of the 1939–43 birth cohort belonging to a family comprising at least three generations. For sake of brevity, the members of this cohort are termed the "pivots." Our current analysis concentrates on the elderly parents of this middle generation—respondents who are distinguished from their peers by virtue of their having living offspring who, in turn, have adult children.

The simultaneous presence of three adult generations requires relative close proximity in age between the generations, however, and this increases the incidence of large families. The earlier one has a first child, the greater the likelihood for a larger-than-average family. This phenomenon is further accentuated by the decision to anchor the survey on the middle generation, in which case elderly with larger families have a higher chance of being sampled.

As the probability of a surviving parent is greater among higher socio-economic strata, a certain overrepresentation of these strata might also be expected. However, this factor is balanced by the fact that women in the relevant age group from lower socioeconomic backgrounds have a greater chance of having an adult child who has already left home, as they tend to have children earlier. Comparison of the socioeconomic backgrounds of the pivots interviewed in the survey with those reflected in a representative national survey shows that the distribution was actually quite representative. The sample of tri-generational families is thus representative of different socioeconomic strata in France.

In comparing the elderly sample in the tri-generational study with the national population of comparable age, the main distinction relates to the fact of the former being parents. One should recall in this respect the considerable percentage of women born at the beginning of the century who did not have children. Moreover, many of this generation—1 in 4 of those born before World War I, and about 18 percent of those born just after the war—had only one child. In our sample, in contrast, the percentage of those having only one child is much lower, approximately 13 percent. On the other hand, almost 70 percent of parents interviewed are aged 75 years or above, thus enabling certain comparisons to be made with peers in this age group.

Regarding place of domicile, the last census in 1990 showed that approxi-mately 3 percent of people aged 75 or above live in communal housing—a level very close to that found among pivots' parents aged at least 75. As for nursing homes, approximately 6 percent of parents aged 75 and over in the survey live in such establishments. This finding is in keeping with the results of the 1988 study on the elderly aged 75 and over, to be discussed shortly, which showed that the rate of institutionalization is higher when there are no surviving children. Of people aged 75 or above without children, 23 percent live in care facilities or nursing homes, as compared to only 9 percent of those who have at least one surviving child.

Initial analysis suggests that elderly survey nonrespondents were somewhat older and more prone to problems of health or old age that require regular daily assistance. The question can be raised, therefore, as to whether the parents interviewed are characterized by a better state of health than their peers. As will be seen later on, in examining the results of both studies, only minor differences emerge concerning the state of health, even in comparison to other representative data. It may therefore be concluded that the traditionally higher level of nonresponse among older and less healthy individuals that is found in most studies is more-or-less equivalent to what we enountered when sampling older people, having started out from their children.

In brief, analysis of this sample shows that the study population of elderly parents differs from its age-peers in the general population primarily in terms of its familial position at the head of a multigenerational unit. In other respects, however, the sample differs only slightly.

The second study to be discussed, which we refer to as "the price of dependence" (Bouget and Tartarin, 1990), was undertaken among a representative sample of 2,136 people aged 75 years or above as of 1 January 1988, in the administrative regions of Doubs and Loire–Atlantique. For persons living at home, health insurance files served as sampling frames. For those in institutions, the sample was drawn from lists of residents provided by these establishments.

Among respondents, 6 percent were "extremely" dependent, 7 percent were "very" dependent, and 10 percent were "considerably" dependent; 6 percent were categorized as "moderately" dependent and 71 percent as "slightly" dependent or not dependent at all.

Among parents interviewed in the framework of the tri-generational study, on the other hand, over one-third noted at least one task from a list of eight activities of daily living (ADL) that they cannot perform alone and for which they require the assistance of another person. Almost 6 percent of those interviewed (of whom 70 percent were aged 75 or above) could not move, eat, or go to the bathroom on their own, thus implying daily assistance from another person. About 9 percent could not leave their home without assistance, and some 13 percent combined at least two tasks that they could not perform without assistance.

THE THEORETICAL BASES OF SOCIAL NETWORKS

Study of the social networks of older people has developed in the context of two categories of social problems frequently encountered in old age: (1) loneliness and isolation, and (2) dependence and need for social support. In both cases precise knowledge of the relationship potentials of the aged individual enables the severity of the actual problem he or she faces to be assessed. However, the functioning of the social network is not exactly the same when the main problem is one of loneliness or loss of health. In the former situation, the issue is the provision of social contacts, whereas in the latter it is the availability of various forms of assistance.

Social isolation has been seen as one of the main problems of old age since the onset of gerontological studies. The struggle against loneliness requires, above all, human contact (even by telephone), company during leisure time and vacations, or having someone in whom one can confide. Usually, this occurs in the context of a reciprocal relationship in which each partner is both recipient and provider of contact. Tools developed for assessing the degree and extent of isolation examine actual contact during a set period, as for example, one day or one week (Tunstall, 1971).

Information on the social entourage of an older person is also consonant with the goal of evaluating the support this person may have in case of need. But simple contacts do not necessarily imply a potential for assistance (Barrera, 1986). An approach based on types of exchange seems more suitable, and this is the approach more frequently adopted. In such a case, the social network is distinguished from the support function; the former refers to the structure, whereas the latter relates to actual practice within this structure (Antonucci, 1990).

Moreover, the network includes people with different roles. A companion for walks or bridge parties may not necessarily be the person who comes to help with shopping or to make meals in the event of illness. It has been shown that only a small part of the network provides support in the event of health problems (Coenen-Huther, Kellerhals, and von Allmen, 1994). The presence of varying kinds of resource persons in the network thus requires that they be differentiated according to the types of interactions and exchanges involved.

The study of social networks may also stem from analysis of role transformation in later life (Dickens and Perlman, 1981; Litwak and Szelenyi, 1969). This goal is less directly linked to an understanding of networks per se, though social networks are an implicit component of a role-based social relations approach. The extension of the network to include relatives, friends, and broader relations, associative or other, is indicative of models of familial or social engagement.

These distinct goals may coexist to varying degrees in the four main approaches usually identified in social network analysis: interactions, exchanges, roles, and affective relations (van der Poel, 1993). In reality, affectivity and instrumentality, escape from solitude, and a desire for social support are all intertwined in relationships. Curtis and Bucquet (1990), quoting numerous sources in the literature, distinguish three dimensions of social support: emotional support, including moral and psychological support through relationships of compassion and friendship; informative support, including help in examining issues more clearly and reaching decisions; and instrumental support, including assistance in activities of daily living.

Instrumental aspects of support can be measured more readily by assessing the proportion of older people in receipt of different types of support and by quantifying their duration and frequency. In the study on the price of dependence, the assistance received by the older person from his or her social network was measured in terms of time and subsequently evaluated in financial terms on the basis of opportunity cost. This calculation enabled the relationship between informal and professional assistance to be compared on a standardized measure. However, the instrumental dimension is vast and includes a large variety of actions for which assistance is sought from different people—such as financial or domestic help.

In reality, social networks include extremely varied and complex relationships and form diametrically varying entities according to the point of view adopted in their examination. It is, thus, essential to define the theoretical background for research on this subject, since this, in turn, determines the practical approach adopted.

A "Lineage-Structured" Social Network Approach

The process used here in identifying the social networks of older people is similar to that of social exchange analysis insofar as it attempts to investigate the dynamics of social support. However, we place a greater emphasis on the field of social relations and leisure and concentrate particularly on the intergenerational axis. Our standing assumption is that this axis shapes the overall structure of older people's social networks.

In the study on the price of dependence we showed that it is primarily adult children who provide active support for elderly parents in the event of health problems, as has been found in other countries (Cicirelli, 1983; Matthews, Werkner, and Delaney, 1989; Stone, Cafferata, and Sangl, 1987). Other members of the network do intervene in the absence of living children or when these do not live in close proximity, but they do so less frequently and less intensively. Our tri-generational study enabled all types of generational transfers to be observed, both in an ascending direction (from youngest to oldest) and in a descending direction (from oldest to youngest). This study also compared parent–child contacts with other types of relations within the family—siblings and more distant relatives—as well as contacts outside the family, with friends or neighbors.

In order to uncover the potential for assistance available to older people, as well as the dynamics of this assistance in the interlocking reality of the biography, this social network study focuses on the intergenerational dimension. The method consists of gathering precise information on each of the children and his or her spouse and relates also to grandchildren and great-grandchildren. In addition, siblings of the elderly focal person and those of his or her spouse are addressed.

Other questions ascertain the identity of companions for leisure time, vacations, and different types of assistance, thus relating both to relational aspects and to mutual support. The involvement of other relatives and friends is also queried in this regard. The results broadly confirm the predominance of intergenerational relationships in the social networks of older people, though they also reveal the importance of friendships and the limited significance of ties with other relatives (Branch and Jette, 1983).

NETWORK SIZE AND COMPOSITION

By definition, respondents stand at the head of a multigenerational unit. On average, they have 3.8 children, 8.8 grandchildren, and 3 great-grandchildren. The mean number of children living with a partner is 3.1, and the mean number of grandchildren living with a partner is about 4. The total number of descendants, including partners of children and grandchildren, ranges from 2 to more than 100, with an average of approximately 22.

Table 3.1: Composition of Respondents' Family Network by Generation

	Youth	Middle Generation	Elderly
	18-36 Years Old	49-53 Years Old	68-94 Years Old
Number	1493	1958	1217
Mean Age	26.1	51.0	77.9
Self	1.0	1.0	1.0
Spouse	0.7	0.9	0.3
Children	0.6	2.6	3.8
Childrens's Spouses	--	1.2	3.1
Parents	2.0	1.3	0.0
Grandparents	2.0	--	--
Siblings	1.6	2.9	1.7
Spouse's Parents	1.2	0.8	0.0
Spouse's Grandparents	0.8	--	--
Spouse's Siblings	1.7	2.8	1.5
Grandchildren	--	1.1	8.8
Great-Grandchildren	--	--	3.0
Total	11.5	14.5	23.3

Source: Caisse Nationale D'Assurance Vieillesse, 1992.

The number of surviving siblings is more limited—1.7 on average; 30 percent have no living siblings, 28 percent have only one, 16 percent have two, 18 percent three or four, and 8 percent more than four. Siblings of the spouse are even less numerous, with an average of 1.5. In terms of the size of the immediate family network, therefore, descendants are much more significant than peers, particularly as the latter belong to the same generation as the elderly, and their number inexorably dwindles. Table 3.1 shows the relative importance of the size of the immediate family network available to older people in comparison to two younger generations.

Leisure Network and Assistance Network

Older people do not meet with the same partners when they engage in leisure activities and when they engage in exchanges of services, according to the "task-specificity" hypothesis (Litwak, 1985). When leisure activities are undertaken with persons other than the spouse, those most frequently mentioned are friends, rather than children or grandchildren. Only very rarely are other relatives mentioned. Children are the most frequently mentioned partners for excursions to the restaurant or for activities in and around the home, such as gardening or household tasks. The same applies to visits to cemeteries—an activity more often engaged in together with relatives than is the case with participation in religious services.

In all other activities, friends are mentioned more frequently than family members, particularly in the case of entertainment, physical activity, fishing or hunting, and social games. In contrast, siblings are slightly more dominant than friends as companions for a weekend or the main holidays: 19 percent mentioned siblings in this case, as compared to 14 percent who mentioned the siblings of spouses, 11 percent mentioned other relatives, and 17 percent mentioned friends. However, 91 percent mentioned children and 84 percent mentioned grandchildren.

The results are quite different when examining services given or received. In these cases, intervention is usually by the spouse or children. Grandchildren are mentioned much less frequently, though more so than friends. Other relatives are rarely involved in these exchanges; for each home service, they are mentioned by less than 1 percent of respondents. This confirms that only a very small proportion of elderly people receive instrumental help from their siblings (Cicirelli, Raymond, and Dwyer, 1992; Connidis, 1994).

In the sphere of services received by older people, we find friends and neighbors assisting with shopping (17 percent), and less frequently with household work (4 percent), or looking after pets and watering plants (6 percent). For other services, friends are mentioned very rarely. Descendants are much more active in assisting with shopping (60 percent children, 22 percent grandchildren), bureaucratic chores (52 percent children, 6 percent grandchildren), house moving or decoration (30 percent children, 6 percent grandchildren), and domestic chores, including care of animals or plants (15 percent children, 3 percent grandchildren).

The same difference is found when elderly persons are the givers of assistance and services. Older people tend to give gifts to children and to grandchildren, while other relatives and friends are rarely recipients. Apart from 8 percent of older people who report helping friends with shopping, the levels of assistance for all other types of services rarely exceed 1 percent when friends or other relatives are involved. For example, financial loans and gifts are given to friends and other relatives by less than 1 percent of older people, whereas financial help by older people to their descendants is particularly notable. One in three provide such help for their children, and the same proportion do so for grandchildren. As some older people help both children and grandchildren, one older person in two provides loans or gifts to descendants. Other financial assistance is given in the form of gift objects, permitting the use of apartments or houses, or transfer of property.

Assistance of a domestic nature is less common and includes primarily help with laundry (11 percent for children and 12 percent for grandchildren), cooking (11 percent for children and 1 percent for grandchildren), or caring for animals and plants (9 percent for children and 2 percent for grandchildren). In addition, very old persons sometimes look after their great-grandchildren or keep them occupied them with activities such as games and storytelling. Other types of services are less frequently provided by these respondents, most of whom are, one should recall, aged 75 and over.

In general terms, almost all the family relationships are with children and grandchildren, whether in the field of leisure, vacations, or different types of assistance. Other relatives are mentioned at least once by only one in four respondents, whereas friends are mentioned at least once by three in four older persons.

How are these familial and friendship relationships assessed by older persons? Family ties appear to remain strong, since 71 percent consider their family to constitute the major part of their social network, and 23 percent consider their familial and friendship relations to be of equal importance. Only 6 percent attach greater importance to friends than to relatives.

Other studies have emphasized the importance of friendships. According to Chappell (1983), contacts with friends are more frequent and more satisfying than contacts with relatives living outside the home. Johnson and Catalano (1983) showed that frequency of contact with children and friends is greater than that with relatives. These studies suggest that ties of friendship are closer than blood ties.

Our study does not confirm these findings in the case of French elderly who have living descendants. For those without children, the social network is indeed comprised mainly of neighbors and friends. However, among those who do have children and grandchildren, intergenerational ties assume primary importance in terms of solidarity, even if friends are dominant in leisure activities and play an important role in combating loneliness.

Reciprocity

Interactions with other generations show a degree of reciprocity, but this is not necessarily reflected in the same types of interaction. Three interaction categories can be distinguished: (1) financial interactions, including gifts and loans of money or objects, or help with housing and furnishing; (2) domestic interactions relating to activities for household maintenance, home, and health; and (3) social interactions, including bureaucratic chores, help in access to public and health services, and professional assistance. The latter introduce the "social capital" of the family (Bourdieu, 1989).

This typology recalls the "three components of the hidden economy of kinship" defined by Dechaux (1994): redistribution of income, domestic support, and social support. Limiting economic support to financial assistance, we measured the degree of reciprocity between older persons and their children for each type of support.

The reciprocity is reflected over the totality of interactions, each generation having its own field of intervention. In general, the different types of interaction of both generations more-or-less balance one another. However, the intermediate generation remains in credit in the context of interactions with its parents, albeit with fluctuations according to socioeconomic class. Interactions with parents are most frequently reciprocal among the self-employed and business people, and less so among the working class. Differences between other classes are relatively limited at this level. On the other hand, financial transactions are on the whole more significant in middle- and upper-class groups (Table 3.2).

We believe it is important in social network analysis to relate to the reciprocal nature of the interaction, rather than concentrating exclusively on the support enjoyed by the older person. Indeed, this support may be seen as an immediate or deferred counterpart to the assistance provided by the older person. The distinction between the social network and social support is also important (House and Kahn, 1985), since the social network includes the concept of reciprocity, whereas social support places older persons in the exclusive position of receiving assistance, obscuring their contribution to members of their network and to those who provide assistance.

SOCIAL SUPPORT

The price of dependence study showed that 53 percent of older persons aged 75 and above receive regular assistance from a relative or neighbor, regardless of their functional health, and some 15 percent receive assistance from an additional person. Findings from the tri-generational study confirm these assistance frequencies.

Many older parents in multigenerational families (88 percent) report receiving at least occasional assistance from their offspring. As for regular assistance, this is noted by 50 percent of these respondents, irrespective of health status or household type (alone, in a couple, or with others). Almost everyone incapable of performing at least one of the eight basic tasks of daily living receives assistance from offspring (94 percent). Regular assistance is closely correlated, moreover, with the need for assistance: 84 percent of those who require assistance for moving around their apartment, eating, going to the bathroom, or leaving their immediate vicinity also receive such assistance. In contrast, just over one-third of those who can accomplish daily tasks alone, even with difficulty, receive assistance.

Whether on an occasional or regular basis, adult children help more often with tasks outside the home, such as shopping, than with household maintenance responsibilities like cleaning, laundry, and cooking. Personal care is the least

**Table 3.2: Reciprocity of Intergenerational Exchange:
Members of the Middle Generation Giving to and Getting
from Noncohabiting Parents**

	Occupational Status[a]						
Type of Assistance	1	2	3	4	5	6	Total
	%	%	%	%	%	%	%
Household Help							
Both gives & gets	36.2	36.5	29.7	30.6	27.9	21.4	28.9
Only gives	56.9	49.0	47.8	51.4	55.5	64.8	54.7
Only gets	5.2	3.1	8.7	6.1	4.7	3.8	5.2
Neither gives nor gets	1.7	11.5	13.8	11.9	11.9	10.0	11.2
Social Support							
Both gives & gets	3.4	3.1	2.2	1.8	1.5	1.4	1.9
Only gives	62.1	53.1	55.8	57.9	62.0	62.9	59.1
Only gets	8.6	2.1	3.6	2.9	0.6	0.5	2.1
Neither gives nor gets	25.9	41.7	38.4	37.4	35.9	35.2	37.0
Financial Aid							
Both gives & gets	3.4	1.0	5.1	3.6	1.5	1.9	2.6
Only gives	10.3	8.3	8.7	5.8	5.3	4.8	6.2
Only gets	19.0	31.3	37.7	30.9	30.3	27.6	30.4
Neither gives nor gets	67.2	59.4	48.6	59.7	62.9	65.7	60.8
Total Assistance							
Both gives & gets	92.1	91.8	82.6	48.6	44.5	38.6	46.8
Only gives	5.3	8.2	16.7	35.3	41.2	50.5	39.2
Only gets	2.6	-	-	8.6	8.9	5.7	7.9
Neither gives nor gets	-	-	0.7	7.6	5.3	5.2	6.0

[a] Occupational categories: (1) farmer, (2) craftsman, merchant, (3) white-collar worker, (4) middle-level professional, (5) clerk, (6) factory worker.
Source: Caisse Nationale D'Assurance Vieillesse, 1992.

common focus of assistance. Nonetheless, the more necessary such assistance is, the more frequently it is given. Personal care is of particular concern to more than 40 percent of the most disabled respondents.

These data relate to the entire range of social support, reflecting its scope and importance. A closer analysis of caregivers in terms of their familial ties underscores the context of intergenerational solidarity. The study on those aged 75 and above, including those without children, allows comparison of the importance of assistance according to family status of the caregiver. A primary caregiver was mentioned by 53 percent of respondents, and a secondary caregiver by only 15 percent. Only rarely were more than two principal caregivers noted, thus reflecting aspects of the substitution hypothesis (Shanas, 1979) and the hierarchical compensatory model (Cantor, 1979).

The spouse, if capable of providing help, is invariably the first source of assistance and is almost never a secondary helper. In fact, spousal support is so commonplace that it is not considered as "aid" per se (Malonebeach and Zarit, 1991), and yet it is the primary deterrent to institutionalization (Forbes, Jackson, and Kraus, 1987). However, since the vast majority of dependent persons are widows, it is the children who are the main caregivers (Chappell, 1991a). Children and their spouses—and, to a minor degree, grandchildren—represent almost two-thirds of primary caregivers and almost four-fifths of secondary caregivers.

A number of differences can be seen between primary and secondary caregivers. Men, and particularly sons-in-law, are overrepresented in the category of secondary caregivers, while daughters-in-law are more commonly mentioned as primary caregivers. Care is provided more often by daughters than by sons, as reflected in the fact that 70 percent of children providing assistance are female.

Single marital status and the lack of children are additional significant factors in the provision of assistance. Of children who provide assistance, 32 percent do not themselves have children, and many (24 percent of primary caregivers and 30 percent of secondary caregivers) are not married. Moreover, the rate of single caregivers is much higher among sons than among daughters, and this difference is even greater when the parent is severely dependent.

These data relate exclusively, of course, to persons living at home. The situation is quite different among those in institutions. Children who intervene on behalf of institutionalized parents are almost all married. Thus it is the presence of never-married or childless children that serves as a safeguard against the risk of institutionalization and as a guarantee of support in case of dependence, rather than the mere presence of any children as reported by Health and Welfare Canada (1982).

The vast majority of caregivers live near the recipient, whether in the same apartment or in the immediate vicinity. Thus, place of residence strongly affects the availability of assistance in case of dependence. When male or female children are the primary caregivers, 36 percent reside in the same apartment as the assisted parent, 18 percent in the immediate vicinity, 17 percent in the same neighborhood, and only 29 percent further away. As for cases when sons-in-law and daughters-in-law are the primary caregiver, only 4 percent live further away, as compared to 44 percent when they are the secondary caregiver.

The high proportion of caregivers who are not otherwise employed is also worth noting: only 47 percent of children and 31 percent of children-in-law who are primary caregivers are employed, and for secondary caregivers the proportions are 58 and 46 percent, respectively. The large number of retired caregivers (37 percent of primary caregivers) and of unemployed women who devote themselves to this task is a strong indication of the level of availability that caregiving requires.

These figures are equally revealing as concerns the age of the children themselves. Slightly under one-quarter of primary caregivers are under 45 years old. The vast majority (69 percent) are in the 45–65 year age span. Moreover, caregivers' age rises along with the intensity of dependence, matching the increasing age of the parents. Nevertheless, the majority of caregivers are not of retirement age, and while they may not be working elsewhere, they are still "potential employees."

A comparison of older persons in terms of the nature of their relationship with the caregiver reflects the dominance of intergenerational support. Assistance is usually provided by other relatives or by neighbors when there are no children living close by or no surviving children. The primary caregiver of almost 12 percent of older persons is a neighbor or friend. Of these respondents, 48 percent have no surviving children, and 25 percent have no children living in the vicinity. Among those who receive assistance from other relatives, 77 percent have no surviving children, and 13 percent have no children living in the vicinity.

In brief, these data reveal not only the extent of social support, but also its limitations: the restricted nature of the network, which rarely comprises more than two active members, the condition that caregivers almost always live in the immediate vicinity, and the high proportion of single or childless caregivers and of those not employed are all indicative of the demands of this function and the difficulties in securing such assistance when professional or parental roles compete for time and attention. For women, who provide the vast majority of informal aid, the task is frequently a lonely one, but this may vary according to familial role—spouse, daughter, or daughter-in-law (Bocquet, Berthier, and Grand, 1994).

Intergenerational Assistance

Characteristics of Care Receivers. The tri-generational study enables the extent of intergenerational assistance to be examined in greater depth and confirms the widespread occurrence of the phenomenon: 39 percent of elderly parents receive regular assistance from a child. In the case of parents aged 75 and above, intergenerational assistance is even more frequent (44 percent), but it is less common among married elderly couples (30 percent). Over two-thirds of those who require assistance with eating, bathing, moving within the apartment, or going out into the immediate vicinity receive such assistance. It is somewhat less common, however, in the case of elderly persons needing help with shopping, housekeeping, cooking, or using public transport (about 60 percent). In the case of parents aged 75 and above who live with their children, four out of five receive assistance from them, including almost everyone who notes at least one ADL that they cannot perform alone.

Of parents who do not receive assistance from a child, four out of five are capable of performing all ADLs, although they may face difficulties. The proportion of those receiving assistance in these cases is half that mentioned above: 28 percent require assistance with eating, going to the bathroom, and moving around—that is, four times more than parents not assisted by a child. Their self-rated health is also less positive: 30 percent consider themselves in poor or mediocre health, as compared to 18 percent of those who are not assisted. The latter consider their health to be very good (46 percent) or good (30 percent). They are twice as likely, moreover, to live in a couple. In four cases out of five, their spouse is able-bodied, as opposed to one out of two among those receiving assistance.

The state of health and level of dependence of older persons varies according to social status, as does the help given by children to elderly parents. The elderly who do not receive assistance from their children live in areas considered more prosperous. They are also more likely to be home-owners than those who do receive such assistance. In addition, parents not in receipt of assistance are less likely to have been engaged in agriculture or labor and are disproportionately male and younger.

Among older parents (75 and above), the socially disadvantaged status of those who receive assistance emerges from the study. These parents are somewhat more likely to be retired farmers (25 percent) living in less comfortable homes (16 percent have neither bath nor shower). While somewhat fewer than half of all parents aged 75 years and above own their own homes and one-quarter enjoy free housing, those assisted by their children are more likely to enjoy free housing (35 percent) and less likely to own their own home (36 percent).

Characteristics of Caregiving Children. Almost three-quarters of children who provide regular ADL assistance for their parents are women (63 percent daughters and 9 percent daughters-in-law). Sons provide help to 29 percent of parents. There is no significance to the mutual genders of caregiver and recipient of care—sons and daughters are each as likely to assist mothers as fathers.

Whatever the composition of the family, the daughter is always more likely to be active than the son. When there is only one child (and therefore a lower probability that assistance is forthcoming), one-quarter of sons help their parents, as compared to one-third of daughters. When families include both male and female siblings, women continue to predominate in caregiving. When there is one son and a number of daughters, the daughters provide assistance in three families out of four; and even when there is one daughter and a number of sons, parents in over half the families still receive assistance from the daughter rather than from the sons. However, there is only a slight difference in the level of assistance provided in families where there are only sons (33 percent) or only daughters (36 percent).

Parents assisted by a daughter are much more likely to be laborers and to live in cities. Parents helped by a son, in contrast, are more likely to be self-employed, farmers, or business people. They are more likely to live in rural areas and to own a home that is likely to be less comfortable than that of parents assisted by a daughter. Daughters-in-law provide assistance most frequently in families with agricultural backgrounds.

Sons who provide assistance for elderly parents are more likely to be unmarried (27 percent, vs. 9 percent of daughters) and to be the oldest sibling. Daughters and daughters-in-law are more likely to live in close proximity to the care-recipient and are much more likely to have children. Daughters-in-law are also more likely not to be employed elsewhere.

Single children who assist their parents differ from other caregivers from larger families. They are more highly educated and are much more likely to belong to the professional or middle class (36 percent, vs. 15 percent for other caregivers). However, the proportion of farm workers is the same among single children as among other caregivers. It should be noted that 38 percent of these children live in the same apartment or building as the parent whom they assist, while the average for other caregivers is 30 percent.

Whatever the composition of the family (daughters and/or sons), geographical proximity appears to play a determining role in establishing caregiving: 57 percent of children who assist their parents live less than 1 kilometer away, as compared to only 14 percent of other brothers and sisters. This fact led us to examine the social logic promoting maximum proximity—that is, cohabitation on the part of approximately one-quarter of parents assisted by their children.

Forms of Cohabitation. The population census enables us to examine the evolution of the rate of cohabitation of parents and children over the past 30 years. Approximately 20 percent of persons aged 60 and above share a residence with a child. Although there has been a significant reduction in this phenomenon, it nevertheless remains fairly widespread. Among widows aged 85 and above—the group where cohabitation was most common—the proportion living in households of two or more people has fallen from 57 percent in 1962 to 30 percent in 1990.

The rate of cohabitation of single older persons aged 75 and above was 17 percent in 1990, according to the census figures. The corresponding rate among the sample is 16 percent, indicating that the sample is quite representative. Analysis of cohabitation based on the results of the tri-generational study reveals two distinct aspects of this practice: (1) in terms of the duration of cohabitation, and (2) in terms of the impact of the characteristics of children on different types of cohabitation—in particular, the importance of social mobility (Attias-Donfut and Renaut, 1994).

When the subject of parents living with their children is raised, it is commonly assumed that parents and children have separated after the children became adults, subsequently coming back to live together after many decades. In reality, this pattern applies to less than half of the instances of cohabitation. In a small majority of cases, parents and children never separate but establish a pattern of cohabitation that continues into old age and, in all probability, until the death of the parents. Parents who live as a couple are more common among those who have always lived together with children, whereas widows and widowers are more common in cases of "recohabitation." Indeed, the death of a spouse appears to be one of the catalysts of recohabitation.

The average age of parents is slightly lower in cases of recohabitation. Moderate or severe dependence is more common, representing one of the main causes. In contrast, dependence has little impact on the process leading to permanent cohabitation. The rural character of permanent cohabitation is confirmed by the fact that 63 percent of such instances occur in villages or isolated places of residence, as compared to 40 percent in cases of recohabitation.

The most significant distinction between families in terms of types of cohabitation relates to social status and intergenerational mobility. The socioprofessional profiles of parents and children suggest that permanent cohabitation is related to social immobility, while intergenerational social mobility is usual in families practicing recohabitation. Former laborers and agricultural workers represent almost 75 percent of parents. However, there is a large majority of former agricultural workers among instances of permanent cohabitation, and of former laborers among instances of recohabitation. Another significant distinction is that unskilled laborers are more common in cases of permanent cohabitation, whereas skilled laborers are more common in cases of recohabitation.

One of the clearest contrasts between these types of cohabitation concerns the respective roles of sons and daughters and their own matrimonial status. The majority of children who have always lived with their parents are sons, whereas the majority of children in cases of recohabitation are daughters. The majority of children who have never left their parents' home are unmarried; the majority in cases of recohabitation are married, although there is also a high number of divorced or widowed children.

The contrast is even sharper in terms of the social mobility of the children. Those who never leave the parental home are much more likely to be agricultural workers or laborers. Those who practice recohabitation are more likely to be salaried employees, and their social profile is more varied, with slightly more self-employed and intermediate professions and 4 percent of white-collar workers—a category absent in permanent cohabitation. Children have the same social status as the father in two out of three cases of permanent cohabitation and in one out of three cases of recohabitation.

A similar trend emerges with regard to schooling and education. Among those who have always lived with their parents, elementary schooling is somewhat more common. In this respect, the subjective opinion of the parents as to their children's social mobility is extremely significant: 72 percent of parents in cases of recohabitation believe that the child has been more "socially successful" than they have been themselves, but this rate falls to 46 percent in cases of permanent cohabitation. These results confirm the return effects of social mobility under conditions of cohabitation (Attias-Donfut, 1993).

In four-fifths of cases of cohabitation where the parents are aged 75 and over, assistance is provided by the children. This includes almost all parents noting at least one ADL that they cannot perform without assistance. Of sons providing regular assistance, 19 percent have always lived with their parents, as opposed to only 8 percent of daughters. In contrast, 17 percent of daughters acting as caregivers are in situations of recohabitation, versus 6 percent of sons. Daughters comprise 43 percent of caregivers who have always lived with their parents, and 80 percent of caregiving children in cases of recohabitation.

Of children who live with their parents and provide assistance, those who have never left home are usually sons (47 percent), unmarried (64 percent), without children (58 percent), agricultural workers (38 percent), and the youngest of the siblings. Assistance by children to parents in cohabitation is more common in all aspects, particularly in housework, laundry, and personal care. Thus, the assistance provided by children is significant: the estimated time devoted each week by children to parents is four times greater than when the child does not live with the parent.

Cohabitation and the Mutuality of Assistance. Cohabitation is frequently perceived as adult children taking charge of their elderly parents after the latter have partially lost their autonomy. In fact, the situation is one of mutuality. Children who take aged parents into their homes were often in receipt of earlier parental financial aid and other supports, which helped them in climbing the social ladder. In these cases, recohabitation benefits the older person, whose living conditions are thus improved, while enabling the children to "repay their debt."

This model of mutual assistance takes the form of a cyclical exchange of gifts and loans throughout the course of life. Hareven (1994) holds that assistance for very old parents must be seen in the context of the relations established since childhood. Bloch and Buisson (1991) underscore the importance of "debt running" in the dynamics of familial ties.

The nature of mutuality in the case of permanent cohabitation is somewhat different. From the patrimonial and material viewpoint, this exchange benefits the child who often gets the donation of the parents' house. The parents gain, in return, the ongoing presence and support of their child.

SOCIAL SUPPORT AND FORMAL ASSISTANCE

The range of practical support provided by the social support network, primarily in its familial dimension, does not cover the entire range of assistance required by older persons living at home. Thus the question of the relationship between informal and formal care emerges as a key area of concern. When older persons are institutionalized, formal assistance is clearly dominant in fulfilling activities of daily living. This does not imply that institutionalization excludes the intervention of the social network. The latter complements formal care in certain practical activities, although its contribution is mostly in the affective and social spheres.

There are two main types of formal home-helpers, distinguishable in both functional and organizational respects. The first are helpers who do housework, cleaning, and cooking in cases where older persons are unable to perform these tasks or have difficulty doing so. It is in this field that the "home-help" intervenes subsidized by social security. Assistance in personal care and health needs, on the other hand, is met mainly through the services of visiting nurses or health visitors. The service may be delivered as part of a public body or on an individual basis.

Results of the "Price of Independence" Study

Almost one-third of persons aged 75 and above living at home are given assistance by at least one formal helper. The average duration of intervention is 28 monthly hours per recipient. A comparison of the respective importance of formal and informal assistance, based on the number of hours per person, shows that at least three times as much help is given by informal caregivers than by paid personnel.

The distribution of formal assistance varies according to the level of dependency, as has already been shown to be the case for informal assistance. Among able-bodied persons living at home, fewer than half enjoy the support of a caregiver, whether informal (from the social network) or from a paid professional. The greater the level of dependence, the fewer the number of persons who do not get some form of assistance.

The ability of very elderly persons to remain at home would appear to be conditional on effective assistance. At middle levels of dependence, only a few persons lack any assistance; when dependence is severe, no such persons are found to be without help. Thus, the higher the level of dependence, the greater the proportion of those who receive formal or informal assistance (or both).

The role of informal help from the social network is crucial. At each level of dependence, informal assistance is more frequent than formal aid. As was mentioned, the ability to remain in the home depends on the availability of assistance. Only rarely is this assistance provided solely by formal caregivers. On the other hand, cases in which assistance is provided solely by informal caregivers are much more numerous. In cases of severe, very severe, and extreme dependence, only 5–10 percent of persons benefit solely from formal assistance, while 40–60 percent of the members of these categories who live at home receive assistance exclusively from the social network.

In fact, the ability to remain at home depends most frequently on the accumulative benefit of both sources of assistance. The more severe the level of dependence, the greater the proportion of persons in receipt of such combined support. In cases of very severe or extreme dependence, for example, about half receive both types of assistance simultaneously.

Formal assistance is also found in cases when there is no dependence, or when the level of dependence is low. In order to understand the factors other than dependence that shape the distribution of formal assistance, in terms of direct hours of work on behalf of respondents, we performed a regression analysis. Four results are of particular interest:

1. Distribution of assistance is greater the higher the level of dependence of older persons living at home: the regression coefficients increased steadily according to the level of dependence.

2. The presence of formal assistance is also highly responsive to the composition of the respondent's household. Such aid is provided primarily to persons who live alone on a daily basis; next is to couples; and much less frequently to cohabiting households of three or more persons. In addition, women—whether living alone or in a couple—are more likely than men to receive formal help. Connidis and McMullin (1994) have shown that never-married and divorced persons are more likely than married individuals to receive formal help, and that the childless are more likely to be in receipt of such aid than those with children.

3. The greater the respondent's resources, the greater the likelihood of receiving formal assistance. This can be explained mainly by the fact that the study included home helps and nurses fully paid for by the recipients.

4. No correlation was found between the receipt of formal assistance and at least one visit to the medical services, but assistance is more frequent among those hospitalized during the year. The findings suggest that hospital discharge is facilitated by one's having a combination of formal assistance and informal support. As well as providing an indication of the state of health, therefore, the hospital serves as an entry point into the network of support and assistance.

Results of the Tri-Generational Study

The tri-generational study provides complementary data on variations in the combination of formal assistance and social support according to caregivers' familial relationship. About one-quarter of the older persons interviewed received formal assistance at home. This assistance was closely related to the need for practical help: 38 percent of those who required daily help received formal assistance, as compared to only 15 percent of those who stated that they do not require such assistance, even if they encounter difficulties in performing certain ADLs. For this latter group, formal assistance is confined exclusively to domestic maintenance. Different types of formal assistance were provided, on the other hand, to more than 20 percent of persons who require assistance in eating, going to the bathroom, and moving around.

Formal assistance is very rarely the only type of assistance available to an older person. In most cases in which paid support is required, it is complementary to informal assistance. The frequency of this combination of formal and informal assistance varies, however, according to the level of dependence. The greater the need for support, the more frequent the appearance of this combination. Thus among the most severely dependent, one parent in three receives both types of assistance, as compared to one in four among the moderately dependent and one in 20 among parents who do not require any assistance.

Recourse to formal assistance is more frequent when the informal caregiver is a son (37 percent) than when it is a daughter (25 percent). The most common type of support is domestic aid. Formal assistance in personal care is much less common (about 9 percent on average), regardless of the identity of the informal caregiver.

Formal assistance is also more frequent in the older age ranges. Among single parents aged 75 and above who are assisted by a child, one-third receive formal assistance (25 percent among parents as a whole). Here, too, the provision of support varies according to need:

- 44 percent among those who require assistance in eating, going to the bathroom, or moving around within the apartment or in the immediate environment;
- 37 percent of those who require assistance in shopping, housework, cooking, or using public transport;
- 21 percent among those who do not require assistance for any of the above activities.

Formal assistance is more frequent among older parents assisted by a son than among those assisted by a daughter or daughter-in-law. Employment of a home help is always more frequent when the son provides assistance for parents aged 75 and above than when it is the daughter who intervenes.

A comparison of informal support from the social network and formal assistance reveals the presence of both an enhancement and replacement effect.

Enhancement can be seen clearly in the cumulative effect of formal and informal assistance. The effects of replacement are more subtle and can only be partial, since the ability to remain in the home is possible only if the social network is mobilized. In most cases of considerable dependency, formal assistance alone is not sufficient to enable the older person to continue to live at home.

Rather than serving as alternatives, the prevalent situation is that both sources of assistance are combined. Within this combination, however, the relative importance of each source may vary. A greater level of dependence and increased financial resources both correlate with a higher measure of formal assistance. Auslander and Litwin (1990) have shown, moreover, that elderly applicants to social services had significantly smaller networks and less affective support.

Situations of cohabitation are interesting in that they enable us to assess the phenomenon of the partial substitution of one source of assistance for the other. Even if both parents living together require assistance, only 18 percent of parents living with a child enjoy paid assistance, as opposed to approximately one-third among parents who do not live in a situation of cohabitation. The assistance provided by children in cases of cohabitation is therefore significant. The estimated time devoted by such children to their parents each week is four times greater than that provided when there is no cohabitation.

Analysis of formal and informal assistance thus shows that one source of assistance does not necessarily exclude the other, as is sometimes feared. It is not an absence of familial support that creates the need for formal assistance. On the contrary, public and professional assistance is necessitated by various considerations in the home and does not lead to a diminution of the social network.

CONCLUSION

The growing interest in the social network as a source of practical support reflects the importance attributed to the care of dependent older persons in France. The public ranks this concern higher than child care, integration of the disabled, and social security. Public authorities and social agencies are even more concerned, as witnessed by their increasing intervention on behalf of the frail elderly. The aging of society as a whole exacerbates the problem, with financial considerations playing an increasingly vital role in the context of dwindling resources.

Interest in the role of the family has been reawakened since the end of the 1970s, when sociologists began questioning the presumed breakdown of social ties and the "death of familial solidarity." Only recently, however, has the importance of family support been seriously considered among researchers and politicians. The economic crisis and the concomitant challenge to the welfare state place a new emphasis upon the limitations of public funding, shifting the spotlight to private sources of support.

Our analysis relates specifically to the intergenerational dimension of the social network. In the circle of exchange, each generation serves simultaneously as helper and recipient. The pivotal generation is the prime regulator of this extended network. Older persons emerge as sources of support for both subsequent adult generations, though the exact nature of such support varies by generation and by socioeconomic status.

Whether an individual is a help recipient or provider varies through the life cycle, and within each stage of life as well. Older persons confronting situations of dependence, for example, are mainly the recipients of support from their family. Yet they may formerly have been the providers of support in the financial realm, and in some cases may continue to be.

Informal practical help provided by the social network is more common than formal assistance. In the absence of familial support, moreover, institutionalization is usually inevitable. Only a small minority of older persons manage to remain in their own homes assisted solely by formal help. This environmental reality is increasingly recognized by professionals, although perceptions of the interrelationship between these two sources of support may vary (Twigg, 1993).

Informal care provided by the family exacts a considerable emotional, psychological, and material burden on the providers (Belford, Gilleard, Whittick, and Gledhill, 1984; Townsend and Poulshock, 1986), particularly if the recipient is cognitively impaired (Bocquet et al., 1993). The dynamics of these support relationships are conditioned, moreover, by prior familial relations and social status.

For example, there is a disproportionate degree of social disadvantage among families in which a child provides support. Larger families, which are more common in disadvantaged backgrounds, are also disproportionately represented among those in which such support is provided. However, two clear groups emerge—a majority typified by upward social mobility, and a significant minority characterized by social immobility or regression.

These data place the public dimensions of familial caregiving in a new light. The ever-growing level of public expenditure on care for the aged seems to be currently less acceptable. This is due to the general improvement in living conditions of older persons, on the one hand, and to the emergence of new and competing social problems, on the other. Consequently, family caregiving is being increasingly invoked as a means for reducing the growth in welfare spending. But informal care is already at a maximum among the more disadvantaged elements of society.

Given this context, what might be the effect of a freeze in public support for assistance provided by informal sources? Affluent families are likely to continue to maintain a sufficient financial margin, enabling them to overcome a partial decrease of public support. However, for disadvantaged families, placing more emphasis on family caregiving will increase an already heavy burden. Would it not be wiser to encourage and assist familial support by means of public policy? The extent of informal support would increase through the availability of publicly financed infrastructures that enable individuals to continue to function independently in their interpersonal and professional life, while simultaneously caring for their relatives.

The significant increase in public funding for care of the aged has been accompanied by a steep rise in the mobilization of familial caregiving. What is the interaction between these two spheres? A comparative intergenerational approach shows no evidence of a reduction in the level of informal caregiving in the event of increased public intervention. On the contrary, the "norm of intergenerational solidarity" continues to apply.

Changing lifestyles, like the decrease in cohabitation and number of siblings and a growing individualism, impact on intergenerational support. A number of hypotheses can be offered regarding possible developments in light of these changes. The pivot generation seems to be close to its adult children. When the pivots reach old age, their children will more often be retired and available to assist them than at present. Can we assume that the latter will offer support, including cohabitation, since they themselves received considerable help from their parents?

Another trend is for young people to leave home later than in the past. We also note a higher level of recohabitation on the part of children who left the parental home at a later stage of their youth. It may, therefore, be predicted that this tendency will continue, leading to a strong trend to move back in with elderly parents weakened by bereavement or dependence.

Beyond these hypotheses, which contradict the claims of a decline in familial support, the fact that generations are surviving longer creates an important basis for prolonged mutual aid. The realization of this solidarity and the questions it raises are important not only in financial terms, but from the viewpoint of social cohesion as well. Family support is no longer solely a private matter—it is increasingly shaped by public policy.

4

The Elderly in Spain:
The Dominance of Family
and the Wherewithal of the State

*François Béland
and Maria-Victoria Zunzunegui*

In this chapter we describe the social networks of a sample of elderly people living in a Spanish city and consider the relationship between social network factors and socioeconomic status variables, health status, and use of formal services. The data for this discussion stem from a study carried out in 1993 in Leganés, a Madrid suburb of 171,400 inhabitants. This analysis is drawn from the first wave of a comprehensive longitudinal investigation of the aged cohort in Leganés, who comprise about 8 percent of the local population (Béland and Zunzunegui, 1995).

We pay particular attention in our discussion to the quantity, density, and content of social relationships (House, Landis, and Umberson, 1988). These factors are operationalized through four aspects of social network: (1) structural features of the network, (2) informal support for daily instrumental tasks (IADL) and functional tasks (ADL), (3) use of formal sources of social and medical care, and (4) evaluation of the quality of interaction with the major social network components and its relation to life satisfaction. The significance of these aspects on long-term care policy in Spain is discussed in the concluding section.

THE SAMPLE

The parameters for drawing the Leganés sample are based on the city registry, in which citizens of all ages must register for receipt of municipal and social services. We stratified the lists by age and gender and then randomly selected subjects by strata. After removing from the lists those who had either died or moved away, 1,542 subjects were identified and visited. Of this group, 82 percent proved to be accessible and agreed to participate in the study, which included both a "social questionnaire" of self-reported items filled out by all respondents with the help of an interviewer and a "medical questionnaire" administered by physicians to almost the entire sample (Léon, Zunzunegui, and Béland, 1995). The results reported in this chapter are weighted in accordance with the size of each of the strata, where necessary.

The study sample is representative of the Leganés elderly population and, to a considerable degree, of older adults in Spain in general. For example, the proportion of elderly women in the 65–74, 75–79, and 80+ age groups in the sample is, respectively, 57, 32, and 11 percent; the corresponding figures for elderly Leganés females are 59, 33, and 8 percent. The relative age distributions of elderly men in the sample and in the larger Leganés community are even closer. Marital status is similarly comparable, with 58 percent of both the sample and the elderly population in the city married and 37 percent of both groupings widowed; 11 percent of study respondents reside alone, as do some 14 percent of all Leganés elderly (Instituto Naciónal de Estadistica, 1992).

A similar picture emerges when addressing the elderly population of Spain as a whole (Instituto Naciónal de Estadistica, 1992). Age distribution rates and marital status are comparable to those reflected in the sample. The rates of those without schooling are also equivalent. On the other hand, nearly three times as many elderly people in Spain were never-married as proportionately in the study sample, and almost twice as many Spanish elderly live alone.

A number of health status indicators further substantiate the representativeness of the sample. For example, 6 percent of study respondents had more than four errors on the Short Portable Mental Status Questionnaire (SPMSQ) (Pfeiffer, 1975), a frequency that falls within the range of results obtained in Madrid (Bermejo and Colmenajero, 1993) and Zaragoza (Lobo et al., 1989). Moreover, severe problems of vision are as frequent in the Leganés sample as reported in Serrano (1990). Finally, self-rated health is ranked similarly by both the elderly respondents in our sample and the elderly population of Madrid (Ministerio de Sanidad y Consumo, 1995).

SOCIAL NETWORK STRUCTURE

Social network characteristics addressed in this analysis include the marital partner, the number of other persons in the respondent's family (that is, children and grandchildren, siblings, nieces and nephews), the availability of friends and, in particular, of a confidant, church attendance, going to a city or neighborhood *"plaza,"* and membership in a voluntary association. The frequency of interaction with family members and friends is assessed as the number of each seen or telephoned over a one-month period. Geographic proximity to network members is considered as the amount of traveling time to each respective residence (measured in minutes).

An additional category of interest to network analysis is the living arrangements of the respondent. This is addressed in four different measures: (1) joint residence with children, (2) joint residence with someone other than spouse or children, (3) being neither head of household nor spouse of head of household, and (4) the number of years without a change in living arrangements. The effect of living alone was found to be colinear with the three first measures taken together and thus is not considered separately.

The results present an interesting picture of the social milieu of elderly people in Leganés. On the whole, their networks are large and comprised mostly of family members. The majority are currently married (60 percent) and have an average of 2.9 children. About 7 percent are childless. Most respondents (85 percent) have living siblings—about 2.5 on average. An even greater percentage (96 percent) report having an average of 7.2 nieces and nephews. An almost equally high proportion (91 percent) have grandchildren—about 4.7 per respondent.

The importance of family in the social networks of elderly Spaniards is underscored by the identification of their confidants. Almost three-quarters of Leganés elderly report having a confidant. Among them, the two largest categories are spouse (48 percent) and daughters (29 percent). Non-kin, on the other hand, account for only about 6 percent of the network members identified as confidants.

However, the social networks of older adults in Leganés also seem to shrink over time: 32 percent of respondents report having lost a person close to them in the two years preceding the interview. The lost network member is most often a sibling (42 percent); somewhat less frequent are the loss of a spouse (10 percent) or of a very elderly parent (7 percent).

Just half of the respondents report having friends, and only four in ten are members of associations. One-third participate in activities of *Centro de Tercera Edad*—a center for third-age adults. On the other hand, more than half attend church regularly, and a large majority go to the central town or neighborhood *plaza* (83 percent).

Respondents report having frequent interaction with members of their social network. Almost all the children are seen at least monthly, and 80 percent of respondents with children receive telephone calls. Grandchildren are seen and telephoned as often as are children. Siblings, nieces, and nephews are seen and telephoned relatively less often. Among those with friends, over 90 percent see at least five different friends monthly, and almost half receive telephone calls. Not unexpectedly, confidants are seen almost daily, as follows from the fact that most of them are either the spouse or daughters.

In terms of geographic proximity, the nearest child and grandchild live about 22 minutes away, the nearest sibling nearly two hours away, and the nearest friend only one-quarter of an hour away. It seems that, on the average, the elderly respondents in our study have a friend in the neighborhood, a child and grandchild within the city of Leganés or in one of the other southern suburbs, and a sibling residing somewhere in the greater metropolitan area of Madrid. The standard deviation in travel time indicates, moreover, that extended family members had the greatest relative dispersion, and friends had the least. The relative dispersion rate of children and grandchildren falls between that of the other categories.

Finally, it should be mentioned that few older adults in Leganés (10 percent) reside alone. Most are at home with a spouse (58 percent) and many live with adult children (44 percent) and/or with grandchildren (33 percent). These categories are not mutually exclusive but nevertheless they allow us to conclude that multigenerational households are still frequent among the elderly cohort addressed in this study. This observation is underscored by the fact that 27 percent of respondents do not consider themselves or their spouse as the head of the household. Among those with a child in the household, furthermore, some 50 percent do not consider themselves as heading the household.

Correlates of Social Network Structure

In order to deepen our understanding of social networks among the Spanish elderly, we considered associations documented in the literature between selected network characteristics and socioeconomic, social network, and health variables (Antonucci, 1990). A logistic regression procedure was implemented to identify and to assess the strength of the correlates.[1] We spell out, first, the control variables applied in this analytic procedure.

The socioeconomic characteristics considered are age and gender, income, education, occupational status, and degree of autonomy on the job held before retirement. *Income* was self-assessed. For those with no personal income (14 percent), household income is substituted. The variable of *education* employed distinguishes four categories of respondents: (1) the illiterate, (2) those with reading and writing abilities but without formal schooling, (3) those with some primary-school education, and (4) those who had completed primary school.

In terms of *occupation*, two variables were set up. First, occupations are classified according to categories from the General British Registrar (1970) Classification: (1) professionals, administrators, and owners of firms (including farm owners), (2) middle management, (3) other white-collar workers, (4) farm workers (excluding owners), and (5) blue-collar workers. Wives who had never been in the labor force are attributed their husband's occupational status. Second is the extent of *autonomy* on the job, as measured by the number of traits accumulated across nine job characteristics on the Wright Social Classes Categorization Scheme (Wright, 1985). In this analysis, the autonomy variable is dichotomized between no autonomy at all and some autonomy or more.

The *social network* features used as control variables are principally structural characteristics (Seeman and Berkman, 1988). They include marital status and the respective count of network members in each of the social network categories described in the previous section.

Several variables were used to measure health status:[2]

- The number of *chronic illnesses,* as drawn from 13 illnesses listed in the United States National Health Interview Survey: hypertension, heart disease, circulatory problems, strokes, diabetes, respiratory diseases, arthritis, cancer, Parkinson's, cognitive deficiency or Alzheimer's, genito-urinary problems, cataracts or glaucoma, and digestive problems (National Center for Health Statistics, 1985). Respondents also had the opportunity to mention up to three additional chronic diseases.

- *Cognitive deficit* was assessed by the Short Portable Mental Status Questionnaire (SPMSQ) (Pfeiffer, 1975) adapted for use with a less educated sample.

- *Depressive symptoms* were assessed by means of the Hispanic Health and Nutrition Examination Survey Translation Form of the CES–D (Moscicki, Looke, Rae, and Boyd, 1989).

- A *functional impairment* measure was developed through correspondence analysis of questions on tasks requiring use of upper or lower limbs. Respondents were, thus, classified into one of three categories: (1) no physical impairment, (2) some impairment, and (3) severe impairment (Nagi, 1965).

- Correspondence analysis brought the measurement of *functional capacities* into greater focus. Respondents were classified on instrumental activities of daily living (IADL) according to three categories: (1) able to do all IADL, (2) able to do IADL with help, and (3) not able to do IADL. The analysis for activities of daily living (ADL) resulted in a four-category scheme: (1) functional in all of the ADL, (2) needing help in ADL requiring physical mobility, such as walking and going to the toilet, (3) needing help in ADL not requiring body mobility, such as eating, and (4) dysfunctional in ADL (Béland and Zunzunegui, 1995b).

- Finally, respondents were asked to self-assess their health status for a measure of *perceived health.*

We should note that not all the correlates are of equal importance in the regression procedure. Thus for some—as, for example, gender—we are interested in their direct effect on social network. Therefore, the gender variable is entered first. However, we are also curious to see how socioeconomic and health status may modify these associations.

Some correlates play a secondary role in the study. Chronological age, which is actually a flawed indicator of social, psychological, or, for that matter, biological age, is a case in point (Marshall, 1995; Schroots, 1995; Yates and Benton, 1995). Accordingly, we consider age as a residual variable and include it last in the regression equations. Variations in social network indicators not explained by other correlates are thus allowed to be associated with age.

The remaining socioeconomic indicators are considered in the regression in the order in which socioeconomic resources are usually accumulated in the life course: first education, then a job and its retribution in a retirement income. Moreover, we test whether middle-income categories have different social network characteristics from those in lower and higher income categories. People with a low income may not have the opportunity to develop and use their social network, while higher-income individuals may replace social network resources with paid resources. Thus, the income variable is squared to take into account a possible nonlinear relationship between income and social network features.

In general, social network characteristics as predictors of other social network features are entered in the regression equations after the socioeconomic characteristics and before health status. The social network factors employed as the main dependent variables are: (1) status as head of household, (2) co-residency with children, (3) co-residency with others, (4) availability of a confidant, (5) availability of friends, (6) going to the *plaza*, and (7) going to church. These network features may be sensitive to the availability of specific social ties, such as spouse, children and grandchildren, siblings, nieces and nephews, and friends.

Finally, it should be noted that our design allows for consideration of associations between various factors and social network characteristics given the socioeconomic context. Health status indicators are a case in point. SES provides resources through which health status is interpreted and social network resources are called upon. The multivariate procedure employed here takes this relationship into account.

In summary, the first variable considered in the regression equations was gender. In a second step, the socioeconomic variables were introduced in the order described above. The health status variables were not introduced at this stage. Some social network structural features, when appropriate, were introduced after the socioeconomic variables and before health status.

The main results of this stage of the analysis, which addresses the correlates of structural characteristics of the network, are presented next. We discuss both the partial results of relevant stages in the stepwise entry of control variables as well as the final collection of significant associations. Tables 4.1 and 4.2 present the regression results.

First, marital status as a network measure is associated with education, occupation, and income, when controlled for sex. The greater the education level, the greater the proportion of married persons: 40 percent among illiterates, as compared to 65 percent among those who completed primary schooling. A similar relationship is observed for occupational status, with 68 percent of professionals married and only 45 percent of former farm workers. These gradients may reflect a different probability for marriage with different schooling level and occupational status, the effect of socioeconomic status on mortality rates, or both.

The association of income level with marital status, on the other hand, is colinear, with more persons in the middle-income categories married than those at either end of the income scale. This partly reflects the consequence of widowhood on income for men and women—widows have a lower income than married women, whereas widowers have a higher income than married men. Finally, married persons with less education and low occupational status tend to have a greater number of children. For example, farm workers have one child more, on average, than do professionals.

Next, we consider the association of socioeconomic status, selected features of social network, and health status on the dependent social network factors of living arrangements and availability of interpersonal relationships. The results are summarized in Table 4.1. The intermediate findings suggest that living with children, living with others, and being neither head of the household nor spouse of head of the household are all associated with gender when this variable is entered first in the equation. However, gender loses its significance when civil status is subsequently considered.

Education, occupational status, and/or income are also related to living arrangements. Generally, the lower the values on these socioeconomic indicators, the higher the odds for sharing housing. The major exception is with income, where a nonlinear relation is evident in each of the living arrangements. Elderly people in middle-income categories have a lower propensity to share a residence with their children or with other people and a higher propensity to head their household.

Leganés elderly who share a household with someone other than a spouse and who are not the head of this household tend to be unmarried—widowed or single. Also, the number of children increases the probability of living with one of them, of not living with other persons, and of not heading a household. Finally, those without friends are also less frequently heads of households. The coefficient for this last association decreases with the introduction of health status variables but remains significant nonetheless.

Few health status variables, on the other hand, enter into the equation. Cognitive deficit is the primary health indicator for living with children—that is, people with no errors on the modified SPMSQ are less likely to live with a child and are more likely to head a household. It seems, therefore, that making a single error on the SPMSQ dramatically affects one's living arrangements. Also, needing help with or being unable to do IADLs is associated with both not heading a household and living with a child. Interestingly, the introduction of health status variables does not strongly affect the coefficient values for the association of social network structural features with the various dependent social network variables.

Availability of a confidant is associated with only a small number of predictors, chiefly with not having a friend. This may well stem from the fact that most confidants are family members. In fact, the social networks of Leganés elderly seem to be largely restricted to nuclear family members. Moreover, the more intimate interactions with family members are, the smaller the role of friends. However, the number of siblings is related to the availability of friends. It may be

Table 4.1: Logistic Regression of Living Arrangements and Availability of Interpersonal Relationships

Characteristics	Non head of household		Living with children		Living with others	
	b Entered	b Final	b Entered	b Final	b Entered	b Final
Gender	-.57*	.05	-.27*	-.02	-.39*	.17
Socio-Economic						
Illiterates	.69*	.19	.48*	.40*	--	--
Farm workers	.96*	.52	.47*	.26	.43*	.48*
Middle managers	-.80*	-.57	--	--	--	--
White collar workers	--	--	--	--	--	--
Autonomy on the job	--	--	--	--	-.35*	-.25
Income	-2.32*	-.25	-2.51*	-1.37*	-1.74*	-.76
Income squared	21.70*	4.29	24.70*	15.60*	17.20*	9.31*
Social Network						
Non-married	1.74*	1.48	.91*	.72*	1.05*	1.05*
# of children	-1.88*	-1.62*	2.91*	3.41*	-1.19*	-1.19*
# of grandchildren	1.16*	.79*	-1.92*	-2.34*	--	--
# of siblings	-.35*	.09	--	--	--	--
Availability of friends	.39*	.23*	--	--	--	--
Health Status						
No error on Pfeiffer	-.60*	-.34	-.38*	-.24	--	--
One error on Pfeiffer	--	--	--	--	--	--
Two errors on Pfeiffer	--	--	--	--	--	--
No depressive symptoms	-.01*	.08	--	--	--	--
Many depressive symptoms	--	--	--	--	--	--
No IADL incapacity	.59*	-.24	--	--	--	--
IADL with help	--	--	--	--	--	--
Age	.12*	.12*	.07*	.07*	--	--

that brothers and sisters are assimilated with friends, or the fact of having many brothers or sisters enlarges the pool of persons available for friendship, as siblings' friends become respondents' friends.

Finally, in relation to friends within the social network, women report fewer friends than men. Former white-collar workers have more friends than average, while former farm workers have fewer. Occupation loses its significance, however, when health status variables enter the equation. The availability of friends

Table 4.1 (*continued*)

Characteristics	Availability of a confidant		Availability of a friend	
	b Entered	b Final	b Entered	b Final
Gender	--	--	.32*	.25*
Socio-Economic				
Illiterates	--	--	--	--
Farm workers	--	--	-.36*	-.17
Middle managers	--	--	--	--
White collar workers	--	--	.26*	.23
Autonomy on the job	--	--	--	--
Income	--	--	--	--
Income squared	--	--	--	--
Social Network				
Non-married	--	--	--	--
# of children	--	--	--	--
# of grandchildren	--	--	--	--
# of siblings	--	--	.34*	.23*
Availability of friends	.27*	.26*	exc	exc.
Health Status				
No error on Pfeiffer	-.48*	-.48*	.19	-.00
One error on Pfeiffer	--	--	.25*	.10
Two errors on Pfeiffer	.54*	.54*	--	--
No depressive symptoms	--	--	.39*	.31*
Many depressive symptoms	--	--	-.57*	-.43*
No IADL incapacity	--	--	.55*	.55*
IADL with help	--	--	.37*	.37*
Age	--	--	--	--

*$p < .05$. exc.: Excluded from the equation.

diminishes with decreasing health, such as having two or more errors on the cognitive deficit scale, being depressed, and being unable to perform IADLs.

We also consider two activities that take place outside the closed family circle: going to the *plaza* and going to church. The results, which are summarized in Table 4.2, show that the former is mainly a male activity, while the latter is primarily a female one. Both activities are also associated in the same direction with education—that is, the illiterate go less often than average to the *plaza* and

Table 4.2: Logistic Regression of Social Network Activities

Characteristics	Going to the Plaza		Going to Church	
	b Entered	b Final	b Entered	b Final
Gender	.32*	.25*	-.51*	-.68*
Socio-Economic				
Illiterates	-.59*	-.36*	-.69*	-.52*
Farm workers	-.28+	.10	--	--
Income	-.14*	-.18*	-.10*	-.12*
Social Network				
# of siblings	.49*	.33*	.33*	.18
Availability of friends	-.23*	-.17*	-.21*	-.13*
Health Status				
2-3 chronic illnesses	.30*	.21	--	--
No error on Pfeiffer	.41*	.09	.32*	.15
One error on Pfeiffer	.27*	.10	--	--
No depressive symptoms	.35*	.29*	--	--
No physical impairment	.78*	.46*	--	--
Some physical impairment	.32*	.18	--	--
Severe physical impairment	-.42*	-.31*	--	--
No ADL incapacity	.55*	.59*	.22*	.22*
ADL incapacity with mobility	-.71*	-.77*	--	--
No IADL incapacity	.66*	.59*	.95*	.95*
IADL with help	--	--	.63*	.63*
Perceived health: bad	-.92*	-.93*	--	--
Age	-.04*	-.04	--	--

$* p < .05.$
+ Overall associations of occupational status with "going to the *Plaza*" was significant though no individual occupational categories reached the .05 level.

to church, associations that remain significant after controlling for the other variables. Low-income individuals are also less inclined to go to both places.

In terms of health status, going to the *plaza* is associated with health indicators, in the expected direction—that is, the healthier go more frequently. On the other hand, going to church is independent of one's health condition, except for those with a cognitive deficit and IADL disability, who attend church less.

Two social network structural characteristics are also associated with going to the *plaza* and/or to church: the number of siblings and the availability of friends. Both variables increase the odds for engaging in these activities. Thus, it seems that, once again, siblings and friends are associated with activities outside the purview of the nuclear family. However, when health status variables are entered into the analysis, they lower the coefficient of these two social network structural features. In the case of going to church, in fact, the network variables lose their significance.

INSTRUMENTAL SUPPORT

We examine the extent of instrumental support available from the social network in terms of help received on IADL and ADL. Respondents were asked whether they receive help on each of the ADL and IADL indicators cited in the social questionnaire and, if so, to name up to three sources. For each respondent, linkages with these sources (family member, friend, neighbor, volunteer, or staff from private or public agencies), frequency and duration of help, and co-residency with caregivers are probed.

A correspondence analysis of these data yielded five categories of frequency and duration of help for IADL: (1) those who do not receive help for any of the IADLs, (2) those receiving help each day for over a one-year period, and (3) those receiving help in the week preceding the interview. Two additional categories are applied separately, according to gender: for men, those receiving help on some IADL activities for at least a year, and those who receive help cooking meals and keeping house; for women, the two additional categories are those receiving IADL help once in a while and those helped frequently for heavy housekeeping tasks (Béland and Zunzunegui, 1995b).

Patterns of frequency and duration of help received for ADL are not viewed separately by gender according to correspondence analysis. Four response categories are utilized: (1) those without any ADL help, (2) those receiving help once in a while for at least a year, (3) those starting to receive help the week before the interview, and (4) those receiving help daily for over a year.

The results of the analysis indicate, first, that caregivers are essentially spouses or daughters; few sons give help, and other sources do not count for much. Of Leganés elderly, 16 percent receive help from at least one source for at least one ADL, while 89 percent do so for IADL. However, the amount of help varies. For example, 10 percent receive ADL help once in a while for a limited number of activities, and 2 percent had started receiving help the week before the interview. The number of persons in the latter group for whom this help is the beginning of a long episode of instrumental support, however, is unknown. On the other hand, 4 percent of Leganés elderly have been receiving daily help on ADL for more than a year.

Viewing the support findings in terms of gender, it is clear that more males (22 percent) receive daily help for more than a year than do females (12 percent), and the same is true regarding help available for no more than a week previous to the interview. However, the important distinction between men and women concerns help available for specific IADL tasks: 44 percent of the women report having had help for more than a year for heavy household chores, while 20 percent of the men have help on tasks usually viewed as "female housework" and on other types of tasks.

It is clear from these results that instrumental social support in IADL and ADL cannot be described appropriately with a simple dichotomous indicator. Receiving help on a daily basis for more than a year is not the same as receiving help for a week, nor is being helped on specific tasks for a number of months the same for men and women, as each are helped on different kinds of tasks.

Who is involved in these caregiving tasks? First is the spouse—in particular, the female spouse. Spouses aid 31 percent of those helped for ADL. Moreover, 74 percent of males receiving help for IADL had their spouse as a caregiver. For females, the corresponding figure is 33 percent.

Among elderly women helped with IADL, 58 percent are aided by daughters. However, in this sample of elderly Spaniards, daughters act less frequently as caregivers for their fathers. They account for 49 percent of the help received by males on IADL. Daughters' share of help for ADL is 40 percent. On the other hand, sons are much less involved: in only 5 percent of cases do they give help for ADL and in only 15 percent to 18 percent of the cases in IADL.

Other family members provide help even less frequently. In fact, the elderly in the sample pay for formal services more often than they receive informal help from family members other than spouse or children. Nevertheless, last among the sources of instrumental support are governmental agencies. They help a mere 3 percent of those assisted on ADL and no more than 4 percent of those receiving help with IADL.

Most of the help for ADL is provided by a person in co-residency with the care recipient (93 percent of those helped with ADL). Help from an external source is available to 10 percent of them, or 2 percent of the total sample. External sources of help, on the other hand, are more relatively available for IADL, and more so for women (35 percent) than for men (25 percent). Moreover, for men, a source of IADL help resides with them in 92 percent of the cases, whereas for women the corresponding figure is 83 percent.

In summary, instrumental support is widely available for IADL, while help with ADL is somewhat less so. This says little, however, about the relationship between the availability of help and the need for help. This topic and other correlates of instrumental support are spelled out next.

Correlates of Instrumental Support

In viewing the correlates of instrumental support, we continue to be interested in changes in the effects of social network features when other conditions are observed. For example, the association of living arrangements with availability of help is clearly documented in the literature (Chappell, 1991a; Tennstedt, Crawford, and McKinlay, 1993). But use of help for ADL and IADL also depends on functional capacity (Béland and Zunzunegui, 1995b; Thouez, Bussiére, Chicoine, Laroche, and Pampalon, 1994). Does health status explain away the association of living arrangements with help for ADL and IADL, therefore? To examine this issue, living arrangements are entered in the regression equations before health status. The results are discussed in the following sections.

The structure of instrumental support in ADL is essentially the same for men and for women. Moreover, we find few correlates of support for ADL in our sample. Only cognitive deficit, physical impairment, and functional incapacities in ADL are statistically significant predictors.

The structure of support in IADL, on the other hand, reflects the gendered distribution of housework: men receive help—that is, they do not themselves engage in meal preparation, doing the dishes, or washing clothes. Women receive help for heavy housework.

Results also reveal different predictors for receipt of help in IADL for each gender. First, although daily support in IADL increases along with educational level in both genders, male non-heads of household are helped more. On the other hand, more of the health status indicators are significant predictors of daily help with IADL among women. That is to say, though males with a health condition receive more help than do females in a similar condition, poor health status is more strongly associated with receiving help in IADL on a daily basis among women. Cognitive deficit, for example, is not associated with daily help receipt in males, while it is highly significant among females.

Frequent help for household tasks in males is associated with only one indicator of health status—that is, the number of chronic illnesses. Otherwise, only quality of interaction with children is positively associated with this type of help. In women, all but the depressive symptom indicators of health status are associated with frequent receipt of help for heavy household tasks, while the quality of relations with their children is negatively associated with help in IADL.

Thus, there is essentially no difference between men and women in help received for ADL. Predictors of such help include only health status indicators. But help in IADL is more gender-dependent. Though health status indicators are the prominent predictors of IADL help for both males and females, they are more powerful for the female respondents.

In order to understand better the correlates of help receipt, we examine the associations with each of five dependent variables: receiving help from (1) spouse, (2) daughters, (3) sons, (4) an external source of help, or (5) an internal source. The analysis utilizes a block logistic regression procedure.

First, comparing external and internal sources of help, the results show that females receive help from outside the home more than do males, while the reverse is observed for internal sources. Elderly illiterates tend to get more help from within the household, but lower-income elderly have less help from internal sources of care and more from outside the home. Middle- and higher-income elderly, on the other hand, have more help from someone living with them.

Social network indicators predict use of internal and external sources of help in different ways. The number of children increases the amount of help received from external sources, while living with children decreases it. However, not being head of household and living with children are positively associated with receipt of help from within the household. Quality of interactions with children is negatively related to receipt of help from internal sources.

Health status indicators are associated with both sources, but more of them significantly correlate with external than with internal sources. Age is also associated with external sources. Finally, all the social network variables, except for quality of interactions, remain significant after health status variables are entered into the equations.

Next is examination of help received on IADL from a spouse, daughter, or son. The small number of cases receiving help for ADL from a spouse or son impedes the use of multivariate procedures; the comparison is thus restricted to IADL. The results indicate that elderly females receive more such help from daughters and sons than do elderly males. Wives, on the other hand, are the main source of help to their husbands.

Illiteracy is a predictor of help received by children for either gender, but only in the case of daughters does this coefficient remain significant after other variables are considered. Elderly people working on a farm before retirement receive more help from children, while low-income elderly get more help from sons than do the higher-income elderly. Men receiving help from a spouse tend not to share a household with a child. However, receiving help from a daughter is more probable among individuals residing with a child. Also, help in IADL is associated with not being the head of household.

Health status indicators are highly associated with help for IADL, though for many of them the introduction of functional incapacity measures minimizes their effect. Similarly, the influence of social network indicators on IADL assistance is reduced after the health status variables are introduced, and some lose their statistical significance.

Finally, the age of elderly respondents is associated with the reporting of children as a source of help with IADL. It may be that age is an important consideration in children's actions toward their elderly parents. An aged parent may have a symbolic meaning over and above his or her actual health status and need for instrumental support. In fact, the parent's age may be an indicator, in the Spanish context, for the need for help from the children.

USE OF FORMAL SERVICES

Spain's social security system covers medical care, hospitalization, social services, and pensions for the elderly (Campos-Egozare, 1993; Rodríguez, and Sancho Castiello, 1995). Physicians affiliated with the National Health System are allowed to practice privately on a part-time basis. Home care and homemaking services for the vulnerable elderly are not yet well developed (Castells and Ortiz, 1992; Rodriguez and Sancho Castiello, 1995). Few firms offer services on a market basis for a paid fee. Paid domiciliary help, on the other hand, is available from freelance cleaning women.

Spain has a universal Medicare insurance system. Only 2 percent of the Leganés respondents have supplemental private medical insurance. A slightly higher proportion of respondents (5 percent) use private medical practitioners, while 97 percent receive their primary medical care at local health facilities known as *Centros de Salud*, which are publicly financed and organized ambulatory care centers.

In the framework of the larger longitudinal study, of which this study is a part, a list of 16 different health-care services was presented to respondents. In this analysis, the five most frequently utilized health-care services are considered. The use of formal services is measured in a dichotomous fashion: use or no use of services. The five health-care services addressed are: (1) visits to general medical practitioners (GPs), (2) GPs' home visits, (3) visits to a hospital emergency room, (4) hospitalization, and (5) visits to a general practitioner by a third party—that is, a visit to a GP made on behalf of the respondent by another individual.

In addition, the questionnaire presents several opportunities to assess the use of social services. First, as indicated earlier, sources of help received for ADL and IADL are available. Second, questions used to obtain an estimate of help received from paid sources, governmental agencies, or voluntary organization are also instructive. These relate to: (1) homemaking, meal preparation, grocery shopping, and transportation, (2) personal hygiene, eating, and dressing, (3) obtaining help for recruiting a nursing aid in the home, (4) obtaining help for bureaucratic procedures such as banking and inquiry regarding pension rights, and (5) solving a family problem. As there were few respondents (4 percent) using social services from a governmental agency, and a little over 10 percent using paid sources, we focus the analysis on use or no use of paid sources for social services.

Looking at the overall distributions, we see that 85 percent of the sampled Leganés elderly use GP services. Physician visits at home are reported by 24 percent of the sample, and 23 percent of them had someone else visit the physician on their behalf (third-party visits); specialists are seen by 28 percent of the respondents. Hospital emergency rooms were visited by 29 percent of Leganés elderly, and 15 percent were hospitalized. A total of 12 percent had used an ambulance. Paramedical services are used by a smaller proportion of our sample: about 6 percent had a nurse visit at home, and 7 percent received physical rehabilitation services. Few respondents used homeopaths (2 percent) or other non-medical therapists.

Help from either governmental agencies, paid sources, or voluntary associations was available to a small proportion of the elderly. Only 3 percent of Leganés elderly were helped in homemaking tasks by a governmental agency, 1 percent by voluntary associations, and 13 percent by a paid source. Help with ADL from these three sources was hardly utilized (0.6, 0.2, and 0.4 percent, respectively). Help from these sources with bureaucratic procedures was used even less.

It is not unfounded to conclude from these data that the main problem facing frail elderly and their caregivers in Leganés is not the coordination of formal sources of care with informal ones, but, rather, the availability of sources of care other than the informal. This is not to imply, nevertheless, that use of medical services and paying for homemaking are unassociated with network structural features and instrumental support. Nor does it imply that Leganés elderly reject help from governmental sources.

We knew that social and homemaking services are few in Leganés, as in Spain in general. We thus felt it important to ask about respondents' preference for source of care. Responses to the preference questions are different for elderly with functional incapacities and those without. Some 88 percent of those without functional incapacities prefer to be helped for homemaking tasks by their spouse. This figure drops to 62 percent among those with functional incapacities. Daughters and sons are also less preferred as a source of care by those with incapacities than those without. However, preference for formal sources of care such as governmental agencies is 45 percent, irrespective of functional capacity. The discrepancy between formal service availability and preference therefore seems to be profound.

Correlates of Use of Formal Services

In examining the correlates of formal service use, we pay particular attention to associations with social network characteristics. Social network structure is one of the foundations on which the use of both informal support and formal sources of help rest (Brody, Litvin, Albert, and Hoffman, 1994; Connidis, 1994; Feld and George, 1994; Freidson, 1970; Logan and Spitze, 1994). Moreover, aspects of social network may be intercorrelated. Thus, use of formal services may be correlated with help given by spouse, family members, or friends.

We apply logistic regression procedures, as before, with the following outcome variables: medical care services, hospitalization, use of paid sources of help for household tasks and social services, and preference for formal agencies in support for ADL, IADL, and social services.

As we learn from the findings, socioeconomic factors are initially significant for access to GPs, visits to a GP by a third party, and GPs' home visits. They lose their significance, however, when other variables are entered into the equations. Nonetheless, it is worth reporting that females, the illiterate, former farm workers, and those at the lowest end of income distribution tend to have more third-party visits to GP's. Educational level is significant in the final model only for emergency room visits—that is, more respondents with noncompleted primary education than average visit the emergency room.

Surprisingly, perhaps, few social network characteristics are associated with use of medical services, and most lose their significance when health status variables are considered. Nevertheless, having few siblings and not being head of household or the spouse of one increases the odds for having third-party visits to a GP. The number of siblings is also positively related to access to the GP's office. It may be that siblings' availability is related to having a peer with whom to discuss health problems, or that siblings provide means of transportation not otherwise available.

The same may be said regarding the positive association between the number of children and use of the emergency room. Adult children may encourage their elderly parents to refer to a medical service when a health problem is reported and/or they may provide transportation. Lastly, the frequency of GP home visits is also related to other help received.

A set of health status variables are related to all the types of use of GP services. These are the number of chronic illnesses, cognitive deficit, physical impairment, and IADL functional status. But not all of these variables work in the same direction. More individuals with cognitive deficit have GP home visits and visits by a third party than individuals without cognitive deficit. Also, respondents with physical impairment and IADL incapacities use more of these GP services.

Finally, age retains a significant association with GP home visits and third-party visits. These findings may not be problematic for GP home visits, but the case is different for those with third-party visits. The latter are generally people of low socioeconomic status with chronic illnesses, cognitive deficit, physical impairment, and IADL incapacities. It is they who receive part of their medical care through a third party—most usually a family member.

Respondents' access to the GP's office is related, in the expected direction, to the number of chronic illnesses. But those with no or few errors on the cognitive deficit scale, with only some physical impairment and able to do IADL and ADL tasks, are more prone to see GPs at their office. Ability to get to *Centros de Salud* would seem to be a main predictor of these visits.

Few variables explain hospital use. Neither socioeconomic status nor gender is related to hospitalization. Only one social network variable is significant: the number of telephone calls to children. Among the health status variables, chronic illness, functional capacity, and perceived health play a role. In sum, hospital use is related almost exclusively to need variables.

Use of paid help, on the other hand, is related to socioeconomic characteristics. The illiterate have lower use of paid help than the other respondents, while those from the highest occupational level have more. Though females use more paid services than males do, this association loses significance when other socioeconomic variables are considered, suggesting that women's socioeconomic conditions rather than their social network characteristics or health status are intervening factors.

Use of paid services decreases with better quality of interactions with children and with help received from daughters. It increases with help received from outside the household. It could be, therefore, that paid sources act as a substitute for the daughters' role as caregiver.

Paid sources of help are also related to physical impairment. This is relevant in that this variable is indicative of the ability to perform tasks, as opposed to the other dimensions of health status related to illness.

Preference for help from formal agencies is lower among the illiterate and former farm workers, and higher among middle-income categories. Formal helping agencies are also preferred by heads of household and their spouses, as well as by those already in receipt of an external source of help. These associations remain significant even after health status indicators are considered. Finally, the health status indicators themselves are highly significant predictors of preference for formal agencies—an insight into the needs for these services among the Leganés elderly.

QUALITY OF INTERACTIONS AND LIFE SATISFACTION

The quality of interactions in the social networks of our respondents is assessed by means of a modified Seeman and Berkman questionnaire (Seeman and Berkman, 1988; Seeman, Berkman, Blazer, and Rowe, 1994). For this analysis, five quality-of-interaction indicators are adopted. However, we apply the original form distinctly to (1) friends, (2) children, (3) spouse, and (4) a mix of other family members, as the Spanish elderly require their separation. Three of the resultant four scales have reliability coefficients over $\alpha = .70$, while the one with friends is a bit lower ($\alpha = .65$).

The results indicate that the quality of relations with spouse, children, family members, and friends is uniformly high. In this sample, the mean quality-of-interaction score with spouse is 18.2 out of a possible maximum score of 20.

Interaction with children was evaluated just as highly. Interactions with friends and other family members received a somewhat lower score, with means in the vicinity of 15.

Life satisfaction is measured by a single question using a five-point ordinal scale. Respondents are asked the extent to which, in general, they are satisfied with their life. Answers to the question on life satisfaction proved to be less skewed than the evaluation of quality of interactions. The mean score on the satisfaction measure is 2.3.

Given the highly skewed scores on the four scales of quality of interaction, we dichotomized the results for purposes of analysis. The first category thus includes respondents with scores in the lowest quintile, and the second category represents those in the next four quintiles. Satisfaction with life responses was also dichotomized, with those satisfied and highly satisfied with life in one category and those somewhat, not, or not at all satisfied in another.

Nevertheless, there are few correlates of quality of interaction. Males rate their interaction with their spouses more highly than do females, but gender is not related to the quality of interaction with the other tie categories. Quality of interaction within the nuclear family is lower than average for the illiterate and higher than average for those with some primary education. Finally, relations with children are better for high-income people.

Interestingly, social network characteristics do not correlate with evaluation of quality of interaction, except for a few noteworthy exceptions. One's relationship with a spouse is found to be better among those heading the household. Interactions with children and with family members are poorer than average for elderly respondents without friends. Use of out-of-household sources of care is negatively correlated with quality of interactions with family members.

The lack of depressive symptoms is associated with quality of interactions with all the tie categories, except for friends. In addition, interaction with children is sensitive to other health status variables indicative of problems with performance of roles such as physical impairment and functional capacities in ADL and IADL. Quality is higher when impairments and ADL and IADL incapacities are not present among elderly parents.

Satisfaction with life is higher for males than for females. However, when health status indicators are considered, the effect of gender is diminished. Autonomy on one's former job is also associated with life satisfaction, though here, too, health status indicators overcome the effect of this occupational variable. Income is the only other socioeconomic indicator found to be related to satisfaction with life. Middle-income people are somewhat less satisfied with life than either low- or high-income elderly.

Only one characteristic of social network is associated with life satisfaction, and that is number of children. Along with autonomy on the job, this variable reflects the influence of earlier occurrences rather than the current dynamics of relationships in old age. As can be expected, health status indicators are positively related to life satisfaction. Older persons in better health in Leganés are also more pleased with their lives.

DISCUSSION AND SOCIAL POLICY IMPLICATIONS

The social networks of older people in Leganés are built around the nuclear family. More than 90 percent of elders have children, almost half live with children, and one-third live with grandchildren. Confidants are mostly spouse or children, help is provided primarily by members of the nuclear family, and satisfaction with spouse and children approaches the maximum on measurement scales. Nevertheless, social life is not limited exclusively to the nuclear family. Half of Leganés elderly have friends, and almost as many are members of voluntary associations. These relationships are less satisfying, however, than those with children and spouse.

Friends are not instrumental in helping the elderly with ADL and IADL tasks. In fact, purchased care is more popular than is turning to friends, neighbors, or even siblings. Within family-provided care, female spouses help husbands more than they themselves are helped in return, but daughters are more supportive of mothers than of fathers. Governmental social service agencies help but a small minority of Leganés elderly, even though they are one of the preferred sources of help.

The social network characteristics of lower-class elderly, specifically the illiterate, former farm workers, and low-income individuals, present a consistent picture. They tend to share households with other people; they have fewer friends and go less to the *plaza* and church. Their use of medical services is also different, due mainly to poorer health: they have more physician visits by a third party, less paid housekeeping help, and less preference for help from formal social service agencies. Finally, illiterate lower-class elderly have a lower quality of interaction with their children and spouse.

The elderly at the lower end of the socioeconomic scale are thus at risk on a number of dimensions, especially since the public long-term care sector is underdeveloped in Leganés, as in Spain in general (Castells and Ortiz, 1993). The combination, on the part of this population, of family-limited social networks, lower-quality interaction, and lack of resources to pay for needed services puts them in particular jeopardy.

Social networks are also quite different according to gender. More females than males live with children or with others. Elderly women have fewer friends and go less to the *plaza*, though they attend church more often. They are helped primarily by a noncohabiting daughter, but they also make greater use than men of paid household assistance. Interaction with husbands is less satisfactory than interaction with wives, and elderly females are less satisfied than males with life in general.

Health status is another important source of variation in social network features. In cases of cognitive deficit, the social network shrinks in size and grows in intensity: confidants and friends are not available, going to *plaza* and church ceases, help increases from all sources, and use of in-home physician visits and third-party visits is greater. Physical impairments and functional incapacities are related to more-or-less the same social network features, while number of chronic illnesses and self-perceived health have more selective effects.

Social network features themselves are related to other social network characteristics and to availability of help, use of formal sources of care, and quality of interactions. First, the greater the number of nuclear family members, the greater the odds for living with one of them, for not being head of the household, and for getting help outside the household. Second, availability of siblings is linked with a more active social life outside the nuclear family: more friends are available, going to the *plaza* is more frequent, use of ambulatory medical care increases, and interaction with children is of a higher quality.

Our data clearly point to illiteracy and former work on the farm as the two main predictors of an almost complete reliance on the nuclear family for social relationship and help with household tasks. These two predictors are cohort linked. Middle-aged adults in Spain today are educated, and few of them are farm workers. Thus, in 25 years, when people 65 years old and over will constitute 20 to 25 percent of the Spanish population (Rodríguez, and Sancho Castiello, 1995), elderly cohorts will bear different characteristics. But in 1995, illiterate older people and former farm workers are a very specific cohort, with needs that have to be attended to.

The second category of elderly in need of attention is women. Here, also, the family bears the brunt of social support. Some older women also use private services, as family and public sources of help are unavailable. However, purchased care cannot be seen as a realistic alternative for women with low incomes.

We have shown that help from the family is mostly synonymous with help from a female spouse, or from a daughter. Given the scarce public resources devoted to institutional and community-based long-term care in Spain (Castells and Ortiz, 1992), it is clear that frail and dependent elderly would be in dire straits without women in their close networks supporting them. The question is, how should scarce public resources be allocated to respond to the needs of the worst off? While the data available here do not answer this question directly, some thoughts can be raised.

First, there is in contemporary Spain a collection of factors specific to this period. As in other western countries, women combine family with work responsibility (Duran, 1986). Elderly people count on traditional support from the family for their needs (Bazo, 1991a). In particular, some move from the countryside to be near their children, while public long-term care services in these areas are still underdeveloped.

Second, we have shown that elderly women are helped more than men from sources outside their household. They also pay for help more often than men, while their incomes are lower. However, it is well known that caregiving is easier when caregivers and care recipients co-reside (Chappell, 1991a; Tennstedt et al., 1993).

Third, the scarcity of nursing homes and senior housing means that the family feels the full burden of taking care of the very frail elderly (Bazo, 1991b). This is reflected in our data as well. The task faced by informal caregivers is huge, to say the least. Thus, Spain has to cope with specific conditions relevant to its transition to an aging society.

The search for solutions cannot but consider the specificity of this transitory period. On the one hand, policy will have to consider the problems families face in supporting their frail elderly, especially those moving from rural areas. On the other hand, the scarcity of actual resources in long-term care should be confronted head on, with policy choices clearly stated.

The rhetoric used by most Western countries in formulating long-term care policy—autonomy of the elderly, role of the family, maintaining the elderly in the community—cannot help formulate policy goals in Spain. These are not goals, but constraints on policymaking in the Spanish context. Unfortunately, this rhetoric has already made its way into major policy documents (INSERSO, 1993).

NOTES

1. The logistic regression coefficients considered here are deviations from the average of coefficients for all categories of a variable. This average is fixed at zero by definition. Thus, coefficient estimates are simply their deviation from zero, statistically significant if they reach the usual .05 level. This procedure was chosen for three reasons. (1) Coefficient estimates are easy to interpret. (2) The polytomous categorical variables were ordinal in this study; coefficient estimates for all of the categories of a single variable may reflect this order. (3) Some of the variables were continuous; odd ratios, though easier to interpret than logistic regression coefficients, do not make sense with continuous variables. Variables with a statistically significant coefficient when first introduced in regression equations were kept in even if they lost significance with the entry of other variables.

2. Health status variables were modeled according to the modified Johnson and Wolinsky Model proposed by Béland and Zunzunegui. The Johnson and Wolinsky work has its sources in the Nagi Model of relations between health status dimensions. The seven health status indicators were entered in four steps. In a first step, the number of chronic illnesses and cognitive deficit were considered; they were followed by depressive symptomatology and functional impairments. These were seen as consequences of chronic illnesses and cognitive deficit. Functional incapacities, ADL, and IADL were entered third, followed by self-perceived health, which was seen as individuals' reading of their health conditions.

5

Profiles of the Social Networks of Canada's Elderly: An Analysis of 1990 General Social Survey Data

Leroy Stone and Carolyn Rosenthal

This chapter presents a typology of the social networks of Canadians aged 65 or over.[1] The typology is based partly on theoretical notions and previous research concerning major features of social networks and partly on an analysis of data from the 1990 General Social Survey conducted by Statistics Canada. The 1990 General Social Survey database provides a representative sample, after record weighting, of the private household population—aged 15 or more—of Canada.

General Social Survey respondents are treated as the focal points of egocentered networks (Minor, 1983; Wellman and Hall, 1986). There is one network for each respondent. This leads to a total of 3,186 sample networks, 1,226 centered on older men and 1,960 centered on older women. These networks are classified according to a six-category network typology, with the help of the Quick Cluster procedure as implemented in SPSS.

For each network type, selected structural features and patterns of contact between elders and certain classes of network members, such as children, are described. The association of network type with the degree of support received by the elders from their non-co-resident children is also reviewed.

Limitations in the available data require that only the class of egocentered networks be addressed in this analysis. Moreover, our review of the theoretical literature on social networks leads to the conclusion that a specific subclass of egocentered networks needs to be defined if the present application of the General Social Survey data is to seem acceptable. We define and propose herein a subclass called *overlapping dyad sets*—all dyads in a network include the person who is the focal point.

An important related issue is how one sets boundaries to a network (Laumann, Marsden, and Prensky, 1983), and this is also discussed. It is proposed that the boundary of an overlapping dyad set is found by enumerating the dyads that are stable and involve recurrent interactions between the network focal point and others in the stable dyad pairs.

The chapter is organized as follows. Selected features of the 1990 General Social Survey are first presented. Then follows a discussion of major concepts and the methods used to develop the network typology. The next section presents the network types and some of their main attributes. The chapter closes with a description of the association of network type with the degree of support received by the elders from their non-co-resident children, and a general discussion of the results of the analysis.

SETTING AND STUDY SAMPLE

As noted, the data for this chapter are drawn from the microdata file of Canada's 1990 General Social Survey (GSS90). A General Social Survey has been taken each year since 1985. Its main purposes are to gather data on social trends and to provide information relevant to major issues of public concern.

The General Social Survey is a national sample of the population aged 15 years of age and older. Excluded from the sampling universe are residents of the Yukon and Northwest Territories, households without telephones, and full-time residents of institutions. Compared with the total population, these are tiny subgroups.

It should be noted, nevertheless, that full-time residents of institutions comprise a significant proportion of the population among older Canadians—about 8 percent at the time of the 1991 Census. More than 30 percent of the population aged 80 and over were residents of institutions. The exclusion of the institutional population means that the GSS90 will yield underestimates of the proportion of seniors that have "thin" social networks (Stone, 1988).

In GSS90, a total of 13,495 individuals were contacted, one per household. An interview response rate of approximately 80 percent was achieved. There was deliberate oversampling of seniors because that year's questionnaire focus module dealt with seniors' kinship ties and the social supports that older Canadians gave and received. The elderly subsample was comprised of 3,186 completed interviews.

The 1990 survey collected the following types of information: (1) existence of, proximity to, and frequency of contacts with parents, grandparents, siblings, children, and friends; (2) help given to and received from relatives and friends who did not reside with the respondent; (3) sharing of work on household chores among the respondent and selected household members.

Questions about sharing of household chores by co-residents of the respondents dealt with meal preparation, meal clean-up, house cleaning, laundry, and household maintenance, as, for example, repairs, painting, lawn mowing, and snow shovelling. These are the only questions that provide a basis for inference about the character of intrahousehold exchanges.

In the 1990 survey, questions about help received from persons not sharing the respondents' homes were in the area of instrumental supports: unpaid housework like cooking, sewing, and cleaning, house maintenance, transportation such as driving to appointments or to shopping, child care, personal care such as bathing and dressing, and financial support. The following format presents typical questions on these matters:

(F18)   During the past 12 months, has anyone from outside your household provided you with unpaid transportation, such as driving you to an appointment or shopping?

(F19a)   Who provided such help?
   [...]   son
   [...]   daughter
   [...]   parent
   [...]   brother/sister
   [...]   other relative
   [...]   friend/neighbor
   [...]   organization/other (specify)

(F19b)   How often did they provide this help?
   [...]   at least once a week
   [...]   at least once a month
   [...]   less than once a month

In 1990, all interviewing for the GSS was by telephone, with probability sampling used to draw the numbers called. The GSS employs Random Digit Dialing sampling techniques.

The microdata file for GSS90 contains a weight variable that allows estimates to take into account the sampling design, including the oversampling of the elderly. The numbers and tables shown in this chapter are based on the weighted data. With these weights, the data can be said to represent the Canadian private household population, which becomes the universe to which the findings of this study can be generalized.

METHOD OF NETWORK IDENTIFICATION

Before discussing any specific technique it is necessary to review the use of certain key concepts, as the phrase "social network" is used in a variety of ways in the literature (Bernard et al., 1990; Dalud-Vincent, Forsé, and Auray, 1994; Milardo, 1992; Sudman, 1985). The alternate ways share some common features; but there are also irreconcilable differences. This is brought out clearly by

McCallister and Fischer (1978, p. 132), who point out that mass surveys that produce data on the general population tend to be inappropriate for structural network analysis in the tradition of sociometry. They see such data as more appropriate for work done in the tradition of British anthropologists, "who use the network metaphor to understand individuals' social milieux."

This study uses the term *social network* to refer to what are often called egocentric social networks (Wellman and Hall, 1986). These networks are seen as having a specific focal point or center (ego). Given this viewpoint, there is dominant interest in sets of dyadic relations, all of which involve the focal point. Ideally, using the notion of a network would also entail consideration of relations among persons linked to the focal point.

The 1990 General Social Survey data were not collected with the purpose of supporting a study of the kind presented here. As a result, they offer no opportunity to portray networks in ways that allow for both the dyadic relations involving the network focal points—survey respondents—and the dyadic relations among persons with whom the network focal point is linked. Thus, the profiles presented here are based on decidedly partial views of the social networks of Canada's elderly. Doreian and Woodard (1994, p. 268) also discuss the issue of the "partial systems fallacy." A review of similar problems in the use of United States General Social Survey data is offered by Burt (1984).

Given more adequate data, we would view the networks differently, and the typology offered here might be altered. Because there is no alternative data source for any remotely similar Canadian sample of survey respondents, however, it is not possible to estimate the ways and the degree to which more adequate data would alter our view of the profiles of the social networks of Canada's elderly.

Overlapping Dyad Sets

Perhaps a useful way to think about the kind of social network that is measurable from the 1990 GSS data is to accept the following notion as a theoretical axiom. A subclass of egocentric networks is definable in the situation where there is no information about the patterns of dyadic relations among persons who are network members but are not in the set of network focal points for the purposes of the analysis in hand. We refer to this subclass of egocentric networks as social networks formed by overlapping dyads, or, to be more brief, *overlapping dyad sets*. An overlapping dyad set is a collection of dyads where a particular person—the network focal point—appears in every dyad.

How Dyadic Relations Are Identified

There are different ways to identify the dyadic relations that are at the core of the concept of social network as used in this discussion. Some ways focus on measuring actual interactions or exchanges taking place between the members of a dyad. Others focus on the focal point's perceptions of the roles and importance of certain individuals with whom he or she has relationships. This includes the person's sense of the reliability of particular persons as sources of specific kinds of help even if the help is not being currently received. Yet other ways rely on measuring patterns of contact that a network focal point has with other persons with whom he or she maintains key relationships, as, for example, spouse, child, and friend (Killworth, Johnsen, Bernard, Shelley, and McCarty, 1990; Sudman, 1985).

Where there are inadequate data to allow consideration of aspects of intradyad interactions beyond mere contacts, it is often necessary to augment the range of observations by eliciting information about whether persons in certain relationships to the network focal point exist at all. For example, are there any children alive, or does the person have any friends? The derived network methodology of the present study is reminiscent of the work of Adams (1968), in which respondents were asked to provide the names and locations of relatives.

Regardless of the kinds of information used to identify dyadic relations, there is major interest in the sizes of the networks (Killworth et al., 1990; Sudman, 1985). Thus, for example, analysts find out not only whether there are children alive, but how many of them there are, or how many friends the network focal point has.

The Network Boundary Issue

The prominent place of network size in the research literature, and in the results presented here, brings up the thorny issue of how one sets boundaries to a network. Ultimately, network boundary setting entails some arbitrary delimitation of the relevant population. Perhaps the classic statement of the orthodox procedure is that of Wellman (1988, p. 26). The first step is to ". . . define the boundaries of a population, compile a list of all the members of this population, collect a list of all the direct ties (of the sort the analyst is interested in) between the members of this population, and employ a variety of statistical and mathematical techniques to tease out some underlying structural properties of the social systems."

When dealing with national-level databases, such as GSS90, it is impossible to gather information on every member of the population and every relevant link for each population member. With this kind of large-sample database, which consists of respondents spread across an entire country, one is forced to set network boundaries somewhat arbitrarily. In principle, for the networks that are formed by overlapping dyad sets, the boundary of a single network is comprised of the set of all stable dyadic relationships—all involving the network focal point—that involve recurrent interactions between the network focal point and another person.

The potential bias in the data that arises from including too many dyads that are either unstable or fail to involve recurrent interactions is reduced by placing reasonable maxima to the counts of numbers of siblings, friends, and children. For this study, the maxima set are 10 for siblings, 15 for friends, and 3 for children. It is clearly understood that these maxima are arbitrary. Such boundary-setting is needed, nevertheless, if we are to remain reasonably faithful to the guiding concept. With networks defined as overlapping dyad sets, the boundary of a network is set by enumerating the dyads that are stable and involve recurrent interactions between the network focal point and others in the stable dyad pairs.

Other Relevant Information
Provided by the 1990 GSS

As indicated by the foregoing discussion, numbers of persons in selected relationships with the survey respondents and contacts with individuals with whom the relationships exist are among the kinds of information provided by the 1990 GSS to assist in delineating social networks in terms of overlapping dyad sets. The other kind of relevant information provided by the GSS pertains to selected instrumental supports given to and received from selected relatives and friends that do not share the respondents' homes, as reviewed earlier.

We have chosen to avoid using the survey data on exchanges of supports in defining the social networks of Canada's elderly. Instead, we raise, and briefly discuss, the question about the extent to which there is systematic association between type of social network—using the typology we introduce next—and the measured degree of social support received by the network focal point. In future analyses, it will be worth while to consider the association of network type with the pattern and degree of supports given by the network focal point, and the nature of the short-term reciprocity that is indicated indirectly when we take into account both the supports received and those given.

Statistical Aspects of Network Typology Development

The statistical phase of network typology development for this study involves the use of the Quick Cluster procedure from methods of cluster analysis (Anderberg, 1973). The choice of this method was influenced by the fact that Quick Cluster has also been used for research on networks in at least one other country where somewhat similar data were gathered (Litwin, 1995b). Once cluster analysis is adopted as the strategy for classification of the networks, it is extremely difficult to avoid using Quick Cluster with a large sample of observations (Anderberg, 1973).

The numbers provided to Quick Cluster for one respondent comprise a profile of features of that respondent's social networks. In the remainder of the chapter we will often use the phrase *social network profile* when addressing as a whole the GSS90 information, as we have synthesized it, about the respondents' social networks.

The features of the social network profile used for this study include:

1. a network-size index;
2. an index of the relative (proportional) shares of the following components of the network size index—children, siblings, friends, parents, and spouse;
3. the presence of a spouse or partner;
4. living arrangement;
5. an index of the frequency of seeing and telephoning each of children, siblings, friends, and parents.

The values for the indices of the frequency of contact with children and parents rise when the respondent resides with a child or parent, respectively. As relatively few respondents had a parent alive, due to the restricted age range of the sample, data for the parent share of network size are not shown in the tables that follow. Also, the parent contact variable has little influence on the cluster results and is not discussed at any length here.

A few remarks about the derivation of numbers for the social network profile criteria are in order. The network size index is a simple accumulation of numbers drawn partly from answers to questions about the existence of certain kinds of relatives still alive and friends. As already noted, certain maxima were set for the numbers of friends (15), siblings (10), and children (3). For respondents whose social networks involve numbers that go beyond any of these maxima, an aggregate of their numbers of friends, siblings, and children is essentially an index number that stands for the real network size.

We assume that this index is valid when it is used for the purpose of separating persons with widely differing network sizes. Toward this end, it is not necessary to know the size of the network precisely. Moreover, the very concept of precise network size needs careful exposition in light of the fact that "there are several possible universes in which one can make estimates of network sizes . . . close relatives . . . more distant relatives, neighbours, coworkers, comembers in organizations, friends and acquaintances" (Sudman, 1985: 133).

In any event, it is quite clear that under a wide variety of approaches to network measurement, precise and accurate measures of network size are generally not available. Sudman (1985) has found, for example, that while, on average, numerical estimates provided by respondents represented a reasonable approximation of network size, there nevertheless existed significant variability in the accuracy of such estimates. It is also the case that the derived network size is quite sensitive to the method used to delineate the network (Doreian and Woodard, 1992; Killworth et al., 1990).

The network composition index (Item 2) is computed from the network size index and its components. These ratios are themselves also somewhat arbitrary index numbers. However, it is assumed that a network with a high value of proportion of children and a low value of proportion of friends is different in kind from one with a low value of proportion of children and a high value of proportion of friends.

The presence of spouse or partner and living arrangements (Items 3 and 4) are drawn from the GSS90 living arrangements variable. The presence of a spouse or partner variable allows identification of both legally married spouses and partners living in a common-law union.

We also took the unusual step of bringing the full range of living arrangement categories into the clustering process. Key categories of the living arrangement variable thus include living alone, living as a couple (2-person household), living with spouse and others, and living with others such as children (no spouse present). It is understood that, given these categories, a spouse has a sort of double weight when the clustering procedure gets under way: the spouse is first reflected in shares of network size and again in the applicable category of the living arrangement variable.

The living arrangement variable was included because GSS90 lacks an appropriate set of variables that directly reflect key interactional aspects of social networks. For those aspects, the household composition is often a major determinant. Thus, in effect, the clusters found by the computer were influenced by the respondents' living arrangements.

The contact index (Item 5) involves categorization of frequency of contact in terms of the following range: daily, weekly (not daily), monthly (not weekly), occasionally, and not at all. The highest level is that of co-residence, and the next-highest is daily contact by seeing or by telephoning (for non-co-residents only). The lowest level is no contact. Persons for whom "not applicable" is the proper response—as, for example, contacts with children for those who have no children—are placed in the "no contact" category for the purposes of this study. This is based on the idea that what matters in network measurement is that there is no contact, and not why there is none, though in other contexts this may be an important issue.

Cautions with the Use of Quick Cluster

Usable output from Quick Cluster requires that the analyst tell the computer the number of clusters to derive; it then finds the best possible allocation of the social network profiles among that number of clusters so as to maximize the intercluster differences, as measured by Euclidean distance, and to minimize intracluster ones.

We experimented with several different numbers before selecting the one used for the analysis presented here. Our choice was based partly upon our preconceptions about appropriate typologies. These preconceptions are based upon current theoretical notions concerning the support networks of the elderly, and on results of past Canadian research (Chappell and Prince, 1994; Connidis, 1989; McDaniel, 1994; McDaniel and McKinnon, 1993; Stone, 1988). Thus, it is important to keep in mind that the groupings we discuss below are partly constructed as well as partly discovered typologies of social network profiles, with older Canadians as the network focal points.

SOCIAL NETWORK PROFILES

In presenting the results of our explorations with the GSS90 data, we are electing to proceed directly to the typology that emerged from Quick Cluster and our interpretations of the data. This means that we are avoiding portrayals of how older Canadians are distributed among categories of the variables that were used as input data to Quick Cluster.

Among these variables, only the network size index would provide a basis for a discussion that would be substantially different from what one encounters in reviews of profiles of Canada's senior population on such variables as living arrangement distribution, or pattern of contacts with children (Desjardins, 1993; Gee, 1995; Norland, 1995; Stone and Frenken, 1988). How the network size index differentiates between the clusters of social networks is, however, important. To that we will turn immediately as we introduce the clusters found.

Table 5.1 displays two sets of six clusters each—one for men and the other for women.[2] We might have shown just one set of clusters and then later asked what proportion of men and women are in each kind. This would facilitate a discussion as to whether a particular kind of structure has the property of being more or less suitable for or attractive to older men (or women, as the case may be). Our view is that it is more useful to begin with the theory-based notion that whether the focal point of the structure is an older man or an older woman will have a great bearing upon the nature of structure that is likely to be observed. Given this fact, the best way to accommodate the powerful force that gender exerts on network structure and functioning is to portray men's and women's clusters separately.

In giving names to the clusters, we have tried to produce short names that can be easily spoken and which bring to mind essential cluster features. In the process, the names oversimplify the nature of each type and its internal variability. This should be kept in mind as the names are used.

"Small: Friendship-Poor and Socially Isolated" Network Cluster. Some 19 percent of older Canadian men and 18 percent of their female counterparts are classified as falling into this kind of cluster. Especially among women, it is a small-family-dominated type. For this type of social network, moreover, the proportion of friends is substantially below average. Its highest level of interaction, among persons not co-residing with the respondent, is with children. Compared to other clusters, however, its rates of interaction with children are well below average. For both sexes, this cluster has the second-lowest rate of inter-

Table 5.1: Structural Features of Network Clusters by Gender of the Networks' Focal Person

Variables	Friendship-Poor, Socially Isolated		Small Child-Focused		Extended Family and Friends-Focused		Medium Balanced		Large Balanced		Very Large Balanced	
	Female	Male	Female	Male	Female	Male	Female	Male	Female	Male	Female	Male
Size Index	3.86	4.19	8.71	8.02	8.31	10.06	14.38	14.43	19.44	19.19	25.50	24.02
Proportion of children	0.38	0.37	0.29	0.32	0.05	0.17	0.16	0.15	0.12	0.11	0.11	0.10
Proportion for spouse	0.07	0.20	0.05	0.10	0.03	0.07	0.04	0.06	0.03	0.04	0.03	0.04
Proportion of siblings	0.27	0.28	0.30	0.30	0.34	0.33	0.30	0.23	0.20	0.19	0.30	0.28
Proportion of friends	0.25	0.14	0.36	0.29	0.58	0.43	0.51	0.56	0.65	0.66	0.57	0.58
Parents contacts index	0.57	0.58	0.50	0.27	2.38	1.92	0.66	1.47	0.52	1.14	1.38	0.63
Children contacts index	0.88	0.76	1.38	1.34	0.11	0.73	1.16	1.00	1.24	1.04	1.23	1.12
Sibling contacts index	0.50	0.60	0.99	0.86	1.25	1.15	1.08	0.86	1.02	1.13	1.17	1.40
Friend contacts index	0.56	0.38	1.05	0.08	1.08	1.28	1.07	1.11	1.17	1.20	1.07	1.23
Percent by sex	17.70	18.70	32.70	18.60	10.00	17.10	24.30	18.60	11.40	18.50	3.60	8.20

Source: Statistics Canada, 1990 General Social Survey.

action with children, and the lowest rates of interaction with both siblings and friends.

The comparatively low rate of interaction with children shown in this cluster is at first surprising when one observes that children form a much greater than average share of the network size in this network type. However, the observation is understandable when one assumes that this share merely reflects a severe lack of other network members, especially friends.

The lack of other network members is particularly notable in the male-centered profiles within this cluster, since a far higher than average 20 percent of network size is comprised of the man's wife. The men in this cluster are thus quite socially isolated, with one important caveat—most are married. Thus they may not be as socially isolated as their female counterparts, where only 7 percent of network size, on average, is comprised of a spouse/partner.

Both the relative and absolute numbers of friends are low for women in this network type. In fact, women in this cluster report only one friend, on average.

It may not be unreasonable, therefore, to characterize these women as "social isolates." They are a vulnerable group because of their small network size and their lack of connections to the few network members they do have. Particularly noteworthy is the lack of contact with children, who often represent the last line of social contact for persons with diminishing social networks. The low rate of contact with children might be due to geographical distance, fewer children compared to other types, or perhaps, in some cases, estrangement.

"Small: Child-Focused" Network Cluster. This type of network is small and child-focused in structure and interaction. It is associated with 33 percent of older Canadian women and 19 percent of the older men. Both men and women have high levels on the proportion of children in the total network and higher levels of interaction with children than is true of the other clusters.

However, there is a systematic gender difference with regard to interaction with siblings and friends. The men show comparatively low rates of contacts with siblings and friends. In the case of women, the rate of interaction with friends is slightly above the average for all women, and that regarding siblings is just slightly below the average.

"Small: Extended-Family and Friend-Focused" Network Cluster. Some 17 percent of older Canadian men and 10 percent of their female counterparts have networks that fall into this cluster. For both men and women, this type is marked by small networks dominated by siblings and friends and characterized by the relative absence of children. Among women only, the relative shares of children are lowest among the network types. For men, the rates of interaction with friends are the highest among the network types, while those with siblings are the second-highest. For women, the rates of contact with siblings are the highest among the clusters.

Women who are focal points of this kind of network are less likely than average to have a spouse/partner. Given the relative absence of children, it may be hypothesized that many of the women at the center of this type of network are lifelong singles. The lack of children is compensated for by the strong presence of siblings in both structure and interactions—in other words, the childless elderly who, in the absence of children, emphasize extended family and friendship ties (Allen and Pickett, 1987; Connidis, 1989).

It is noteworthy that women at the center of this type of network have by far the highest rate of contact with parents, though the absolute level of contact is very low, since so few persons still have a parent alive. This adds support to the general picture of greater extended family contact among never-married and childless women. A relatively high rate of contact with parents, in comparison with the other clusters, is also shown for the networks of this type that are centered on men.

However, the networks that are "small: extended-family and friend-focused" with men at their focal points exhibit some systematic differences from those with women at their focal points. Among these differences are the observations that the male-centered networks have a greater proportion of both children and spouses in their networks.

"Medium: Balanced" Network Cluster. Compared to the network types already discussed, the remaining three kinds may be said to be balanced in the sense that they fail to show levels of dominance of either family or friends similar to those indicated earlier. The balanced networks are also distinctly larger than those discussed previously. Although the network size variable does not support ratio calculations, it may be suggested that the balanced networks tend to be at least twice as large as any of the others already mentioned.

The "medium: balanced" network type contains 19 percent of older Canadian men and 24 percent of senior women. It is the second-most-common kind of network for older Canadian women. Compared to the network profiles already discussed, moreover, contact rates with children and friends are neither strikingly low nor strikingly high—they are "in the middle."

"Large: Balanced" Network Cluster. This network type is distinguished from the "medium: balanced" profile not only in size, but also in the relatively greater presence of friends and higher rate of interaction with them. In fact, the relative share of friends in the network centered on women is greatest for this type. In addition, among the networks with women as the focal point, this type has the highest rates of interaction with friends. Over half of these women also have a spouse/partner. This network type represents 11 percent of older Canadian women.

Among men, on the other hand, 19 percent of whom are at the center of "large: balanced" networks, there are higher-than-average rates of interaction with friends, children, and siblings. This subgroup of older men has the third-highest rate of interaction with both friends and siblings.

"Very Large: Balanced" Network Cluster. This is the class with extensive networks. It represents relatively few older Canadians—4 percent of Canadian women aged 65 or more and 8 percent of their male counterparts. Networks of this type exhibit high rates of contact of each kind—contacts with children, siblings, and friends. The great majority of women at the center of these networks live with a spouse or partner.

Although the measurement scales for most of the components of the network size index are arbitrarily truncated, there are strong indications that networks of this kind genuinely have relatively large numbers of ties of each kind. Given this situation, these networks might be expected to show patterns of interaction that show no great concentration on any specific type of contact. This pattern is especially evident for the networks centered on women.

Among networks of this kind centered on men, there are much higher than average rates of interaction with siblings, friends, and children. Among these male-centered networks, we find the highest rates of interaction with siblings and friends and the second-highest rate of interaction with children.

PATTERNS OF INTERCLUSTER VARIATION

In turning to a brief review of intercluster variation with regard to variables that are not integral to the discussion of network size or frequency of interaction, we have elected to review living arrangement and help received from children who do not live with the respondent.

The choice of living arrangement is important, because the full picture on social supports received cannot be constructed from the 1990 GSS. This is because the range of supports covered for intrahousehold exchanges is far narrower than is the case for interhousehold exchanges. Also, the content of the questions asked differs fundamentally. The best one can do, therefore, is offer the discussion on living arrangement as the next-best alternative to a proper discussion of intrahousehold exchanges of supports.

Table 5.2 shows distributions for the clusters of network profiles with regard to living arrangement, with separate panels for men and for women. Living with a spouse, and possibly with others such as children, is by far the dominant pattern among the *balanced* network types. In these clusters this pattern represents far more than one-half of the network profiles, when men and women are aggregated. Also, for both sexes together, and among the balanced clusters, the larger the clusters' average network size, the greater is the predominance of living with a spouse or partner, including possibly children in the home. In none of the remaining three kinds of cluster is as much as 50 percent of the network profiles comprised of living with a spouse, for the two sexes taken together.

Table 5.2: Distributions of Respondent Living Arrangements by Cluster

Living Arrangement	Friendship - Poor, Socially Isolated			Small Child - Focused			Extended Family and Friends - Focused		
	Both	Female	Male	Both	Female	Male	Both	Female	Male
Alone	38.1	53.2	18.9	28.7	38.0	11.6	49.9	61.0	33.8
Spouse only	43.7	22.0	71.2	48.6	39.0	66.1	31.6	20.7	47.4
Spouse, children[a]	4.6	5.1	4.0	7.7	4.8	13.1	6.3	3.0	11.0
Spouse, others[b]	1.1	1.5	0.6	0.5	0.2	1.0	2.1	1.8	2.7
Children, others[c]	8.2	12.6	2.5	11.5	14.8	5.4	0.0	0.0	0.0
Parent, others[d]	2.0	2.7	1.0	1.6	1.7	1.6	7.2	9.8	3.5
Non-relative	2.3	2.7	1.8	1.4	1.5	1.3	2.8	3.7	1.5
Total	100.0	100.0	100.0	100.0	100.0	100.0	100.0	100.0	100.0

Table 5.2 (*continued*)

Living Arrangement	Medium Balanced			Large Balanced			Very Large Balanced		
	Both	Female	Male	Both	Female	Male	Both	Female	Male
Alone	26.5	35.3	11.1	20.9	33.2	11.1	14.1	20.5	9.3
Spouse only	52.9	46.8	67.0	59.3	49.5	67.0	51.4	41.9	58.6
Spouse, children[a]	9.4	4.2	16.6	10.4	2.6	16.6	22.9	25.0	21.3
Spouse, others[b]	1.6	2.1	2.8	1.9	0.9	2.8	6.1	0.0	10.7
Children, others[c]	6.5	8.7	1.9	6.3	11.8	1.9	4.2	9.7	0.0
Parent, others[d]	1.6	2.0	0.5	0.9	1.3	0.5	1.3	2.9	0.0
Non-relative	1.5	1.0	0.1	0.4	0.7	0.1	0.0	0.0	0.0
Total	100.0	100.0	100.0	100.0	100.0	100.0	100.0	100.0	100.00

[a] possibly others   [b] no children   [c] no spouse   [d] no spouse, no children.
Source: Statistics Canada, 1990 General Social Survey.

It seems that men are primarily responsible for the pattern just outlined. By adding the figures for all lines that use "spouse" in the row heading of Table 5.2, it can be seen that among men, more than three-quarters of the network profiles show residence with a spouse. In the case of the "very large: balanced" cluster, the percentage goes above 80 percent. The corresponding figure for women is 66 percent in the "very large: balanced" network type.

Although living alone or with others excluding a spouse is not rare among the balanced clusters, it is much more prevalent among the remaining clusters. Particularly notable are the "small: extended-family and friend-focused" and the "small: friendship-poor and socially isolated" clusters, in which living alone comprises 50 and 38 percent, respectively, of the network profiles. Women are primarily responsible for this pattern, as it is not shown among the male-centered network profiles. However, in the "small: extended-family and friend-focused" profiles, one-third of the male-centered ones involve living alone, and among the "small: friendship-poor and socially isolated" profiles, close to 20 percent of the male-centered ones involve living alone.

The "small: child-focused" cluster is notable for having over 10 percent of the respondents living with a child and no spouse present. Living with nonrelatives is most common in the "small: extended-family and friend-focused" and "small: friendship-poor and socially isolated" clusters, while living with a parent is most common in the "small: extended-family and friend-focused" cluster. These patterns are shown more sharply in the case of the female-centered network profiles than the male-centered ones.

The foregoing remarks suggest that when one is faced with a gap in network interaction data as severe as that of Canada's GSS90, a detailed living arrangements variable should be considered in designing clusters of social network profiles. This conclusion is strengthened when we look at cluster differences in patterns of help received from children.

Table 5.3 shows two sets of distributions for the clusters of network profiles with regard to frequency of help received from a child who did not live with the respondent. As listed earlier, the kinds of help considered in the index of frequency of help fall in the class of instrumental supports. The levels of the index range from none to very high. A person is rated as having very high help when he or she receives weekly help from a son or a daughter on at least two of the five kinds of supports measured. The next level, high, means weekly help of one type or monthly help of two kinds. As we move from high toward none, either the number of kinds of help received, the intensity, or both, decline.[3]

One set of distributions in Table 5.3 is for persons living as a couple in two-person households. The other set is for persons who live alone. These sets are specially chosen so that help from co-residents of the respondent other than a spouse would be held constant at zero across all the clusters.

In the households occupied by a couple and no other person, high or very high frequencies of help received from children are most likely to be found in the

Table 5.3: **Distribution of Cluster Members by Frequency of Help Received from a Child Who Lives Elsewhere**

Help Frequency	Friendship-Poor, Socially Isolated		Small Child-Focused		Extended Family and Friends-Focused		Medium Balanced		Large Balanced		Very Large Balanced	
	Living as a couple	Living alone	Living as a couple	Living alone	Living as a couple	Living alone	Living as a couple	Living alone	Living as a couple	Living alone	Living as a couple	Living alone
None	75.5	57.5	75.2	51.3	73.6	84.5	76.0	66.8	75.6	64.3	80.2	41.4
Low	6.0	7.7	6.4	8.6	17.3	7.4	9.7	7.9	9.2	3.3	4.6	5.7
Medium	5.8	12.4	9.1	18.5	0.0	8.1	6.8	10.2	8.6	15.8	7.9	12.3
High	11.2	19.0	8.8	18.6	9.1	0.0	6.9	13.1	6.5	12.6	7.3	31.9
Very high	1.5	3.5	0.5	3.0	0.0	0.0	0.6	1.9	0.1	4.1	0.0	8.8
Total	100.0	100.0	100.0	100.0	100.0	100.0	100.0	100.0	100.0	100.0	100.0	100.0

Source: Statistics Canada, 1990 General Social Survey, with index developed by Leroy Stone based on Payne and Strain (1990).

"small: friendship-poor and socially isolated," "small: extended-family and friend-focused," and "small: child-focused" clusters. Among these network profiles the "small: friendship-poor and socially isolated" one stands out in terms of having a substantial percentage of networks in which there is high-frequency help received from children (just over 12 percent of the cases in this cluster) where there is a couple-only household.

Across all the clusters, the couple-only households have a fairly similar level of reporting no help received from children. The range is from 74 percent for the "small: extended-family and friend-focused" network to 80 percent for the "very large: balanced" type. The same is not true for the set of persons living alone, however. Here the range starts as low as 41 percent for the "very large: balanced" type and reaches 85 percent for the "small: extended-family and friend-focused" network cluster.

The rate of receiving high-frequency help from children is far more impressive for persons living alone than for couples. In the "very large: balanced" network clusters just over 40 percent of persons who live alone have high-frequency help from children. Rates close to 20 percent are estimated for both "small: friendship-poor and socially isolated" networks and for "small: child-focused" ones. Two of the remaining three clusters have rates of high-frequency help from children well above 10 percent. The "small: extended-family and friend-focused" profile is a striking exception, with zero percent estimated as the rate of receiving high-frequency help from children. As this cluster consists of by far the highest percentage living alone, it can be hypothesized that it has an unusually large proportion of childless older women.

The foregoing remarks suggest that the clusters have meaningful patterns of variation as regards aspects of instrumental supports exchanged by the persons designated as the social network focal points. This finding is reasonable in light of the systematic variation among clusters in terms of size, scope, and interaction patterns. Thus general morphological and functional features of network clusters are pointers to actual and potential rates of involvement in the exchange of social supports (Chappell, 1983; Stone, 1988; Wellman and Hall, 1986).

This finding is supported by the work of Litwin (1995a), which considers the social networks of elderly recent immigrants to Israel. He examined four types of support—emotional, instrumental, affirmational, and advocacy assistance—and found that, overall, family-intensive social networks were the most supportive.

CONCLUSIONS

As this analysis demonstrates, there are gender differences in the frequency with which individuals are distributed among the six types of network profiles. Men are comparatively evenly distributed, with five of the six profiles each comprising between 17 and 19 percent of the male population. One cannot, therefore, point to one or two typical network patterns for older men. Women, in contrast, show more irregular distribution, ranging from 4 percent to 33 percent. The two most prevalent profiles characterize 57 percent of the female population, making it possible to discuss common patterns.

A gender difference that runs through all the network profiles is that the great majority of men in all network types are married, whereas for women the proportion married varies markedly among network types. As rates of widowhood are higher for women (Martin-Matthews, 1991), a consistent gender difference across network types is that higher proportions of women live alone. Higher proportions of women also live with children but no spouse, with the exception of the "small: extended-family and friend-focused" profiles, in which neither men nor women live with children in the absence of a spouse. These differences point to the greater vulnerability of older women, because they live alone—an issue which we discuss further.

When living alone is no longer a viable option—for example, when needs for care become great or when income is insufficient to support independent living—some women move in with a child. Although this is not usually a desired solution, given the North American preference for independent living arrangements (Connidis, 1983), which facilitate intimacy at a distance, it is an arrangement that characterizes between 8.7 and 14.8 percent of women in five of the six types.

In the largest network type ("very large: balanced"), a fairly high proportion of both men and women—21 and 25 percent, respectively—live with a spouse and children. It is very likely that these children are still living in the parents' home, since married couples do not typically move in with children (Rosenthal, 1986; Speare and Avery, 1993). Moreover, the children who are living with their parents are most probably the youngest in large families. These children have not yet reached the "leaving-home" stage of adulthood. This also implies that the parents, although 65 years old or older, are still in the early years of later life.

A much higher proportion of women than men has a "small: child-focused" network type—33 percent versus 19 percent. This is likely to be related to the greater prevalence of widowhood among women and the concomitant increase in contact with children (Martin-Matthews, 1991; Rosenthal, 1987).

Among people who have children, those who live alone are much more likely to get help—and high levels of help—from children than those who live with a spouse, with the exception of persons in the "small: extended-family and friend-focused" network type. This pattern has been commonly identified in other research, wherein a spouse is the first line of assistance in the event that assistance is needed (Shanas, 1979; Stone, 1988; Stone et al., 1987).

Close to one in five older Canadian men and women have a "small: friendship-poor and socially isolated" network type. Especially among women, a high percentage of such persons live alone. These older adults are a vulnerable group. They have small networks and tend to lack connections with the few network members they do have. Many men with this network type are married, placing them at somewhat less of a disadvantage than their female counterparts. Nonetheless, an old isolated couple is in a vulnerable situation with advancing age and age-related needs for social support (Johnson and Catalano, 1981a).

It is interesting that men and women in the "small: friendship-poor and socially isolated" network type who live alone and who have children do, in fact, get help from children, despite the fragility implied by the structural characteristics of their networks. It seems likely, however, that given the small size of these networks, there may be fewer children—perhaps only one—again underlining structural fragility. Moreover, high levels of help may reflect high levels of need; poor health might both catalyze help from children and diminish network size and interaction.

The absence of children in the "small: extended-family and friend-focused" network type serves as a reminder that some older Canadians do not have children to whom they can turn in time of need (Connidis, 1989). This is a very important consideration, given the current thrust in so many developed nations to shift some of the state's responsibilities "back" to the family. Social policies that have the effect of placing increased responsibility for care of the elderly on families may leave such older adults in situations of enhanced vulnerability because they have little or no family.

While childless elderly may substitute interaction with siblings and friends for interaction with children, this substitution effect (Shanas, 1979) does not necessarily extend over the whole range of helping patterns where children can be found as caregivers. Help from siblings or friends to impaired elderly is typically less common, less intensive, and of shorter duration than help from a spouse or child (Johnson and Catalano, 1981a). Thus, older people who do not have children are at increased risk of institutionalization, compared to persons with children (Carrière and Legaré, 1993; Gee, 1995; Pelletier, 1992; Shapiro and Tate, 1989; Stone, 1988).

Women in the "small: extended-family and friend-focused" network type are particularly at risk since such a high percentage of them (61 percent) live alone, indicating that they do not have a spouse to whom they might turn should help be needed. With the very low number of children in their network sizes and the correspondingly extremely low degree of interaction with children, it means that we should be cautious in accepting without qualification Gee's (1995, p. 110) statement that ". . . older people are not isolated from family members living outside their household. . . ." While this statement refers to the overall pattern describing the majority of older Canadians, the construction of network types such as those presented in this analysis illuminates the variety of patterns that exist among Canada's seniors. Some of these patterns imply greater social isolation than others.

In closing, it must be remembered that the social network profiles we have identified in this study are snapshots of people's lives at one point in time. Our depiction cannot capture the dynamics of change over the later years of the life course. Some features of social networks do, no doubt, show some continuity over time; for example, a person who enjoys having many friends is likely to seek to maintain such interactions, perhaps by acquiring new friends as death diminishes the network availability of old ones. Similarly, a person who has a lifelong pattern of frequent contact with children and other kin will try to maintain that pattern over time. Nonetheless, it is equally as likely that age-related losses have an impact on the social networks of elderly Canadians.

NOTES

1. The authors thank Howard Litwin for advice concerning selection of a technique for achieving network typology and Vincent Dale for assistance with literature review and style editing.

2. The size index is an index number for network size, not the real average number of persons per network. The proportion of children, siblings, etc. constitutes the percentage shares of each kind of relation in the size index. Each respondent contributes at most 1 to the numerator for proportion for spouse, 3 to that for proportion of children, 10 to that for proportion of siblings, and 15 to that for proportion of friends. The contacts figures are based on index numbers that reflect frequency of contact (by seeing or by telephone) with selected relations. Each number here is a transformation of the original index numbers and represents the position of a given cluster relative to the average for all clusters (by sex). Thus, 0.57 in the line for parent contacts index means that the cluster's rate of contact was far below average. The figure 2.38 in the same line represents a cluster for which the corresponding rate of contact was far above average (average is 1.00 in this scale). Finally, percentage by sex shows the relative number of cases within a given cluster among the total for a specific sex.

3. The construction of the index is quite complex, since it summarizes information about multiple kinds of supports received from either son or daughter at varying daily rates. Full documentation in plain language would require a long appendix (even the programming involves many lines of code). Interested parties should contact Leroy Stone.

6

Social Network Characteristics
and Social Network Types
among Elderly People in Finland

Tuula Melkas and Marja Jylhä

In Finland there has been very little research to date on the social networks of elderly people. However, there are many reasons why the configuration and significance of social ties in old age need to be understood in greater depth. As in other Western countries, the expectation in Finland has been that the role of informal networks as a source of help for elderly people will continue to increase in the future. It is only reasonable, therefore, to base these expectations on current empirical data as to the importance and the functioning of social networks.

In addition, there are several studies that indicate that elderly people in Finland live alone more often but report feelings of loneliness less often than their age peers in Central and Southern Europe (Jylhä and Jokela, 1990; Vanhuusbaro-metri, 1994). These results raise important questions about the nature and meaning of social interaction between elderly people and their significant others.

In this chapter we examine the composition of social networks of elderly people in Finland. Five network types are differentiated on the basis of the breadth, intensity, and nature of social interaction. The availability and sources of formal and informal help as well as feelings of loneliness and satisfaction in the different network types are also examined. Finally, we discuss implications for future policy and research regarding the social networks of the old.

STUDY SAMPLE

The empirical data for our study come from a survey of living conditions carried out in 1994 by Statistics Finland. The basic population consists of the noninstitutionalized adult population of Finland, 15 years of age or over. The systematic random sample of respondents was drawn using stratification by home municipality, occupational class, and income. An additional sample was drawn from the capital area using the same stratification criteria. Subjects who participated in a panel survey begun in 1991 and were again sampled using the same criteria are also included in the sample (Ahola, Djerf, Heiskanen, and Vikki, 1995).

The data were collected using a structured questionnaire comprised of some 140 items or sets of questions. Like the studies preceding it, the 1994 living conditions survey covered several broad themes, such as family and other social relationships, working life and unemployment, leisure activities, physical health, and psychic and social well-being. The interviews were conducted by trained staff members of Statistics Finland during the winter and spring of 1994.

The overall sample size of the living conditions survey was 11,843 persons, and the number of completed interviews was 8,650, giving a response rate of 73 percent. In this particular analysis only persons aged 60 years or over—altogether 1,655 respondents—are included.

The response rate among persons aged 55–74 years was roughly the same as that of the whole sample (about 73 percent), but it was only 66 percent among the "old–old" (75 years old or over). The response rate was also higher in rural areas (78 percent) than in urban areas (71 percent). With the oldest age groups and urban people being underrepresented in the data, the unweighted results may give too positive a picture of the social life of elderly people in Finland. Therefore, weighting was employed to correct the complicated sampling frame and the systematic differences in the response rate as well. As a result of corrections, the data used here are, indeed, representative of the noninstitutionalized population of Finland aged 60 years or over.

It should be mentioned that the survey was not specifically designed for the analysis of social networks. We will thus not be able to give the exact size of the network or to comment on its exact structure (e.g., uniplexity vs. multiplexity, tightness vs. looseness). That would require a design in which subjects are asked to name the members of their network and where they are then classified into different categories (Fischer, 1982). However, the data employed here do provide abundant information concerning the existence and number of close kin (parents, children, and siblings) and friends, contacts, social support, and the quality of the relationship between the center of the network and the different categories of kin and non-kin. By means of composite variables, it is also possible to describe the size of networks and the intensity of social interaction.

COMPOSITION OF THE SOCIAL NETWORK

The most immediate social network consists of people who live in the same household. For elderly people in Finland this network is not very large: 41 percent of all people aged 60 or over live alone, 49 percent live with their spouse only, and only 10 percent live with more than one other person. However, the situation is different for men and women: 21 percent of men and 55 percent of women live alone. Among women aged 75 years or over, two out of three live alone.

As households consisting of extended families of three or more generations are rare, respondents' living situation mainly reflects marital status. The percentage of married men is twice as high as the proportion of married women (74 vs. 37 percent) and the proportion of widowed persons among men is only one-third of the figure among women. This discrepancy is mainly due to the fact that the husband is usually older than the wife, and life expectancy is longer for women.

Kin play an important but not a predominant role in the lives of elderly people in Finland. We shall first describe the size and then the composition of the kin network. The indicator of the size of kin network includes (1) the number of children, siblings, parents, and parents-in-law living either in the same household or outside the household, (2) the number of other people living in the same household, and (3) the number of other relatives in the exchange network. The mean size of the resultant kin network is 6.3. One-third of the sample has a kin network consisting of 4 members or fewer, one-third report 5–7 members, and another third 8 members or more. The kin network is smaller for women (6.0) than men (6.6), and somewhat smaller for the old–old than for the young–old. In particular, women aged 75 years or over have fewer members in their kin networks than others. The mean figure is 4.9, and 50 percent in this group fall in the smallest kin network category.

Immediate kin—children and siblings—are particularly important. Eight out of ten persons have children, and one in two meet at least one of their children at least once a week. Although siblings are roughly as prevalent in the network as children, on the other hand, contacts with them are not as frequent. Only every sixth person meets his or her siblings every week, and more than 40 percent do so less than once a month.

Moreover, children are met frequently even if they do not live in close proximity, while siblings are not met very often, even if they do live close by. This difference probably reflects both the nature of the relationship and the difficulties that elderly siblings have with mobility. Interestingly, around 10 percent of persons aged 60–74 still have parents or parents-in-law in their social networks, and 2 percent of all elderly people meet their parents at least once a week.

The indicator of total network size utilized in this analysis includes (1–3) the three components of the kin network just mentioned, and the existence of (4) a friend, (5) a neighbor, and (6) a colleague in the exchange network, or some other contact with them that occurs at least a few times a year. Thus, the network size indicator is a mixed one consisting of the number of close relatives and the number of categories of non-kin ties in the network. The mean of the total network size indicator is 8.1. Men have somewhat larger networks than women, and younger–old people have larger networks than the old–old. As is the case with the kin network, the size of the total network of women aged 75 or older is considerably smaller than that of other groups.

Friends are a predominant category in the non-kin network. They are even more prevalent than children in the social network and, among women, are met more often on a weekly basis. On average, elderly Finns have about four or five friends. Three-quarters have a friend residing at a distance of 4 kilometers or less, and 86 percent at a distance of 20 kilometers or less. Neighbors are also often included in the network, but colleagues are included as network members in only one out of ten cases. In Finland, most people retire by age 60, and virtually everyone is retired by age 65. Against this background, it is understandable that colleagues play a role mainly for the young–old, who are still working or who have only recently left work.

A frequency-of-meetings measure indicates how often different member categories of the social network—that is, children, parents, siblings, neighbors, colleagues, and friends—are met. "Almost daily" meetings are given a score of 5 points, while meetings that take place "about once a week" are scored as 1. The mean value of the frequency is 5. This value refers either to daily meetings with only one category—for example, children—or to weekly meetings with five categories—for example, children, siblings, neighbors, parents, and friends. The frequency of meetings is lower among men than women, and lowest among men aged 75 or over (4.3).

The composition or size of the network is not, of course, a direct measure of its significance to the individual. Although social networks often provide support and help, they may also be causes of stress. Some relationships may be emotionally neutral and of no major personal importance. In this study, respondents were asked to mention the number of intimates they have outside the household, regardless of whether or not they are kin. They were also asked if they have a real confidant.

Over two-thirds, or 70 percent, of older people have a real confidant outside the household. Both intimates and confidants are less frequent among the old–old than among the young–old. However, it was interesting to find that men mention more intimates than women, but women report having a confidant more often than do men. Feelings of loneliness are more frequent among women and among the old–old.

Marital status is an important indicator of life situation and in many ways influences the composition and functioning of the social network. Among elderly people in Finland, regardless of gender, the network is smallest among single persons and largest among the married, while the widowed fall in-between these two groups. The differences are mainly due to the number of kin, but it is worth noting that even for singles the lower number of kin is not compensated for by non-kin.

The frequency of meeting with other people is also dependent on one's marital status, reflecting the importance of the family institution in Finland. Single persons tend to lead a more isolated life than do others. Married people have relatively large circles of friends but meet people outside the household less frequently when compared with widowed persons, because of the fairly privatized way of life in Finland. Widowed persons maintain their contacts not only with children, but also with other people, probably taking advantage of the "cultural capital" acquired in the former family.

The number of children also influences the frequency of meetings with other people, reflecting the significance of children in social intercourse. However, the personal consequences of the family situation seem to be different for men and women. Single men report feelings of loneliness twice as often as do single women, and the figure is also higher for widowers than for widows.

Deteriorating health and functional capacity often make it difficult for aging people to maintain their social contacts. This applies particularly to non-kin relationships. In our study both kin and non-kin networks are smaller among people with functional disabilities. A person is defined as having a functional disability if he or she has (1) a disease or injury affecting activities of daily living, or difficulty in at least one of the following tasks: walking briskly for 5 minutes, using stairs, carrying a load of 5 kilograms, and (2) difficulty in at least one of the following: housecleaning, washing clothes, buying food, cooking, washing, or dressing and undressing. The mean number of intimates among those with good functional ability is 5.4; the corresponding figure for those with a disability is 4.0. Disability is also related to increased feelings of loneliness.

In terms of social class, the network size is smallest among white-collar employees and largest among farmers. This is mainly due to the size of the kin network and particularly the number of children. The mean number of children for farmers is 3.1, for blue-collar workers 2.3, and for white-collar employees 2.1. However, white-collar men and women are at opposite poles in the sense that, compared with other social groups, the proportion of childless people is lowest among white-collar men (11 percent) and highest among white-collar women (22 percent). The non-kin network, however, is slightly larger among white-collar employees than in other groups.

The function and meaning of social relationships also seems to differ between social classes. Farmers have the most frequent meetings with significant others outside the household, and white-collar employees have the fewest. But white-collar employees have a confidant more often than do the other social groups.

Some differences in the composition of social networks can also be found between rural and urban areas. The most significant difference regards the proportion of people living alone: the figure for men in rural areas is 20 percent, whereas for women in urban areas it is 60 percent. In rural areas, the number of children and the size of the kin network tend to be larger than in urban areas. In contrast, people living in urban areas have more intimates that people in rural areas. This is true for both men and women.

NETWORK TYPES

The variables for the construction of different network types were drawn from the following conceptual dimensions: (1) the breadth of the network, (2) the depth of the network, or the closeness between network members, (3) a dimension of everyday interaction in the form of meetings—that is, whether a person shares daily life with other people or lives mainly alone, and (4) practical support.

These dimensions follow the typology of measurement strategies presented by Milardo (1988). According to this typology, networks can be studied from the point of view of (1) the existence of significant others, (2) the rate of interaction, or (3) the extent of social exchange. The first two of our four dimensions refer to the first parameter in Milardo's typology, and the latter two dimensions to the second and third parameters, respectively.

But why are two indicators necessary for the existence of significant others? In the literature, two different types of friendship are discussed. Thus, the value of friendship can lie in either one's attachment to the other part of the relationship and in being together as such, or in the common activity itself (Allan, 1979; Bensman and Lilienfeld, 1979). The first type, called a "communal type," consists of confidentiality and taking care of each other. The other, called the "agentic" type" consists of a common interest in some valuable or enjoyable activity (Rawlins, 1992).

Because the communal type of friendship is highly demanding, one person cannot have many such relationships, insofar as it involves spending a lot of time together. Having a large number of significant others thus refers to agentic rather than to communal friendship. However, having a small number of significant others does not necessarily reflect the communality of friendships. Therefore, separate indicators are needed for tapping both the breadth and the depth of the social network.

As for friendships among elderly people, several different styles have been identified in the literature. The independent style, which resembles agentic friendships, refers more to circumstances than to specific individuals and fulfills the need for autonomy that many elderly people are known to exhibit. The discerning style, which resembles communal friendship, reflects deep attachment to specific individuals regardless of changing circumstances. The acquisitive style maintains bonds with old friends while at the same time keeping open the option of forming new friendships (Rawlins, 1992). Moreover, by combining the existence of significant others and frequencies of interaction, two kinds of co-presence can be distinguished—namely, concrete face-to-face meetings between people and imaginary co-presence if the members of the network are there only in one's thoughts and memories (Urry, 1991).

Given the limitations in the measurement of network size in this study, the breadth of network is operationalized as the number of friends. The depth of the network, or the closeness between network members reflecting communality, is operationalized as whether or not respondents have at least one confidant. The everyday interaction is measured by the frequency of meetings with members of the network, using the frequency indicator described earlier.

The exchange of practical help includes both help received and help provided between the person in the center of the network and nine member categories (mothers or mothers-in-law, fathers or fathers-in-law, sons or sons-in-law, daughters or daughters-in-law, siblings, secondary kin, neighbors, colleagues, and friends). "Help received" consists of the number of categories from which help has been received during the past 12 months or from which help can be asked for if needed. "Help provided" comprises the number of categories the person has helped during the past 12 months.

Network types were constructed by using the SAS FASTCLUS procedure, where the number of clusters must be specified. The best solution was sought by comparing the homogeneity of the clusters among the alternatives of 2–6 clusters. The 5-cluster solution proved to be the best. In the alternatives of 2–4 clusters, the clusters remained quite heterogeneous, as indicated by the within-cluster standard deviations as compared with the overall standard deviation. On the other hand, the addition of the sixth cluster did not significantly reduce the within-cluster standard deviation.

Variation in the number of friends and in the frequency of meetings were the most important factors producing clusters. Although significantly correlated, they showed relatively highest variation independently of each other. The variable indicating the existence of a confidant covaried quite closely with the number of friends ($R = .29$), whereas the exchange of practical help was most strongly correlated with the frequency of meetings ($R = .20$ with both "help received" and "help provided").

The positive correlations between all the cluster variables indicated the cumulative nature of the phenomena included in the cluster analysis. In fact, three of our five clusters—Clusters 1, 4, and 5) form a continuum in terms of the cumulation of positive characteristics, with Cluster 1 representing the most positive end of this dimension. As opposed to this dimension of cumulative well-being, the dimension underlying Clusters 2 and 3 is the great variation in the contacts of daily life—that is, the frequency of meeting with other people.

As for the friendship typologies discussed earlier, the communal, discerning type, which is characterized by a high degree of confidentiality but a small number of significant others, was not found in our data. On the other hand, we did identify (1) the *agentic, independent type* in the sense of exhibiting a high frequency of meetings but only an average level of confidants, (2) the *acquisitive type,* which we call in the coming sections the "endowed" type, and (3) a type described by Urry (1991) as *imaginary* and here referred to as the "perceived" type.

In the five-cluster solution, the network types are structured as follows: one-quarter of all elderly people belong to a cluster with characteristics that approximate the average in all respects (Cluster 4); a large cluster representing one-third of all respondents is characterized by poor social life in all dimensions (Cluster 5); and three smaller clusters, representing 11 to 15 percent of the elderly, reflect a richer social life in one or more respects (Clusters 1–3). These and other statistics are summarized in Table 6.1.

The clusters produced by the five-cluster solution are internally homogeneous. Some of them can be interpreted as typical of a certain sociodemographic group, while others seem to represent special types of individual life-style that are not dependent on one's sociodemographic background.

1. The *endowed network* (Cluster 1) is characterized by a large number of friends, having a confidant, frequent meetings with non-kin, and active exchange of practical help. Half of the persons representing this network type meet their neighbors daily, but fairly many—about 40 percent—also meet their children or friends on a daily basis. The persons who are met weekly, on the other hand, form a more heterogeneous group and are divided between many different categories.

While the dominant category of daily social contact tends slightly towards neighborhood ties, weekly contacts are most often between friends. However, while interaction with non-kin is active in this network type, the most intensive interaction takes place with children who live outside the household, as is the case in other network types. Only 5 percent of those belonging to this type have a passive parent–child relationship—that is, meetings less often than once a week and having no exchange of practical help.

The endowed network is also heterogeneous in terms of marital and social status, age, and urban–rural residence. This means that the richness of the social network in this network type cannot be explained by reference to sociodemographic characteristics such as high social class. This network type may be considered a lucky but not very probable possibility among different people in different parts of Finland.

2. The *perceived network* (Cluster 2) is quite different from the endowed network with regard to the frequency of meetings. Even though in principle they have many network resources, hardly anyone in this network type meets people outside the family on a daily basis. As for weekly social contact, it is about as usual to meet only one category of people as it is to meet combinations of different categories. Weekly contacts are mainly between friends and/or parents and children. Although the people representing this network type have one of the largest family circles consisting mainly of children and their families, activity in parent–child interaction is only on an average level.

Table 6.1: Network Types as Expressed by Clusters and the Variables Included in Cluster Analysis

Cluster	Network Type	Elderly People Belonging to the Network Type	Number of Intimates	Having a Confident	Frequency of Meetings	Practical Help		The Help Recipients
		(%)	(mean)	(%)	(mean)	Number of Helpers (mean)		(mean)
1	Endowed	12	9.7	84	8.0	2.1		1.9
2	Perceived	11	8.7	77	1.6	1.6		1.5
3	Agentic	15	3.7	74	11.9	1.9		1.6
4	Family-intensive	26	3.1	74	6.0	1.8		1.5
5	Defective	35	2.5	57	1.2	1.4		1.1

The perceived network is dominated by young–old, relatively healthy married people with an urban middle-class background. It is also noteworthy that although the endowed and the perceived networks are the smallest of all types, comprising together some 23 percent of the elderly in the sample, one-third of elderly men belong to one or the other of these two types. Some of them are probably married to a younger wife.

3. In the *agentic network* (Cluster 3), the number of friends and the proportion of those with a confidant are near the average, whereas contacts with people outside the household are far more frequent than in any other cluster. Social intercourse in the agentic network type is characteristically everyday interaction: there are daily meetings with many kinds of people, and the number of weekly contacts is relatively small. The prevalence of helpers is second only to the endowed network type, and being a helper is as frequent as in the perceived network type, although the average age is higher. This characterizes the practical nature of social intercourse in the agentic network.

The emphasis in daily social intercourse is on contacts with neighbors and friends. One-fifth of those representing the agentic network also meet siblings daily, which is extraordinary in Finland. However, the significance of children varies within the network. On the one hand, almost half the members of this network type meet their children daily. On the other hand, the proportion of passive parent–child relationships is one-fifth—the second-highest rate among all the network types.

The agentic network differs from the former two network types in terms of its sociodemographic characteristics. Most of those belonging to the agentic network are women, many of them widows, with a working-class or agricultural background and resident in nonurban environments. In terms of age and functional capacity, the agentic network comes close to the average, which means that people in this network type are older and not as healthy as those representing the endowed or perceived network type. The only noteworthy similarity to these network types is the large number of children.

4. The *family-intensive network* (Cluster 4), the second-largest grouping, is very similar in terms of its composition to the general elderly population of Finland. But, there is one important exception: the exceptional significance of children. This network type is particularly active in maintaining ties between parents and their children. However, the family-intensive type differs from the endowed type in the status of the other parts of the network, which are more highly active in the endowed type.

5. The *defective network* (Cluster 5) is characterized by a small number of friends. Furthermore, almost every other person in this network type lacks a confidant. Together with the perceived network type, it differs clearly from the other network types with respect to its isolated way of life. None of those belonging to the defective network meet people outside the household on a daily basis, and only three-quarters do so on a weekly basis. In weekly social intercourse, friends and/or children are met most frequently.

Moreover, every second person in the defective network type lives alone. Both total and kin networks are smaller in the defective network than in any other network type. Kin network is small because of the very high proportion of childless people (23 percent); the non-kin part of the network is small because of the relative lack of neighbors in the network. With the exception of the small number of children in the neighborhood in this network type, its sociodemographic characteristics do not significantly differ from the average.

The defective network (Cluster 5) is the most prevalent network type among elderly people in Finland. It is also the most prevalent type in all the sociodemographic groups examined, with just one exception: among parents of larger-than-average families, the family-intensive type (Cluster 4) is most prevalent. These two types come first or second in prevalence in all sociodemographic groups, but the prevalence of other types varied according to the group.

RECEIVED FORMAL AND INFORMAL AID

The exchange of practical help was already addressed as one of the variables by which the different network types were constructed. The following discussion looks in closer detail at questions of receiving practical help and the sources of help.

Respondents were asked whether, during the past 12 months, they had received help in the following six activities: (1) domestic work, (2) small services (e.g., watering flowers, lending or borrowing tools or perishables), (3) shopping or running errands, (4) personal care due to old age or illness, (5) rides or other kinds of transport, and (6) building or repairs. Informal help provided by the social network was queried separately for each item. There were four possible responses: (1) have received help during past 12 months; (2) have not received help, but know someone who can be contacted for help, if necessary; (3) do not know anyone who can be contacted for help; and (4) do not need type of help concerned.

The receipt of formal help was addressed by means of a global measure—that is, whether the person had received any formal help with these kinds of activities. A question was also included to identify the sources of formal help (municipalities, voluntary organizations, and the private market).

Finland has traditionally shared the welfare-state ideology that is common to all Scandinavian countries—the view that the main responsibility for guaranteeing the welfare of citizens and for providing the services they need lies with the public sector. The services provided by voluntary organizations and the market have thus been of minor importance. In recent years, however, there have been increasing efforts to transfer the production of services from the public sector to other service producers.

Nonetheless, the public sector remains the major formal service provider in Finland; this, at least, was the situation in 1994, when the data were collected. However, when only the noninstitutionalized population is considered, as in our analysis, informal social networks are the most prevalent source of help. From 18 to 25 percent of respondents whose functional capacity is good said they did not need help with any of the activities queried. Therefore, help received by functionally disabled people is examined separately.

As is evident in Table 6.2, about eight out of ten persons with functional disability received informal help, and one in three received municipal help. About every other elderly Finnish person with some disability relied solely on informal sources, mostly close kin (family members or grown-up children in a different household), for practical help. The second-most-common alternative was a combination of municipalities (public sector) and social networks. Almost one-third of those with functional disability received practical help from both the municipality and from people belonging to the network. About one tenth used services

Table 6.2: Receipt of Municipal, Other Formal, and Informal Help during Past Twelve Months by Functional Capacity and Network Type

	Proportion of those who received		
	Municipal Aid	Other Formal Aid[1]	Informal Aid
	%	%	%
Functional Capacity			
good	6	6	73
poor	36	10	78
Network Type			
Endowed	10	7	84
Perceived	7	9	74
Agentic	16	4	78
Family-intensive	12	6	77
Defective	15	8	68
All	13	7	74

[1] Aid provided by voluntary organizations or the private market.

produced by voluntary organizations or the private sector, mostly in combination with informal sources.

It is quite unusual for disabled people in Finland to be left completely without help or for them to rely entirely on formal sources. Of persons with disability, 3 percent live without any help, and a further 3 percent rely entirely on formal sources. However, the help provided may not fully satisfy the needs. For instance, one in five of those with functional disability report that they did not receive any help with domestic work.

In all the network types, an overwhelming majority receive informal help, but Table 6.2 reveals that for the endowed network type this is far more common than for the defective type. In all network types, informal help usually comes from more than one source (from 61 percent of those representing the endowed type to 45 percent of those representing the defective type). The second-most-common pattern is the combination of municipal services and informal help. As regards the sources of help, the only major difference between the network types is the relatively heavy dependence of those representing the agentic type on municipal services and the corresponding low proportion of other formal sources of services, probably explained by their rural living environment. Municipal services have been more readily available and commercial services less so in rural municipalities.

As for the sufficiency of help provided by the social network, the differences between the network types are largely consistent with their general situation as portrayed earlier. Almost all of those representing the endowed network type had either received help or know someone who can provide all the different kinds of practical help mentioned in the interview (86 percent). The endowed network is followed in this regard by the agentic network type (81 percent), the perceived type (72 percent), and the family-intensive type (75 percent). The situation is worst among those representing the defective type of network, where more than one of every two people lack at least one kind of informal help, most typically for domestic work, building or repairs, or personal care. Even so, only 4 percent of them remain completely without practical help when formal care is also taken into account.

FEELINGS OF LONELINESS AND SATISFACTION

We now move on to discuss experiences of well-being in different life situations and in different network types. The indicators used in this section of the analysis are: (1) the frequency of feelings of loneliness, (2) satisfaction with the emotional support provided by other people, and (3) satisfaction with life in general. Different dimensions of experienced well-being are connected, of course, with different life situations. As far as social interaction and social support are concerned, for example, living alone represents a special situation—one that is very common among elderly Finns. Moreover, quality of life is often challenged not only by own's one deteriorating health and functional capacity, but by that of the spouse as well. Our data thus include information on whether someone else in the respondent's household also needs daily care because of a disability or illness.

People who live alone report feelings of loneliness much more often than do elderly people on average. But in terms of satisfaction with emotional support provided by others or satisfaction with life in general, they do not differ from the rest of the elderly population. This is demonstrated in Table 6.3.

Functionally disabled elderly people who live with healthy family members (mostly disabled husbands with healthier wives) report satisfaction with emotional support. However, they also report feelings of loneliness somewhat more often than do those with good functional capacity. On the other hand, persons with good functional capacity but who live with a family member in need of daily care (mostly wives with disabled husbands) are most dissatisfied with the emotional support they receive and are also relatively dissatisfied with life in general. Nevertheless, they do not often feel lonely themselves.

Not surprisingly, the small minority of respondents amongst whom both the subject interviewed and a family member—usually a spouse—are disabled, show the greatest dissatisfaction with life in general. However, they still report the second-highest satisfaction with emotional support received—more so than persons with good functional capacity. Perhaps it is easier to appreciate social relations when one can no longer take them for granted.

All the different life situations described here are present to a greater or lesser degree in all the network types. The frequency of risk situations in which one or more family members are disabled varies from one-fifth of those representing the perceived network type to one-third of those in the defective network type. A slight majority of the members of the endowed network (52 percent) and two-thirds of the perceived network are parties to couples with good functional capacity. This is the case in but a minority of people in the other network types.

The fortunate situation of those representing the endowed type of network is also reflected in their experiences of well-being—that is, in the absence of loneliness and in satisfaction with emotional support and life in general. This good fortune is largely due to the nature of the interaction between network members, as the most immediate life situation in this network type is by no means unproblematic. Those living alone and those with functional disability constitute a significant minority within this network type, but they are nevertheless better placed than the elderly on the whole to share their life with other people.

The experiences of well-being among those representing the perceived network type differs from the experiences of those representing the endowed type. The relative absence of loneliness among those in the perceived network has to do with the large proportion of family members and the small proportion of those living alone. When family situation is controlled for, the feelings of loneliness approximate the average rates. In spite of the family situation, the existence of a

Table 6.3: Feelings of Loneliness and Satisfaction with Emotional Support Provided by Other People and with Life in General by Functional Capacity of Subject and a Family Member, and by Network Type

	Seldom or Never Lonely	Very Satisfied		Proportion of Elderly People
		With Emotional Support	With Life in General	
	%	%	%	%
Living Alone	47	41	34	41
Living with Family Members				
All with good functional capacity	77	43	36	42
Subject with disability	64	54	35	10
Subjects with disability and a family member in need of daily care	72	35	24	5
Family member in need of daily care	63	47	14	2
Network Type				
Endowed	74	60	39	
Perceived	71	42	33	
Agentic	62	48	36	
Family-intensive	61	44	35	
Defective	59	34	31	
All	63	43	34	

spouse, and mostly a good relationship between spouses, the proportion of those who are satisfied with their emotional support (and with life in general) is only average. One probable explanation is that a very private family life style does not satisfy social needs, at least among retired people with good functional capacity.

Compared with the perceived network type, the agentic type has more feelings of loneliness, but a higher level of satisfaction with emotional support (and also with life in general). This is consistent with the life situation of people in this network type: almost one in two people live alone and have good functional capacity. It seems that feelings of loneliness are more-or-less unavoidable consequences of living alone, even when other people are met frequently.

However, frequent meetings with other people do seem to contribute to emotional support and also to the meaningfulness of life. The family-oriented type of network was described earlier as the average type of network, and indeed the experienced well-being of those representing this network type is at an average level.

Over one-third of all elderly people and between one-third and almost half of those who either themselves have some disability or who live with a person needing daily care belong to the defective network type. The relative dissatisfaction expressed by people in this type of network indicates that the defects of the network are not without consequences. Irrespective of the immediate family situation, feelings of loneliness and dissatisfaction with emotional support are more prevalent in the defective type of network than in any other type. In this network type, the nuclear family seems to be almost the only source of emotional support. For example, every other married person with disability is very satisfied with the emotional support they receive.

However, only one-fifth of the caregivers representing this network type are satisfied with the emotional support they receive, even though they report warm relationships with their spouse more often than average. The situation of the people representing the defective type of network implies that urban life in Finland can be quite lonely and cold and does not provide adequate support for elderly people.

IMPLICATIONS FOR THE FUTURE

Our analysis has shown that social networks among elderly people in Finland are quite diversified, reflecting a wide variety of life situations and ways of life. In general, the configuration of social networks also reflects what may be regarded as traditional basic values in Finnish culture and social interaction, such as the importance of family life and the nuclear family in particular, as well as an emphasis on individual independence. This value of independence is illustrated by the large number of elderly people who live alone and by the very small number of those who live together with their grown-up children. It is also consistent with the official emphasis on community care in social and health policy.

The modern pension system in the welfare state allows elderly people to go on living in their own household and to retain economic independence from their children. On the other hand, Finland is a sparsely populated country, where distances are long. During the 1960s and 1970s, large numbers of young adults moved from the rural North and East into the cities in the South, while their parents stayed back home. Successive living conditions surveys have shown that even without these waves of migration, geographical distances between elderly parents and their grown-up children have continued to increase.

Although the majority of elderly people in the 1990s live in urban environments, Finland has the second-largest rural population in the European Union (38 percent—the figure is higher only in Portugal), and a large proportion of them are elderly. Furthermore, the proportion of women with full-time jobs outside their own household is higher in Finland than in any other European Union country. All these factors contribute to the cultural model of intergenerational relationships that, as many opinion polls have shown, is largely shared by Finnish people.

The model of independent living does not imply lack of intimacy or social exchange between elderly parents and their children. It is evident that for the majority of elderly people children have an essential role in their social networks and are also a source of help. However, it is important to realize that the elderly, particularly the young–old, are themselves important providers of help, not only to their spouse, but frequently to the families of their children as well.

The division of labor between formal help and help given by children and friends to older people is often a complex puzzle. The main task of grown-up children in securing the well-being of their elderly parents is often thought to be provision of emotional support. Children will usually be willing to provide occasional help and to take care of minor errands, but when more serious and regular help is needed in the form of daily care in the household, preparing meals, etc., that is usually understood to be in the purview of formal sources, primarily municipal organizations.

Many surveys have shown that even elderly people themselves prefer formal help in such situations (Jylhä, 1993, *Omaisten Suhde Ikäihmisten Palveluihin*, 1991). However, it is worth noting that help by children or other relatives is often needed in order to get this formal help. Indeed, formal help by the welfare state is heavily concentrated among those in poorest health, which may cause problems for people with reasonably good functional capacity but in need of some help to cope with their daily life. If they do not have children, to whom can they turn?

What about the future? Finland has recently joined the European Union, but it is still too early to predict the implications of this move for the economy, for family life, and for cultural values. We do not know, for example, how migration patterns will change with the right to free movement of labor, and, accordingly, how this will affect interaction between the generations.

As in other European countries, there are currently heavy political pressures in Finland to cut public expenditure. If this development continues, the availability of formal help will probably be reduced. In 1994, every fourth Finnish elderly person in the middle class purchased welfare services provided by the private market, but only 8 percent in the working class and 2 percent of farmers did so. In all, if the role of the state and local municipalities in the provision of practical support to elderly people will decrease, there is bound to be a corresponding increase in social inequality among the members of the elderly cohort. This will, in turn, curtail the possibilities for independent living outside of institutions and threaten the continuity of the Finnish cultural model that is described in this chapter.

However, the expected increase in the number and the proportion of elderly people in Finland does not only mean an increase in the number of persons in need of help. Along with the improvement of living conditions and rising levels of education, the number of relatively healthy and active young–old people will be much higher than it is today. The vast majority of elderly people within the foreseeable future will continue to be women. There are studies that suggest, moreover, that new life-styles are developing among elderly people, character-ized by an active social life involving continuing education and new hobbies as well as lively friendship networks.

At the same time, relationships between generations are becoming more and more diversified. The continuing development of communication technology is also creating new means and new forms of contacts between individuals. Both old age policy and old age itself are undergoing significant change in Finland, creating challenges both to formal policy and to social networks. To be able to respond to the needs of new generations of elderly people, we will need to under-take not only the kind of large-scale surveys we have reported here, but also qualitative studies. Approaches such as narrative analyses or ethnographies (Gubrium, 1993; Silverman, 1993) may help us to capture and illustrate in-dividual meanings of different types of social relationships, as well as their functions in different people's individual way of life.

7

Support Network Measurement and Typology Development in England and Wales

G. Clare Wenger

This chapter describes the development of a support network measurement technique based on a longitudinal study in rural North Wales and discusses its subsequent application in the City of Liverpool, England.[1] It shows how the availability of funding over a period of 12 years and the combination of both quantitative and qualitative methodological approaches led to the design of a robust measurement instrument, which has been shown to have both research and practice applications.

The measurement technique described in this chapter was developed over 12 or more years of network research. Each phase of the research built on the former, using earlier findings to raise and test hypotheses in subsequent phases and adapting and refining network measurement techniques in the process. Each phase had a slightly different focus, and at each stage the requirements of the funding agencies influenced the breadth and scope of the work undertaken.

The research has been based on successive grants, with funding primarily from the Department of Health and Social Security (DHSS), which subsequently became the Department of Health (DoH)—a government department. Additional funding came from the Economic and Social Research Council (ESRC), a government-funded academic research funding body, and the Joseph Rowntree Foundation (JRF), a charitable trust.

The development of the measurement technique from a small intensively studied sample made it possible to identify support network type in a large epidemiological screening sample in the City of Liverpool. In the next section of this chapter, the different research periods are discussed, showing how findings led to changes and development in our understanding of support networks and the method of network measurement. The subsequent sections of the chapter report on the findings from the Liverpool study and discuss other uses of the typology and the measurement technique by researchers and practitioners.

DEVELOPMENT OF A TECHNIQUE
FOR MEASURING SUPPORT NETWORK TYPE

Phase One

The first phase of the research was carried out between 1978 and 1982 with funding from the DHSS and focused on elderly people living in rural Wales and their access to services and formal and informal help. It consisted primarily of a survey, conducted in 1979, based on an interviewer-administered questionnaire. Interviews were conducted in the home of the respondent. Respondents were aged 65 and over, living at home in a cross-section of community types existing in the region. The achieved sample size was 534 and was representative of the aged in the area. The researcher was particularly interested in the informal networks of support.

It was felt important that the unit of study should, in addition to the elderly respondent themselves, be the support network as an entity. For this reason an adaptation of a measurement technique developed by McCallister and Fischer (1978) was adopted. This technique elicits the membership of partial or purposive networks by asking for the names of network members who fill particular roles. By asking for names, it is possible to control for multiple roles in the network and to count each member only once. By focusing questions on the domain in which the researcher is interested, it is possible to arrive at a listing of all those who are active or perceived to be potentially involved in that domain. It is also possible to measure the size of the active network rather than the number of needs that are met or roles that are filled. This is important because some respondents will have more needs to fill than others, and double counting of network members providing more than one type of support needs to be avoided.

The elicitation of support network members was based on a series of questions, including some beginning, "Who . . ." which asked about both real and hypothetical instances where help was likely to be needed. Those mentioned in the following contexts were identified as members of the support network:

1. all members of the respondent's household;
2. the relative seen most often (more than one counted only if seen equally often);
3. confidant;
4. people who could be asked to do favors (up to 5);
5. real friends in the local area (up to 5);
6. anyone needing the respondent to care for them;

7. anyone dependent on the respondent's friendship;

8. all those providing informal help with personal care (excluding paid professional caregivers);

9. the person the respondent would turn to in case of illness (excluding medical practitioners);

10. the person the respondent would ask for financial advice (excluding paid professionals);

11. the person the respondent would talk to about a personal problem;

12. the person the respondent would talk to if they were feeling "down";

13. the person the respondent would ask for a lift (excluding commercial companies);

14. the person the respondent would borrow small things from;

15. people, including home helps, providing regular help with domestic tasks and property maintenance.

On the basis of responses to these questions, it was possible to ascertain the size and composition of the support network and the functions performed by its members. These were ego-centered networks; no information other than relationship to the respondent was collected on the characteristics of network members. It was a purposive network—that part of the larger social network involved in help and support.

Findings from this first phase of the research demonstrated that support networks ranged in size from 2 to 22, but the modal size was in the 5–7 range (Wenger, 1984). The overall distribution of network size was as follows: small (< 5) = 25 percent; average (5–7) = 43 percent; and large (> 7) = 32 percent. Large networks were most common amongst those who were still married, and never-married people were more likely than others to have small networks.

Network size was also related to gender. Small networks were most common amongst never-married men, followed by widowed men, but married men were those least likely to have small networks. For women, network size was unrelated to marital status, and though married men's networks tended to shrink on widowhood, women's networks tended to remain the same.

Differences in the distribution of support and help tasks within networks also became apparent. It was clear that those who were or had been married tended to focus most of their dependency needs on one person in the network. For married people, this was their spouse; for widowed people, it tended to be the most proximate adult child. Those who had never married tended to spread their needs throughout the network and not to rely too much on any one person.

Not surprisingly, it was found that who one turned to for help was determined by who was available in the support network. Some tasks fell clearly in the kin domain and others in the non-kin domain. However, for those without local kin, friends and neighbors played a much more central part in the support network. Some networks were composed of mainly kin and others primarily of non-kin.

It also became clear that support network structure varied along a number of other parameters. Some respondents identified all network members as living in the same community, others named members who lived over 100 miles away but who were obviously important to their well-being. The proximity of network members was obviously important in emergencies and for face-to-face contact. It also seemed that a large proportion of network members were themselves over 60 years old, and an equally large proportion seemed to be female. It was not apparent immediately how these differences might affect the nature of support.

At the end of Phase 1, it was possible to report findings on the size, content, and functions of support networks. It was clear that variation between networks on several parameters was quite extensive, but it was not possible to identify any patterns of variation. It was also not possible on the basis of one survey to say anything about the stability of network relationships, nor whether the help described or expected would materialize in a predictable way.

Phase Two

The second phase of the research, 1982–1986, involved a follow-up study of the survivors of the older 1979 respondents—that is, those aged 75 and older in 1979. This project was initiated to test the stability of support network size and membership over time, to monitor the reliability of informal help, and to collect standardized data on the radius of networks and the proportions of members who were women or over 60. In order to limit costs, the funding agency (DHSS) was prepared to support the re-interview of only the older respondents, whose situations were deemed those most likely to be subject to change. The achieved survivor sample was 105.

In addition to a repeat survey, which replicated all questions related to support networks, plus additional questions whose relevance was indicated by findings from the 1979 survey, the second phase of the research included an intensive qualitative study of 30 survivors aged 79 and over. This intensive study continued for four years and was carried out by the author, who visited each of the randomly selected participants 2 to 4 times a year. Additional visits were made where the network was in a state of flux or under pressure. During this phase, the principal researcher became increasingly interested in variation in support networks.

On the basis of the quantitative data, the second phase demonstrated considerable stability in support networks (Wenger, 1986). The findings showed that: (1) the mean size of support networks remained stable, although nearly all networks experienced changes in membership composition; (2) more networks increased in size than shrank; (3) networks adapted to meet the needs of the older person at the core; (4) kin replaced both kin and non-kin in the performance of specific tasks, but non-kin only replaced other non-kin.

It was observed that support networks appeared to maintain an equilibrium; those with small networks in 1979 were likely to have small networks in 1983, and those with large networks in 1979 tended still to have large networks in 1983. Gains in network membership were, most frequently, adult children or children-in-law (often associated with widowhood or failing health), nieces and nephews (often associated with the death of a sibling), grandchildren, friends, neighbors, and professional caregivers. The largest increases were in numbers of neighbors and professionals.

The quantitative data showed that the radii of support networks followed a bimodal distribution: more than 40 percent of networks were made up of members who all lived within a 5-mile radius, and an equal proportion included members who lived more than 25 miles away. For most respondents, more than half the membership of their network was made up of women. Those without children were likely to have support networks made up primarily of others over the age of 60. Seven out of ten respondents, however, had three or more network members living within one mile.

The qualitative study made it possible to test the reliability of the network elicitation technique, and it was found that no support network member was identified who had not already been picked up by the survey methodology. This finding reinforced confidence in the methodology.

Because of the small size of the intensive sample, it was possible to collect personal data on all network members and to measure the density of the support networks. It was also possible in the course of intensive interviews to gain a fuller picture of the respondents' larger social networks. Over the four years, it became clear that recruitment to the support network took place from those in the social network who were already known to the respondent but not previously involved in a supportive role.

On the basis of the qualitative findings, it was possible to identify five different types of support networks based on: differences in the availability of local family; the proportions of kin and non-kin; frequency of face-to-face contact with family, friends and neighbors; and involvement in community groups, such as religious or voluntary organizations. The network types identified were as follows:

1. The *local-family-dependent support network* has primary focus on local family and close family relationships, with few peripheral friends and neighbors. This type of network tends to be small, of high density, and homogeneous. The larger social network is made up primarily of other, more distant kin not involved in the day-to-day support of the older person at the core of the network.

2. The *locally integrated support network* includes relationships with local family, neighbors, and friends. Many neighbors are also friends. Usually this type is associated with long-term residence and involvement in community groups. High levels of reciprocity are typical. These networks are larger and less dense and less homogeneous than the family-dependent type. The larger social network includes more distant family and friends but tends primarily to be composed of additional local family, friends, and neighbors who do not fulfill support functions.

3. The *local self-contained support network* is associated with less active involvement with close kin and a household-centered life-style. Primary reliance is on neighbors, although contact is not necessarily frequent. Community involvement tends to be low. These networks also tend to be small and of moderate density. The social networks associated with this network type tend to be smaller than others and to be characterized by low levels of contact.

4. The *wider-community-focused support network* is typically associated with an absence of local kin but active relationships with distant kin, especially children. This network is friendship-centered and includes some neighbors. Involvement in community and other voluntary groups is usually high. Those with this network type are more likely to be middle-class. Networks are typically large, heterogeneous, and loose-knit. Associated social networks are large, active, and heterogeneous.

5. The *private restricted support network* is also associated with an absence of local kin. Contact with neighbors tends to be minimal or arms-length, and friends tend not to be evident in the immediate community. Usually this type is associated with a lack of community involvement. Networks are very small and diffuse.

On the basis of qualitative data it was also possible to identify a consensus of normative expectations attaching to the different network relationships. It was clear that not only were specific responsibilities and expectations associated with each type of relationship, but that these were hierarchically ranked. At the top of the hierarchy came spouses, from whom both emotional and instrumental care was expected to the limit of physical capacity; next came daughters and sons, from whom both emotional and instrumental care were expected (more expressive and personal support from daughters and more instrumental help from sons), on the understanding that the children's families would not suffer unduly.

After children came sisters and brothers, from whom expectations were primarily expressive although, where distance allowed, emergency help was also taken for granted. Expectations for friends were comparable. Next came neighbors, where expectations were primarily for instrumental help with long interval needs and in emergencies, together with a general concern and awareness of one's well-being. Grandchildren, nieces, nephews, and cousins followed, but for each of these relationships responsibilities were mainly symbolic—keeping in touch, recognizing the blood-tie, but little else unless an unusually close relationship had predated old age.

The understanding of support networks had been substantially enhanced by the second phase of the research. It had been shown that size remained stable although the membership changed and that losses to the network tended to be replaced. It had been shown that different network relationships are associated with different levels of expectation. Further variance in network structure had been identified in terms of the radius within which the members were located and further evidence existed of the interaction between demographic variables and network structure and content. In addition, it had been possible to identify five different types of support networks.

The differences in network type made it possible to speculate about the significance of network type for support and instrumental help in old age. Different types of networks had different combinations of relationships. It was hypothesized, therefore, that different types of networks would provide different types of support and that they would have different strengths and weaknesses. However, the network typology was based on a small sample of 30, and it had not yet been validated with a large sample. It was possible that the different types were artifacts of the particular sample or that different types of network existed which had not been identified. It was necessary to look at a larger sample to test for correlations between support network and other variables and outcomes.

Phase Three

The third phase of work was conducted between 1986 and 1989 and involved a follow-up of all survivors of the 1979 survey in 1987. Application for funding from the DHSS initially failed, and an amended, less policy-driven grant application was then made to the ESRC. This second application was successful, but days before this news was received by the research team the DHSS agreed to fund the research. This meant that more research could be done, and each funding agency gained for less cost. This phase was, therefore, jointly funded by the DHSS and the ESRC and involved a further survey of survivors, including those in long-term care facilities. The original study had now become a longitudinal study. The questionnaire again replicated all questions related to support networks and asked additional questions which findings from the previous phase indicated would be relevant. An interviewed survivor sample of 198 was achieved.

On the basis of total interviews, which were quite extensive (and took between one-and-a-half and two hours to administer), and detailed interviewers' descriptions of respondents' overall situation, trained assessors identified the network type of each respondent based on the typology developed on the small intensive sample of 30. Assessments were sampled blind for reliability and consistency, and all borderline cases were discussed by the research team before decisions on network type were made.

Identification of network type for this larger sample made it possible not only to run correlations with network type, but also to identify for the first time the distribution of support network types in the community. It was found that distribution of network types was skewed, but that distribution was related to community. This finding is comparable with that of Warren (1981) in the United States, who found that help-seeking behavior was related to neighborhood type. However, in all communities more than half of respondents had either locally integrated or local-family-dependent networks. In all communities, local self-contained and private restricted networks were minority adaptations. Analysis also showed that network type was correlated, at high levels of statistical significance, with all demographic and outcome variables: age, marital and parental status, household composition, proximity to adult children, migration history, social class, income, health, mobility, loneliness, social isolation and morale (Wenger, 1991; Wenger and Shahtahmasebi, 1990). This finding reinforced our conviction of the validity of the typology.

The 1987 findings also reinforced the stability of support networks over time in terms of size and core membership, but it was not possible to say whether network type remained stable. In order to look at the stability of network type, all earlier interviews, conducted in 1979 and 1983, were assessed for network type. On the basis of these data it was possible to examine stability and shift in network type over time. It was found that most network types remained stable and that while shifts occurred, only some possible shifts were recorded. It was found that where shifts did happen, they were predominantly from a stronger network type to a less independent network type and were associated with a deterioration in physical or mental health or, in some cases, a change of residence. Few shifts occurred in the opposite direction, and these were mainly associated with residential moves, recovery from serious illness, or the release from caregiving responsibilities on the death of a spouse (Wenger, 1990).

Phase Four

The fact that network type was associated with all outcome variables indicated that identification of support network type might have practice applications as a predictive tool. Subsequently, funding was granted by the DoH and the Joseph Rowntree Foundation for a pilot study for the development of an instrument for the practitioner assessment of network type (PANT).

The practitioner study was conducted with six community care teams providing care for elderly people. These included: two specialist elderly social work teams; two social work teams working with elderly and physically handicapped people; one hospital social work team; and one multidisciplinary mental health support team working with elderly people. The project included the testing and refinement of a measurement instrument for use by practitioners. In addition to assessing for network type, participants in the study also recorded basic demographic details of those assessed and their presenting problems.

This phase of the work resulted in the development of a tested assessment instrument based on only the following eight questions:

1. How far away, in distance, does your nearest child or other relative live? (Exclude spouse.)

2. If you have any children, where does your nearest child live?

3. If you have any living sisters or brothers, where does your nearest sister or brother live?

4. How often do you see any of your children or other relatives to speak to?

5. If you have any friends in this community/neighborhood, how often do you have a chat or do something with one of your friends?

6. How often do you see any of your neighbors to have a chat with or do something with?

7. Do you attend any religious meetings?

8. Do you attend meetings of any community/neighborhood or social groups, such as old people's clubs, lectures, or anything like that?

The findings from this phase of the work demonstrated that the distribution of support network types on case loads was distinctively different from that in the community. The dominant network type on case loads was the private restricted support network, which is a minority adaptation in the community. It was also shown that the local-family-dependent and locally integrated network types were underrepresented on case loads (Wenger, 1994a).

In addition, it was clear that different network types were associated with different patterns of presenting problems. For example, the most common pattern in family-dependent networks was caregiver stress in the context of cognitive impairment of the dependent elderly person and a need for help with personal care or respite care coupled with caregiver support. In contrast, those with local self-contained networks were most likely to be living alone and to present with poor physical health and a need for help with day-to-day household tasks.

Some problems were more common in some network types than others. For example, problems associated with mobility and physical health were most common amongst clients with local self-contained and wider-community-focused support networks, although the need for help with personal care was highest in family-dependent and private restricted support networks.

It was also found that responses to interventions were affected by support network type. Some interventions worked well in one network type but were rejected or exacerbated the problem in others. Those with private restricted support networks tended to be more likely than others to make poor adaptations to residential care, despite the fact that they were more likely to need such care. Although paid good-neighbor schemes were acceptable to those with locally integrated and local self-contained networks, they were often anathema to those with wider-community-focused networks or to the caregivers of those with local-family-dependent networks. The predictive strength of the network typology was thus further extended (Wenger, 1994a).

The development of a mechanical assessment instrument had distinct advantages over assessor identification of network type. It was standardized and consistent, with no margin for differences of interpretation. However, while assessors could in most cases make a decision—however difficult—the instrument could not do this for borderline cases. In approximately 75 percent of cases an unequivocal identification was made; in 5 percent of cases the network was unclassifiable; but in approximately 20 percent of cases a borderline between two network types was identified. As a result, some means had to be found to deal with borderline cases.

On closer examination it became clear that not all possible borderlines occurred. Those that did were those that had previously been identified as pairs of types between which shifts occurred. In other words, there appeared to be an affinity between certain pairs of network types. It is likely that some borderlines represented true hybrid network types. On the other hand, particularly on the case loads of community care teams, it was possible that the support network was under pressure, in flux, and in the process of shift. For most analytical purposes, therefore, borderlines were recoded to the predictable destination of a shift.

Funding for a fourth round of the longitudinal study, planned for 1991, had not been achieved. It was felt by the DoH that after the passage of 12 years, an insufficient number of survivors would be found to make a further survey worth while. This was disappointing because the research team had seen it as an opportunity to test the PANT instrument on a population sample of comparable age with those on case loads. This was seen as important because it was necessary to validate the instrument in this way to ensure that the different distribution on case loads was not merely the result of the introduction of a new measurement technique.

In the event, unavoidable delays in another project made it possible for a minimal survey to be carried out in 1991. Data collection was limited to those demographic variables that could have changed, contact with formal domiciliary and some secondary health-care services, and the eight questions making up the PANT instrument. Because the survey instrument was short, it was possible to mail copies to those who had moved outside the study area for self-completion. A survivor sample of 127 was achieved. A computer algorithm based on the PANT instrument was designed to minimize error.

On the basis of the 127 surveyed, it was possible to compare network type as identified by assessor in 1987 with network type as identified by the PANT methodology in 1991 (Wenger, 1994b). This was, of course, not straightforward, since shifts in network type could be expected over time. Detailed scrutiny of the files of all cases demonstrating change in network type was necessary. The outcome of this exercise showed that in most cases changes were due to predictable shift in network type. However, in several cases where assessors had made a decision between locally integrated and wider-community-focused support networks, it was felt on reassessment that the PANT algorithm probably gave a more objective or consistent typing.

THE LIVERPOOL DEMENTIA STUDY

By 1989, funding had been awarded by the Medical Research Council (MRC) to the Department of Psychiatry, University of Liverpool, and by the DoH to the Centre for Social Policy Research and Development, Bangor, for a large epidemiological study of the prevalence and incidence of dementia, based on the screening of a population sample. The identification of network type was included in this project with the intent of monitoring the impact of the onset of dementia on support networks.

The development of the PANT algorithm made it possible to type support networks for large samples. Identification of network type was therefore undertaken for the total achieved screening sample of 5,222 people aged 65 and over, of whom 4,736 were not living in any type of residential-care facility. The sampling frame was based on the age/sex registers of general practitioners in the City of Liverpool and was stratified for age and sex. Respondents were recruited into the project over two years (1989–91) and were interviewed primarily in their own homes.

In the remainder of this chapter, the results from this Liverpool study are presented and discussed. For the purposes of the analyses reported here, the stratified data are weighted in order to approximate a population sample. Weightings are based on the 1989 midyear population estimate for England and Wales (Registrar General, 1991). In most respects, the elderly population of Liverpool is comparable with most other urban areas of similar size in the United Kingdom. At 3 percent, the proportion of members of ethnic minorities is comparable with that for the elderly population in the United Kingdom as a whole.

In addition to the screening survey, a subsample was randomly selected for intensive network study. This study involved an achieved sample of 612, who were re-interviewed in depth about their sources of support and the membership of their networks. This additional study made it possible to identify sources of help with a range of domestic and personal care tasks.

Findings from the Screening Study

The distribution of support network type in Liverpool was found to be as follows:

1. local-family-dependent: 22 percent;
2. locally integrated: 46 percent;
3. local self-contained: 11 percent;
4. wider-community-focused: 4 percent;
5. private restricted: 12 percent;
6. unclassified: 5 percent.

In contrast with earlier rural studies, more respondents had local family and locally integrated support networks, and fewer were identified as having wider-community-focused support networks. This reflected two particular factors: the low level of migration into Liverpool after middle age and the largely working-class character of the sample (Wenger, 1995c).

Support network was correlated with age, gender, marital status, household composition, social class, education, type of neighborhood, place of birth, duration of residence in the city, religious affiliation, and ethnicity, as shown in Table 7.1.

Age. As discussed above, shifts in network type are more frequent with increasing age, and for those aged 75 and over they tend to occur at the rate of 2.5 percent per annum (Wenger, 1990). Shifts are predictable, and for each network type there is a dominant destination type (Wenger and Scott, 1995). Local-family-dependent and private restricted support networks are the most likely destination for shifts. Higher proportions of these two types would, therefore, be expected with increasing age. As Table 7.1 shows, with increasing age the proportions of local-family-dependent and private restricted networks increase, and the proportions of locally integrated and wider-community-focused networks decrease.

Gender. Women made up 60 percent of the sample. Despite the fact that women are on average older than men, women were found to be more likely than men to have locally integrated networks, and men were more likely to have private restricted networks. This was in contrast to rural findings (Wenger, 1995c) and reflects the urban tendency for preferred neolocal residence following marriage to be near the wife's mother. Women, then, are more likely than men to remain in their natal neighborhood and to be more integrated into the urban community. Network type distribution is also likely to be influenced by the largely working-class elderly population of Liverpool and the greater local integration of working-class women (Cornwell, 1984).

Marital Status. Most respondents were or had been married: 43 percent were still married or cohabiting; 42 percent were widowed; 3 percent were divorced or separated; and 12 percent had never married. The relationship between marital status and support network is primarily due to differences between the never-married and the ever-married. Those who never married were twice as likely as others to have private restricted support networks, more likely to have local self-contained or wider-community-focused networks, and less likely to have family-dependent or locally integrated networks. However, the differences are largely due to differences in parenthood. If parents and nonparents are compared, the distributions of network types for those who never married and those who married but had no children are similar.

Table 7.1: Correlates of Support Network Types (Pearson χ^2)[a]

Variables		Family dep %	Local int. %	Local s.c. %	Wider c.f. %	Private restr. %
All		26	41	12	7	15
Age ***	65-69	28	49	11	5	8
	70-79	23	46	12	8	11
	80-89	26	35	13	7	18
	90+	30	29	11	4	27
Gender**	Male	25	39	13	6	16
	Female	26	43	11	7	13
Marital Status ***	Never married	19	24	17	10	30
	Mar./coh	26	45	12	6	11
	Widowed	27	42	11	6	13
	Div./sep.	26	43	13	4	15
Household Composition***	Lives alone	14	43	16	9	19
	Spouse only	23	46	13	6	12
	Younger gen.	65	30	2	1	2
	Same gen.	44	37	5	4	10
	Other	10	35	16	9	30
Social Class ***	I	18	43	10	14	15
	II	19	38	15	11	17
	III	26	41	13	6	14
	IV	30	42	11	4	13
	V	32	45	9	3	12
Length of F/T Education ***	< 9 years	35	32	11	7	16
	9-12 years	26	42	12	6	14
	> 12 years	17	39	10	14	20
Neighborhood***	Inner city	29	38	10	6	17
	Old w.c. sub.	27	43	12	6	13
	Mid. cl. sub.	24	38	13	9	17
	Periph. est.	26	44	12	5	13
Place of Birth ***	Liverpool	26	43	13	6	13
	Within 20ml.	26	42	11	6	13
	Over 20 ml.	26	32	10	11	22
	Overseas	26	36	3	7	29
Religious Affiliation ***	None	29	34	15	3	19
	Roman Cath.	24	52	8	7	10
	Anglican	27	37	13	6	16
	Other Chr.	20	42	13	11	14
	Other	22	38	12	12	16

[a] Percentages are totaled by row for each variable value.
** $p < .01$ *** $p < .001$

Household Composition. Eight out of ten respondents were either living alone (40 percent) or with their spouse only (39 percent). Only 15 percent were living in households with members of a younger generation; 4 percent in households with relatives of the same generation; and 2 percent in other types of households—that is, non-kin households. The relationship between household composition and support network type is fairly predictable.

As might be expected, those who live with children (or other younger-generation relatives) and those who live with siblings (or other same-generation relatives) are more likely than others to have family-dependent networks. Those living with younger-generation kin are least likely to have locally integrated networks, reflecting the fact that they are more likely to be able to remain in the community in the face of impaired health and mobility. They tend, therefore, to be older, more impaired, and more likely to be housebound. Local self-contained networks are more common amongst those who live alone or with a spouse only. "Other" household types, reflecting a variety of non-kin-based households, are more likely than others to have wider-community-focused and private restricted networks and "unclassified" networks.

Social Class. The social-class categories used in this study are those adopted by the government Registrar-General: professional (I); managerial and qualified (II); skilled workers (manual and nonmanual) (III); semiskilled workers (IV); and unskilled workers (V). Those who spent all their working lives in military service are classified separately. As mentioned earlier, Liverpool is largely a working-class city (Social Classes III, IV, and V). In the elderly sample, only 17 percent were classified as middle class. Most of the respondents fell into Social Class III.

Support network type was clearly related to social class. Locally integrated networks were the modal network type for all social classes. However, working-class respondents were almost twice as likely to have local-family-dependent support networks as middle-class respondents. Middle-class respondents were more likely than others to have local self-contained support networks and were two to four times more likely to have wider-community-focused networks than working-class people. Private restricted networks were twice as common amongst those whose main occupation had been in the armed services. This is likely to reflect the fact that they moved around frequently during their adult lives and may explain the finding that men are more likely to have private restricted networks.

Education. The large majority of respondents had received only a basic education (90 percent) or less (5 percent). The number of years respondents had spent in full-time education was also related to support network type. Those with the least education were most likely to have family-dependent support networks. Those with a basic education were most likely to have locally integrated networks and more likely than others to have local self-contained networks. Those with most education were more likely than others to have wider-community-focused or private restricted support networks. In other words, the better-educated were less likely to rely on kin and more likely to adopt independent lifestyles and have loose-knit networks. Similar findings have been reported by Fischer (1982) in the United States.

Neighborhood. Earlier work had demonstrated that network type correlated highly with village, community, or neighborhood (Thissen, Wenger, and Scharf, 1995). In the Liverpool study, only postal district was available as a proxy for this variable. Postal district and network type were correlated at the highest level of significance. However, the large number of postal areas made this a cumbersome variable. These were, therefore, aggregated to reflect the predominant neighborhood types existing in the city: inner city; older working-class suburbs; middle-class suburbs; and peripheral postwar housing estates. The analysis of relationships between support networks and neighborhood types is based on these categories and so is comparable with findings on social class.

Locally integrated support networks were most common in the older working-class suburbs and wider-community-focused networks in middle-class suburbs. Local self-contained networks were most common in middle-class suburbs. Private restricted networks were most common in the inner city and in middle-class suburbs.

Place of Birth. The elderly people of Liverpool are a very homogeneous and stable population: 85 percent were living within 20 miles of their place of birth, 12 percent were born elsewhere in the United Kingdom, and only 2 percent had come from overseas. This reflects population trends which demonstrate a net of loss of population for Liverpool (*Regional Trends*, 1989, Table 4.6). The city has a postwar history of slum clearance, rehousing to the periphery, high levels of unemployment, and the collapse of traditional industries—particularly the shipping and port industries—and a high level of social problems. It is perceived as a problem city by outsiders. People move out, but few move in. This is reflected in the fact that 97 percent of respondents had lived in the city for more than 30 years.

Place of birth was significantly related to support network type. Those with locally integrated and local self-contained networks were most likely to have lived in Liverpool all their lives. Those with wider-community-focused networks were more likely than others to have been born more than 20 miles away. Those born overseas were more likely than others to have private restricted networks.

Religious Affiliation. The modal religious affiliation was Anglican (or Episcopalian) (44 percent), followed by Roman Catholic (28 percent), and Other Christian (11 percent), making 83 percent of the older population of Liverpool

Christians. Only 3 percent belonged to other faiths, but 15 percent stated that they were agnostic or atheist. Network type was clearly related to religious affiliation.

Locally integrated support networks were most common amongst those who were Roman Catholics. This is likely to reflect larger family size, more regular church attendance, and predominantly working-class status. Family-dependent support networks were more common among those who reported that they were atheist/agnostic or who said they were "Church of England"—that is, Anglican. Those who are only nominal Christians, not affiliated with any church, tend to be recorded as Anglican as a residential category. This suggests that those who are not church members are more likely to have family-dependent networks. This finding, together with the finding that those who identified themselves as atheist/agnostic were most likely to have private restricted networks, suggests that membership of a religious group may be an important integrating factor in urban environments. While religion and support network type are also correlated in rural areas, the nature of the correlation is different, and religious membership does not appear to be important for community integration. In the rural context, local provenance seems to be more important (Wenger, 1995c).

Ethnicity. The study sought to identify differences between ethnic groups represented in the city. The categories used to identify ethnic group, based on U.K. Census categories tailored to represent the ethnic mix in the city, were: English/Irish/Scottish/Welsh; other European; Jewish; Afro–Caribbean; other African; Chinese; other Asian; and other. The numbers of members of minority ethnic groups in Liverpool are small but it was clear that, even allowing for this, members of ethnic minority groups were underrepresented in the study: 95 percent of respondents were identified as English/Irish/Scottish/Welsh; 2 percent were other Europeans; 1 percent were Jewish; and less than 1 percent each were African and Afro–Caribbean, Chinese, and others.

There were relationships between ethnic group and support network type, but the small numbers suggest tentative discussion and are not included in Table 7.1. The majority of Chinese and other Asians had family-dependent networks, reflecting patterns of migration in which two- and three-generation families emigrated to the United Kingdom. Afro–Caribbeans and other Africans were more likely than other ethnic groups to have private restricted networks. Members of these groups had primarily come to Britain as young single adults. High levels of separation and divorce and the matrifocality of these black families results in a high proportion of the men becoming socially isolated in old age. The Jewish population is longer established and is more integrated. Jews were those most likely to have locally integrated networks and were more likely than others to have local self-contained networks. Jews and other Europeans (reflecting their largely middle-class status) were more likely than other ethnic groups to have wider-community-focused networks.

Determining Variables

The eight variables used in the network identification algorithm were presented earlier. The assessment instrument (and thus the algorithm) was based on predicted response(s) to each question in the case of an ideal type network. These are the determining variables for network type. Respondents do not have to give the ideal response to every question; however, it is the modal network response that determines network type. It is therefore of interest to look at the distribution of responses by network type. These are summarized in Table 7.2.

It can be seen that nearly all those with local-family-dependent support networks lived within a mile, and virtually all lived within 5 miles of a relative, as did 86 percent of those with locally integrated networks. In contrast, 58 percent of those with private restricted networks and 67 percent of those with wider-community-focused networks had no relative within 15 miles.

Those with both family-dependent and locally integrated support networks were more than twice as likely as others to be parents, although those with family-dependent networks were more likely to be living within a mile of an adult child. Approximately one-third of those with local self-contained or wider-community-focused networks were childless, as were more than half of those with private restricted networks. Those with children in these network types were also more likely to live at some distance from their children.

It might be thought that those without children would be more likely to live nearer to their siblings. However, the findings for Liverpool do not support this unequivocally. Those with family-dependent support networks are not only more likely than others to live near an adult child, they are also most likely to live near a sibling: 49 percent of those with family-dependent and 43 percent of those with locally integrated support networks lived within 5 miles of a sibling. Those with local self-contained networks were those most likely to have living siblings, but 52 percent lived more than 5 miles from their nearest sister or brother, and only 4 percent had a sibling within a mile. In contrast, 54 percent of those with wider-community-focused and 70 percent of those with private restricted networks had no living sister or brother.

Of those with family-dependent support networks, 94 percent had a relative living within a mile; most saw a relative every day, and 96 percent at least twice a week. In addition, 74 percent of those with locally integrated networks saw a relative at least twice a week, and 72 percent of those with local self-contained networks saw a relative at least weekly. In contrast, 70 percent of those with wider-community-focused networks saw a relative less often than weekly (4 percent never did) and 27 percent of those with private restricted networks never saw a relative.

Those with locally integrated and wider-community-focused networks have most frequent contact with friends: 81 percent of the former and 74 percent of the latter see friends more than twice a week; however, so do 52 percent of those with local self-contained networks. In contrast, 36 percent of those with local-

Table 7.2: Network Characteristics by Network Types[a]

Variables		Family dep %	Local int. %	Local s.c. %	Wider c.f. %	Private restr. %
Nearest	1 mile	94	34	8	11	12
child/relative ***	1-5 miles	6	2	27	15	23
	6-15 miles	<1	3	48	4	7
	> 15 miles	0	1	17	67	41
	No relative	<1	0	<1	4	18
Nearest child ***	< 1 mile	71	25	2	3	1
	1-5 miles	13	43	5	5	12
	6-15 miles	1	16	34	1	4
	>15 miles	4	4	25	59	27
	No children	11	12	35	33	55
Nearest sibling**	< 1 mile	24	12	4	2	3
	1-5 miles	25	31	26	6	4
	6-15 miles	7	20	31	4	5
	> 15 miles	17	12	21	35	19
	No siblings	28	26	19	54	70
Freqency see	Daily	83	42	5	8	9
children ***	2-3 per week	13	32	8	4	9
	Weekly	3	19	59	19	15
	< weekly	1	6	28	66	39
	Never	<1	1	1	4	27
Frequency see	Daily	25	50	30	39	34
friend***	2-3 per week	15	31	21	35	13
	Weekly	10	14	18	22	8
	< weekly	14	1	13	2	8
	Never	36	5	19	3	38
Frequency see	Daily	35	60	44	52	44
neighbour ***	2-3 per week	17	28	21	23	17
	Weekly	8	8	23	17	8
	< weekly	16	2	7	6	8
	Never	25	2	6	3	23
Attends religious	Regularly	7	40	10	55	11
meetings ***	Occasionally	20	11	13	21	4
	Never	73	50	77	23	85
Attends community	Regularly	6	52	11	70	9
groups***	Occasionally	7	5	7	10	2
	Regularly	87	42	82	20	89

[a] Percentages are totaled by column for each network characteristic.
*** p < .001.
Note: 4 percent of the subjects had an inconclusive network type and are excluded from the table.

family-dependent and 38 percent of those with private restricted networks never see a friend. This is related to the greater average age and poorer average health of those with these types of networks.

Contact with neighbors is highest amongst those with locally integrated and wider-community-focused networks, more than half of whom are in daily contact with neighbors. Approximately one-quarter of those with family-dependent or private restricted networks never have a chat with neighbors, again reflecting their generally poorer health.

Those with locally integrated and wider-community-focused networks are more likely to attend religious meetings and neighborhood groups than others. Membership is highest amongst those with wider-community-focused networks. Over 80 percent of those with family-dependent, local self-contained, and private restricted networks never attend meetings of neighborhood groups.

While the outcomes for the determining variables are predictable, Table 7.2 shows the degree of difference between the different network types. The findings emphasize the differences between networks and show that some types depend primarily on family, and others on friends, neighbors, and voluntary groups.

FINDINGS FROM THE NETWORK SUBSAMPLE

On the basis of the subsample of 612 who participated in a detailed interview about their support networks, it is possible to demonstrate what the above findings mean in terms of the different sources from which older people with different types of networks can expect help or support.

Respondents were asked whether they had a confidant and, if so, the nature of their relationship to their confidant. The importance of marital status and in the absence of a spouse or children comes across very strongly here. Those with local-family-dependent support networks named adult children most commonly (40 percent—24 percent daughters); 20 percent named their spouse, but almost as many (19 percent) said that they had no one in whom to confide or that they did not confide. This is surprising, given the dependency on the family but, on the basis of the qualitative data, is likely to reflect the unwillingness of dependent old people to burden their caregiver with their problems and worries. Adult children were also the most likely confidant (32 percent—21 percent daughters) for those with locally integrated networks; spouses were named by 26 percent; friends by 13 percent (9 percent female); and 12 percent said there was no one in whom they confided. Childlessness is highest in local self-contained networks, and this is reflected in the choice of confidant. Most frequently mentioned were spouses (30 percent), followed by adult children (22 percent—17 percent daughters) and "other" relatives (12 percent); 15 percent had no confidant. In all three of these network types, more than half of confidants were either spouses or children.

A different pattern is shown by those older people with either wider-community-focused or private restricted networks. The most frequently mentioned confidant amongst those with wider-community-focused networks was a friend (30 percent—27 percent female), followed by a spouse (23 percent) and children (17 percent—13 percent daughters); 13 percent said they had no confidant. However, for those with private restricted networks the commonest response was no one (28 percent); an adult child was named by 21 percent (17 percent daughters), a spouse by 18 percent, and a friend by 17 percent (14 percent female).

The centrality of spouses and children, especially daughters, and the importance of female friends is also evident in the responses to the question as to whom the respondent relied on most. These were the two categories mentioned most often for those with family-dependent, locally integrated, and local self-contained support networks (accounting for 78 percent, 67, and 58 percent, respectively). More than twice as many of those with local self-contained networks reported that there was no one in particular on whom they relied (10 percent). For those with wider-community-focused networks, spouses were mentioned most frequently (33 percent), followed by a friend or neighbor (20 percent) and a niece or nephew (10 percent); only 3 percent mentioned a child. Amongst those with private restricted networks, 46 percent mentioned a spouse (24 percent) or child (22 percent), and 23 percent named a friend or neighbor; 10 percent of those with wider-community-focused networks, but only 2 percent of those with private restricted networks, named no one.

Respondents to the detailed network questionnaire were also asked to whom they would turn for help with a range of situations or tasks. The responses to these questions were coded differently: spouse or relative in the same household, relative in another household, friend or neighbor, professional, other.

Spouses and relatives were the most usual sources of help in the event of illness for all network types. In local-family-dependent networks, 70 percent of helpers were either spouses (29 percent) or relatives in the same household, and another 19 percent were relatives in another household. In locally integrated networks, help came primarily (69 percent) from spouses (29 percent) and relatives in other households, with 11 percent from a relative in the same household. Spouses were more important for those with local self-contained networks (36 percent), where 71 percent received care when ill from either spouses or a relative in a different household, but 16 percent depended on a neighbor or nearby friend.

Apart from spouses, the sources of help when ill for respondents with wider-community-focused and private restricted networks were more likely to be non-kin. Friends (and neighbors) were mentioned most frequently by those with wider-community-focused networks (33 percent); in combination with spouses, they were named by 60 percent. Those with private restricted networks were most likely to name neighbors (or friends) as those to whom they would turn for help when ill (30 percent), and one-quarter mentioned their spouse, making more than half dependent on this source of help. However, 17 percent in both these network types named a relative in another household, often living some distance away.

Overall, spouses and relatives comprised the main source of help in illness: for 90 percent of those with local-family-dependent networks, 80 percent of those with locally integrated, 72 percent of those with local self-contained, 50 percent of those with wider-community-focused networks, and 59 percent of those with private restricted networks. What seems clear is that in the case of illness, in the absence of a spouse, relatives are expected to care if they live close enough, but in the absence of kin, older people will turn to friends or neighbors before seeking professional or commercial help. Professional, commercial, or "other" sources of help when ill were mentioned by small proportions of respondents ranging from 5 percent in the case of family-dependent networks to 10 percent in the case of wider-community-focused networks.

Respondents were also asked about the help they received with shopping and cleaning. Many of them did not need help with either of these tasks and were independent of helpers. Most independent with shopping were those with wider-community-focused networks (57 percent), followed by those with locally integrated networks (47 percent) and locally self-contained networks (44 percent). Most dependent were those with family-dependent networks (29 percent) and private restricted networks (23 percent).

Help came primarily from spouses and relatives in the same household for those with family-dependent and private restricted networks; spouses and relatives living in another household for those with locally integrated and local self-contained networks; and spouses and friends (or neighbors) for those with wider-community-focused networks. However, as a proportion of help received, those with wider-community-focused networks were most likely to receive formal paid help (39 percent of help), followed by those with local self-contained and private restricted networks (each 23 percent). Only 7 percent of help with shopping came from formal sources for those with family-dependent or locally integrated networks.

Similar patterns of independence were found for help with cleaning. However, sources of help were quite different. In addition to informal sources of help, formal helpers were far more significant. These were either provided by the local authority or privately contracted by the older person or their family. In local-family-dependent networks, the main sources of help were a relative living in the same household or a spouse, followed by a formal paid helper (14 percent). In all other network types, formal helpers were the most frequently mentioned source of help.

As a percentage of those receiving help, formal sources provided 69 percent of all cleaning help to those with wider-community-focused networks; 46 percent to private restricted networks, 44 percent to those in local self-contained networks, and 42 percent to those in locally integrated networks. However, in family-dependent networks only 6 percent of cleaning help received came from formal sources. The proportions of those receiving formal help with shopping and cleaning in wider-community-focused networks reflects their largely middle-class status and ability to pay for help. The receipt of formal help with cleaning was significantly related to network type, but other statutory domiciliary services were unrelated to network type.

Home visits from ministers of religion were also related to network type. Those with wider-community-focused and locally integrated networks were most likely to be visited (45 and 22 percent, respectively). In other words, those most likely to be able to attend religious meetings were more likely to receive visits. Those whose network types are most associated with social isolation—the local self-contained and private restricted—were least likely to be visited at home by a religious practitioner (7 and 12 percent, respectively).

SOCIAL POLICY IMPLICATIONS

The network typology described in this chapter was developed over the course of continuous research funding over a number of years. At each stage, it was possible to build on the findings of earlier work and to test out new techniques and hypotheses. The resulting typology has benefited from the continuity of the research. The resultant measurement algorithm seems to be a rigorous instrument and produces consistent results with high levels of correlation with the majority of variables of interest.

The Liverpool study made it possible to test the algorithm in use with a large sample and to compare the distribution of networks in an urban environment with those recorded earlier in rural areas. Contrary to conventional wisdom, which suggests rural villages as idyllic places in which to retire, the findings in Liverpool showed that the critical factor is population stability; more of the Liverpool elderly population had robust network types than had been identified in rural Wales and the rural Netherlands (Thissen, Wenger, and Scharf, 1995).

The importance of recognizing differences in support network type lies in the identification of variation of the strength and weakness of available informal help and support. With increasing age, people are faced more often with health and mobility problems, which mean that they have to rely on others more frequently. Much that has been written in the social policy and practice fields, while not denying differences in household composition and the availability of adult children, has been couched in generalizations that appear to assume a relatively homogeneous elderly population. Assumptions are made about the availability of informal help, irrespective of what expectations can realistically be held about different types of relationships. The fact is that if there is no one in your network for whom cultural expectations of commitment to care exist, it is unlikely that help (particularly at high levels of dependency) will be forthcoming.

As discussed, different types of networks reflect different combinations of proximate relationships and hence the availability of different levels and sorts of informal help. Once network type has been identified, it is possible to predict the likely pattern of help that will emerge in a specific situation. The hierarchy of responsibilities and expectations identified in an early phase of the research has been reflected in the sources from which different types of help come. Sources of help reflect the same hierarchy. If there is a spouse, most reliance will be put on them in all support network types. In the absence of a spouse, help comes first from another member of the household. Where a person lives alone, help will come first from a relative living in another nearby household. Where there are no close relatives living nearby, the person in need may receive help from a friend or a neighbor.

Depending on their life history, some people are less likely to ask for or accept help from others. Those who have moved out of the area in which they were born are more likely than others to have developed an independent lifestyle. For a few people, no source of any informal help may be available. In the absence of informal helpers, formal services will be sought. However, the findings suggest that formal help is in most cases a last resort.

It has been recorded elsewhere that the more intimate or personal the care domain, the more likely it is that the older person will turn to a relative; but for certain other types of help friends and neighbors may be preferred or be more appropriate (Wenger, 1984, 1990). For instance, health and money concerns fall squarely in the family domain. There is some evidence to suggest that personal care is most likely to be provided by family living in the same household. Some sorts of help come more frequently from a friend or neighbor, including lifts, company, and conversation, and borrowing small items. Nonmarried women are more likely to turn to friends, and men are more likely to turn to family.

Differences in age and levels of impairment between network types reflect primarily the capacity of certain network types to make it possible for frail old people to remain in the community. In subsequent phases of the North Wales study, all those receiving personal care who had short interval needs (for example feeding, washing, toileting), had family-dependent support networks (Wenger, 1992). In Liverpool, it has been found that those suffering from cognitive impairment who were still living in the community had either family-dependent or private restricted support networks (Wenger, 1994c, 1994d), and in another study it was found that networks on the family-dependent/private restricted borderline were often associated with being housebound and with high levels of mental or physical impairment, which confined the old person to the house (Wenger, 1994a). Where there is no family member available and willing to assume the role of caregiver, admission to residential care is the usual outcome.

It has also been found that the most common network type—locally integrated—is most adept at supporting older people at increasing levels of disability in their own home. In contrast, those with local self-contained and wider-community-focused support networks are likely to place a very high value on independence and to resist help until they are unable to cope without it (Wenger,

1993). In the absence of a spouse, in local self-contained, wider-community-focused, and private restricted networks, residential care is often the only alternative to self-care.

From the findings of the Liverpool study, it seems clear that formal services are the residual choice as a source of help, although there are indications that formal help with cleaning is more acceptable than are other types of service. It is also shown that some network types have more need to turn to formal services than others. It has been suggested elsewhere that the interface between formal and informal services will be different for different network types (Wenger, 1995c). In some network types, cooperation between formal and informal helpers is possible and may be preferable; in other network types there are no informal helpers with whom formal workers can collaborate. Different styles of working, therefore, need to be adopted depending on network type.

The predictive capacity of network type in terms of a wide variety of outcomes, including morale, social isolation, loneliness, presenting problems, sources of help, appropriate service interventions, and hospital discharge outcome, means that the identification of support network is a useful practice (Swinford, 1995) as well as a research tool. The typology is increasingly being adopted by practitioners. Amongst their independent findings are the fact that network provides one of the best indicators for mental health interventions and predictors of mental health outcomes (Goudie, 1995). Identification of the network type of caregivers of dementia sufferers has also proved to be useful in decisionmaking about packages of care (McNeely, 1995); network type has also been found to be predictive of uptake of benefit entitlements (Arwyn, 1995).

In terms of future social policy, it seems evident that variations in available networks of support need to be taken into consideration when making policy for the provision of supportive services for older people. Household mobility undermines the strength of informal networks. Where high levels of geographical mobility occur, those networks most likely to need formal service responses will be common. Local and national governments introducing policies that emphasize the mobility of labor will need to take account of this. High labor mobility will increase the need for formal support for old people.

Subsequent cohorts of elderly people are likely to have moved around more during their lifetimes, and thus patterns of mobility need to be taken into account when projecting service needs in the next decades. Social mobility is also likely to have an impact. Those in middle-class occupations are more geographically mobile. With an increasingly technical and mechanized workforce, a larger proportion of occupations are classified as middle class, and greater proportions, therefore, are moving not just within the country but within the European Community and farther afield. It is probable that greater proportions of older people in following cohorts will have less robust informal support networks. In other words, the proportions of wider-community-focused and private restricted networks may increase. However, requests for formal help may also be mitigated by greater emphasis on independence.

In addition to the growing numbers of old people, especially in the over-80 age group, the likelihood that because of changes in network distributions more of them will need to seek formal rather than informal help in the future suggests that policymakers need to start to take these shifts on board as they plan for the next century. For instance, these suggested shifts may also be reflected in a higher salience being attached to independence. More sophisticated and/or more independent generations of old people may be prepared to use much higher levels of electronic and technical aids with both instrumental help and communication. It is difficult to preguess the future, but it is likely that variation in lifestyle and sources of help will increase. The network typology described in this chapter has shown the potential in the identification of patterns of adaptation in the increasing complexity of the postmodern world.

NOTE

1. I am indebted to Anne Scott and Vanessa Burholt for help with data handling and the preparation of data and tables in the writing of this paper. I would like to express my thanks and appreciation for all their support.

8

Assessing Social Support Networks among Older People in the United States

James Lubben and Melanie Gironda

The relationship between social integration and health and well-being among elderly populations is an area of increasing importance in gerontological study and practice in the United States. The theory and evidence on the topic approximate that available at the time of the U.S. Surgeon General's 1964 report on smoking and health, with similar implications for future research and public policy. Whereas routine health examinations now increasingly inquire about past and present smoking behavior, similar inquiry regarding an elderly person's social support network remains rare.

Inadequate social support has been associated among people of all ages with an increase in mortality (Berkman and Syme, 1979; Blazer, 1982; House, Umberson, and Landis, 1988; Zuckerman, Kasl, and Ostfeld, 1984), morbidity (Berkman, 1985; Ell, 1984; Torres, McIntosh, and Kubena, 1992), and psychological distress (Hurwicz and Berkanovic, 1993; Turner, 1981; Williams, Ware, and Donald, 1981), and a decrease in overall general health and well-being (Bloom, 1990; Chappell, 1991; Chappell and Badger, 1989; Cutrona, Russell, and Rose, 1986; Minkler, Satariano, and Langhouser, 1983). Although few large-scale empirical studies have been conducted among elderly populations, a significant relationship also appears to exist between an elder's level of social networks and health risk (Kaplan, Seeman, Cohen, Knudsen, and Guralnic, 1987; Lubben, Weiler, and Chi, 1989). Furthermore, studies of stressful experiences, social support, and mental health among elderly populations conclude that various forms of social support may also provide stress-buffering effects (Cohen and

Wills, 1985; Cutrona, Russell, and Rose, 1986; Krause, Herzog, and Baker, 1992; Krause and Jay, 1991, Mor-Barak et al., 1991).

Gerontological researchers clearly need to expand their investigation of the nature and consequences of social isolation and social integration among elderly populations and to relate such findings to questions of social care policy. Accordingly, this chapter addresses the factors that account for the apparent health risk of social isolation among a sample of older adults in California. The study presents an overview of attempts to assess elders' social support networks and suggests strategies for future research.

THEORIES FOR THE APPARENT RELATIONSHIP OF SOCIAL SUPPORT NETWORK AND HEALTH

A buffering effect provided by strong social ties that serves to reduce the susceptibility of an individual to stress-related illnesses is probably the most common explanation for the apparent link between health and social support networks (Cassel, 1976; Cobb, 1976; Thoits, 1982). This theory suggests that an elderly person with a nurturing social support network is more equipped to manage the stress associated with major health events as well as other stressful situations common in old age. This is especially important in geriatric practice, where many practitioner–patient encounters are inherently stressful, increasing the relevance of this theory to assisting in desired clinical outcomes.

A theory similar to the stress-buffering hypothesis suggests that social isolation can have a direct physiologic effect, increasing an elderly person's vulnerability to morbidity and mortality (Berkman, 1985). It is suggested that social ties may serve to stimulate the immune system to ward illnesses off better. Although there is less hard evidence to support this theory, some very current research involving persons with immune disorders (e.g., cancer, AIDS, etc.) should further clarify the veracity of this theoretical assumption.

A third theory suggests that health promotion behaviors can be enhanced by a strong social support network through encouraging an elder to practice health promotion behaviors and to quit bad practices (Berkman, 1985; Cohen and Syme, 1985a; Crawford, 1987). For example, support from family and/or friends may facilitate better nutrition and exercise practices. Furthermore, family or friends may help an elderly person to seek timely medical attention for a specific health condition before it becomes a larger, more difficult problem to treat.

A fourth theory, which is almost as common as that of the stress-buffering hypothesis, posits that social networks provide essential support needed during times of illness, thereby contributing to better adaptation and quicker recovery time (Cohen and Syme, 1985a). Those elders without an adequate social support network are at increased risk for illness-related complications and are more likely to have a slower recovery time. This is an especially important consideration in today's managed health-care arena in the United States, which relies heavily upon outpatient medical care. Outpatient care requires the presence of a functional social support network to provide the supportive services to elders that previously would have been delivered by nurses or nurses' aides in a hospital setting.

Although gerontological research increasingly substantiates the importance of social support networks to health and well being among the elderly, considerably more research is needed before successful interventions can be generally prescribed and implemented to change an elder's social network in a positive direction. To address these deficiencies, the present chapter compares and contrasts three related but slightly different constructs of social integration: (1) loneliness, (2) social support, and (3) social networks. For each of these constructs, a commonly used measure is presented.

Distinguishing Three Aspects of Social Integration

Social networks, social supports, and loneliness are not identical constructs. Of the three, social networks and social supports are confused most often. A review of social network theories reiterates the necessity to differentiate between the two concepts (Auslander and Litwin, 1987). Generally, social networks refer to the structural aspects of social integration, whereas social supports consider functional aspects.

A metaphoric definition of social networks is to view them as a web of social ties that surround a person and then focus on the nature of the various strands of a person's grid of social relationships (Ell, 1984). Structural dimensions of social networks include size, density, source of ties, member homogeneity, frequency of contacts, geographic proximity, durability, intensity, and opportunity for reciprocal exchange of supports (Ell, 1984; Vaux, 1988). Social networks function as a way for an individual to influence the environment and also for the environment to influence the individual.

Social supports are generally considered a subset of one's total social network. Thus, an adequate social network precedes the existence of social support. For example, Berkman (1984) defines social support as "the emotional and instrumental assistance that is obtained from people who compose the individual's social network." This functional nature of support is distinguished from the structural nature of social networks by the presence or perceived availability of specific dimensions of support (Sherbourne and Stewart, 1991). Emotional support can consist of caring, affection, love, sympathy, understanding, esteem, and empathy. Instrumental assistance consists of more tangible support such as information, financial aid, help with medical needs, help with household maintenance or other daily living tasks, and so on. The assessment of social support should be done within the context of need, however, as an absence of support may be merely due to the absence of need rather than the unavailability of support.

Loneliness is distinguished as a construct distinct from both social networks and supports. Indeed, one may feel lonely while in the midst of a crowd. For example, Weiss (1973) states that "loneliness is not simply a desire for company, any company; rather it yields only to very specific forms of relationships." Perlman (1987) claims that loneliness is a discrepancy between one's desired and achieved levels of social contacts. It has been suggested that there are two types of loneliness: emotional and social (Weiss, 1973). Emotional loneliness is a lack of truly intimate ties, whereas social loneliness is a lack of a network of involvement with family, peers, friends, and neighbors.

Although not identical, there is likely to be some overlap between social support, social networks, and loneliness. Because social networks are the source of social support, the two are not totally separable from one another. Similarly, because loneliness may result from deficiencies in one's social environment, loneliness is likely to be correlated with social networks or social supports. Thus, the three constructs are related to the extent that they are aspects of a person's total social milieu.

Scales Representing These Three Aspects of Social Integration

Social Networks. One composite measure of social networks, developed explicitly for the elderly population, is the Lubben Social Network Scale (LSNS) (Lubben, 1988; Luggen and Rini, 1995; Rubinstein, Lubben, and Mintzer, 1994). The LSNS is a refinement of the Berkman-Syme Social Network Index (Berkman and Syme, 1979) and consists of an equally weighted sum of the following 10 items:

LSNS 1: How many relatives (including in-laws) do you see or hear from at least once a month?

LSNS 2: Tell me about the relatives (including spouse) with whom you have the most contact. How often do you see or hear from that person?

LSNS 3: How many relatives (including spouse do you feel close to? That is, how many of them do you feel at ease with, can talk to about private matters, or can call on for help?

LSNS 4: Do you have any close friends? That is, do you have any friends or neighbors with whom you feel at ease, can talk to about private matters? If so, how many?

LSNS 5: How many of these friends do you see or hear from at least once a month?

LSNS 6: Tell me about the friend with whom you have the most contact. How often do you see or hear from that person?

LSNS 7: When you have an important decision to make, do you have someone you can talk to about it?

LSNS 8: When other people you know have an important decision to make, do they talk to you about it?

LSNS 9: Does anybody rely on you to do something for them each day? For example: shopping, cooking dinner, doing repairs, cleaning house, providing child care, etc.

LSNS 10: Do you live alone or with others?

Scores for each item range from zero to five, with zero indicating minimal social integration and five indicating substantial social integration. According to Lubben (1988), factor analyses suggest that the LSNS represents three distinct structural dimensions of social networks: family, friends, and mutual support, including confidant relationships.

Social Supports. A scale that has been developed to measure social support is the RAND Medical Outcome Study Social Support Survey (MOS–SSS) (Sherbourne and Stewart, 1991). The MOS–SSS is an 18-item scale designed to measure four dimensions of functional support: (1) emotional/informational, (2) tangible, (3) affectionate, and (4) positive social interaction. Each item is associated with a Likert-type response option describing availability of support (1 = "none of the time," whereas 5 = "all of the time").

The RAND Medical Outcome Study Social Support Scale asks how often the following kinds of support are available to the respondent:

MOS–SSS 1: Someone to help you if you were confined to bed?

MOS–SSS 2: Someone you can count on to listen to you when you need to talk?

MOS–SSS 3: Someone to give you good advice about a crisis?

MOS–SSS 4: Someone to take you to the doctor if you needed it?

MOS–SSS 5: Someone who shows you love and affection?

MOS–SSS 6: Someone to have a good time with?

MOS–SSS 7: Someone to give you information to help you understand a situation?

MOS–SSS 8: Someone to confide in or talk about yourself or your problems?

MOS–SSS 9: Someone who hugs you?

MOS–SSS 10: Someone to get together with for relaxation?

MOS–SSS 11: Someone to prepare your meals if you were unable to do it yourself?

MOS–SSS 12: Someone whose advice you really want?

MOS–SSS 13: Someone to help you with daily chores if you were sick?

MOS–SSS 14: Someone to share your most private worries and fears with?

MOS–SSS 15: Someone to turn to for suggestions about a personal problem?

MOS–SSS 16: Someone to do something enjoyable with?

MOS–SSS 17: Someone who understands your problems?

MOS–SSS 18: Someone to love and make you feel wanted?

Loneliness. A commonly used measure for loneliness is the UCLA Loneliness Scale (UCLA–LS: Russell, Peplau, and Cutrona, 1980). The UCLA–LS is a 20-item self-report measure. To safeguard against response-set bias, half of the items are positively worded, reflecting satisfaction with social relationships, and half are negatively worded, reflecting dissatisfaction with social relationships. Respondents are asked to indicate how often they feel the way described in each of the statements that make up the UCLA–LS. The following statements are those used in the present analysis:

UCLA–LS 1: I feel in tune with the people around me.

UCLA–LS 2: I lack companionship.

UCLA–LS 3: There is no one I can turn to.

UCLA–LS 4: I feel part of a group of friends.

UCLA–LS 5: I have a lot in common with the people around me.

UCLA–LS 6: I am no longer close to anyone.

UCLA–LS 7: My interest and ideas are not shared by those around me.

UCLA–LS 8: I am an outgoing person.

UCLA–LS 9: There are people I feel close to.

UCLA–LS 10: I feel left out.

UCLA–LS 11: My social relationships are superficial.

UCLA–LS 12: No one really knows me well.

UCLA–LS 13: I feel isolated from others.

UCLA–LS 14: I can find companionship when I want it.

UCLA–LS 15: There are people who really understand me.

UCLA–LS 16: I am unhappy being so withdrawn.

UCLA–LS 17: People are around me but not with me.

UCLA–LS 18: There are people I can talk to.

UCLA–LS 19: There are people I can turn to.

Scoring on each item ranges from 1 to 4 (never, rarely, sometimes, and often). Scores are reversed on the ten negative items. A low score indicates loneliness.

METHODOLOGY

The purpose of the present analysis is to examine the psychometric properties of the LSNS, RAND MOS–SSS, and the UCLA–LS concurrently among a community-dwelling population of older adults in California. Data come from the UCLA Medicare Screening and Health Promotion Trial (MSHPT) funded by the Health Care Finance Administration.[1] MSHPT was designed to test the feasibility of providing disease-prevention and health-promotion services to Medicare beneficiaries in a cost-effective manner. This screening and health-promotion study was one of five demonstration projects mandated by the U.S. Congress under the 1985 Consolidated Omnibus Budget Reconciliation Act.

Elderly participants were recruited by contacting physicians affiliated with UCLA Medical Center in Los Angeles, California. These physicians were asked to provide names of patients in their practices who would be suitable for participation in the study. Enrollment criteria included being at least 65 years of age, a Medicare participant, English-speaking, having a telephone, and having no terminal or dementing illness.

Comparisons were made between the participants in the MSHPT study and those elderly who were included in the Los Angeles subsample of the Supplement on Aging (SOA) of the 1984 U.S. National Health Interview Survey. Both the SOA data and those of the MSHPT elders were collected among community-dwelling elderly populations. These data show that MSHPT elders were, indeed, similar in age (both groups had a mean age of 74), race (85 percent of both groups were white), and the number of offspring (both groups had an average of two children).

However, there were slightly more males in the MSHPT sample than in the LA–SOA sample (42 and 35 percent, respectively). Also, the MSHPT respondents were more apt to be married than the LA–SOA sample (60 and 46 percent, respectively). Finally, the MSHPT elders were more highly educated (13.3 mean years) than their LA–SOA subsample counterparts (11.2 years). Additional details regarding sample recruitment and random assignment to experimental and control groups have been reported elsewhere (Hirsch et al., 1992).

As part of the MSHPT, a Screening and Health Promotion Clinic was conducted for the purpose of providing health screening, health assessments, health promotion, and counseling targeted to experimental group participants' risk status (Atchison, Mayer-Oakes, Schweitzer, Dejong, and Matthias, 1993; Dorfman et al., 1995; Mayer-Oakes et al., 1992). Accordingly, some experimental participants received counseling by MSHPT social workers for problems related to apparent limited social contact.

As experimental participants might previously have received counseling by the MSHPT social workers for problems related to limited social contact, only the control participants who attended the annual screening and health promotion clinic in April, 1991, are used in the present analysis (*n* = 429). Unlike the experimental group, the control participants did not participate in the previous health day screening and health promotion clinics.

Shortly before seeing the MSHPT clinical social worker, control participants were asked to complete a self-administered questionnaire containing the Lubben Social Network Scale (LSNS), the MOS Social Support Survey (MOS–SSS), and the UCLA Loneliness Scale (UCLA–LS). These data are used to conduct individual scale analyses and scale-to-scale analyses, as shown in the following five steps.

In *Step 1,* we determined the intercorrelation among individual scale items and item-to-scale total scores. A high degree of intercorrelation between items in a particular scale indicates that the items are measuring a common construct (Devellis, 1991). Item-to-scale total score correlation assesses the strength of relationship between each item and the total score. The rule of thumb, according to Streiner and Norman (1995), is that an item should correlate with the total scale score above 0.20. Therefore, individual items are expected to correlate highly with the total scale score.

One commonly used summary measure of interitem correlation is a Cronbach alpha. This statistic measures the proportion of the variance in the scale score that is attributable to the true scale score, or the percentage of the score that is information (signal) as opposed to random error (noise). A high Cronbach alpha indicates strong internal consistency.

In *Step 2,* we obtained semipartial regression coefficients by regressing scale items on total scale scores in a multiple regression analysis. This analysis assesses the unique contributive value of each item to the total scale score. The semipartial coefficient associated with each scale item reflects the unique contribution that each item makes to the total scale score.

In *Step 3,* we factor analyzed the individual scales. This is done to determine whether the original factor structures reported in the literature for each scale can be replicated among the current elderly population. Factor analyses using varimax rotation are employed to examine underlying factor structures. A low factor loading of a scale item on all factors indicates that the item does not contribute much to the overall scale and may suggest that the item might be omitted from the scale.

In *Step 4,* we conduct interscale correlational analyses by examining the pairwise correlations among the three scales. This set of analyses is done to determine the amount of discrimination or similarity between the scales. Small interscale correlations suggest that the scales are relatively distinct, whereas high interscale correlations suggests that the three scales measure relatively similar constructs. In addition to examining the correlations among the total scale scores, we also conducted interscale correlational analyses among the various subscales of the three main scales.

In *Step 5,* we factor analyzed combined items from the three scales. This is done to determine further the nature and number of distinct and unique constructs among the total set of items from all scales. Overlap is demonstrated when items from two or more scales load onto a common factor. Factors made up of items overwhelmingly from one scale imply a singular construct, whereas factors made up of items from two or more scales reflect overlapping of constructs between scales.

STUDY RESULTS

First, it should be noted that we found some significant demographic differences in social networks, social supports, and loneliness among respondents, but these differences are not entirely consistent. There were no differences, for example, between men and women on the social networks scale and the loneliness scale. However, men did report significantly higher social support scores than women (mean of 74.4 vs. 70.9). Octogenarians had lower social network scores than their younger counterparts. There were no differences by age on the social support and loneliness scales, however.

Poverty was associated with social networks and social support scores, but not with the loneliness measure. Using Medicaid status (welfare recipient) as a measure of poverty, poor elderly were found to be significantly lower on the social networks scale (mean of 30.3 vs. 33.3) and the social supports scale (65.4 vs. 73.6) than elders with higher economic status.

Turning to the results of the intrascale and interscale analyses, we present the results according to the five stages of the analytic procedure.

Step 1: Interitem Correlations. A wide range of interitem correlations was observed among the LSNS items. The Pearson correlation coefficients among the LSNS items ranged from .02 to .81. Two clusters of moderately correlated LSNS items include those that address friendship and those that address family. However, the set of family items have weak intercorrelations with the set of friendship items, suggesting a possible substitution effect between family relationships and friend relationships.

The MOS–SSS items show much higher interitem correlations than the other two scales. The Pearson correlation coefficients among the MOS–SSS items ranged from .43 to .86. Two clusters demonstrating especially high correlations include those MOS–SSS items dealing with availability of instrumental support and emotional support. For example, "help if confined to bed," "availability of someone to prepare a meal," and "help with chores" were all correlated with each other in a range from .82 to .86.

Only 19 UCLA–LS items are used in the present analysis, because an inconsistent correlation of one item with other UCLA–LS items suggested a poorly understood question. Furthermore, some MSHPT social workers reported that the response options of "never, rarely, sometimes, or often" to the statement "I do not feel alone" often confused elderly participants in the present study. Factor analyses of the UCLA–LS further documented the apparent confusion caused by this double negative expression. Accordingly, this item was dropped from the present analysis. The remaining UCLA–LS items are moderately correlated with one another. The Pearson correlation coefficients for these UCLA–LS items ranged from .17 to .72.

Item-to-scale total score correlations (Table 8.1) show that most items of the LSNS are correlated with the total scale score in the .55 to .65 range. The MOS–SSS items are more strongly correlated with total scale score, with most correlations being in the .75 to .85 range. This suggests an especially strong unifying construct. The UCLA–LS has item-to-scale correlations that are more similar to those of the LSNS than to the MOS–SSS item-to-scale correlations. Most item-to-scale correlations for the UCLA–LS range from .52 to .75.

Cronbach alphas are necessarily consistent with both interitem and item-to-scale correlation coefficients. Scales with higher interitem correlations and higher item-to-scale correlations have higher Cronbach alpha scores. The LSNS shows moderate reliability with a standardized alpha of .76, compared to standardized alphas of .97 and .92 for the MOS–SSS and UCLA–LS scales, respectively.

Step 2: Semipartial Regression. An examination of the unique contribution of each scale item to the total scale score as measured by the semipartial regression coefficients shows that all the LSNS items are important to the total scale score (Table 8.1). More modest semipartial coefficients found for UCLA–LS items suggest that few of these items contribute uniquely to the total scale score. Redundancy of items is highly problematic with the MOS–SSS. Very low semipartial regression coefficients among most MOS–SSS items indicate a very high similarity among items, thereby reducing an individual item's unique contribution to the total scale score.

Step 3: Factor-Analyzed Individual Scales. Factor analyses using varimax rotation demonstrated multidimensionality among all three scales. An examination of scree plots for each scale indicated the number of factors to retain in a factor analysis. Similar to results previously reported by Lubben (1988), the present analysis identified three factors in the LSNS: relationship with friends (LSNS Items 4, 5, and 6), relationship with family (LSNS Items 1, 2, 3, 9, and 10), and confidant relationships (LSNS Items 7 and 8).

Although the developers of the MOS–SSS reported four factors for this scale, the present analysis only found three factors in the MOS–SSS: emotional support (MOS–SSS Items 2, 3, 7, 8, 12, 14, 15, and 17), affectional support (MOS–SSS Items 5, 6, 9, 10, 16, and 18), and tangible support (MOS–SSS Items 1, 4, 11, and 13). Only two factors were identified in the UCLA–LS: emotional loneliness (UCLA–LS Items 2, 3, 6, 7, 10, 11, 12, 13, 16, and 17), and social loneliness (UCLA–LS Items 1, 4, 5, 8, 9, 14, 15, 18, and 19).

Table 8.1: Item Analysis of Three Social Integration Scales

Scale and Item Number	Mean	SD	Item-to-Total	Alpha if Item Deleted	Semi-Partial R^2
Lubben Social Network Scale					
LSNS 1	3.32	1.39	.60	.72	.014
LSNS 2	4.14	1.39	.64	.71	.016
LSNS 3	2.89	1.18	.65	.71	.100
LSNS 4	2.68	1.25	.55	.73	.007
LSNS 5	2.89	1.26	.57	.72	.008
LSNS 6	3.28	1.31	.34	.75	.022
LSNS 7	4.10	1.35	.51	.73	.022
LSNS 8	3.10	1.18	.47	.73	.016
LSNS 9	3.51	1.76	.60	.72	.031
LSNS 10	3.27	2.27	.63	.74	.041
RAND Medical Outcome Study Social Support Scale					
MOS-SSS 1	3.88	1.37	.80	.97	.001
MOS-SSS 2	4.23	1.05	.78	.97	.001
MOS-SSS 3	4.14	1.13	.75	.97	.001
MOS-SSS 4	4.16	1.20	.71	.97	.002
MOS-SSS 5	4.38	1.02	.80	.97	.001
MOS-SSS 6	4.17	1.05	.83	.97	.001
MOS-SSS 7	4.13	1.10	.84	.97	.001
MOS-SSS 8	4.09	1.17	.81	.97	.001
MOS-SSS 9	3.99	1.26	.81	.97	.002
MOS-SSS 10	3.97	1.07	.80	.97	.001
MOS-SSS 11	3.82	1.46	.77	.97	.001
MOS-SSS 12	4.01	1.17	.83	.97	.001
MOS-SSS 13	3.79	1.46	.81	.97	.001
MOS-SSS 14	3.91	1.35	.86	.97	.001
MOS-SSS 15	4.06	1.16	.84	.97	.001
MOS-SSS 16	4.15	1.05	.83	.97	.001
MOS-SSS 17	4.05	1.17	.85	.97	.001
MOS-SSS 18	4.22	1.16	.83	.97	.001

(*continued*)

Table 8.1 (*continued*)

Scale and Item Number	Mean	SD	Item-to-Total	Alpha if Item Deleted	Semi-Partial R^2
UCLA Loneliness Scale					
UCLA-LS 1	1.33	.57	.52	.91	.002
UCLA-LS 2	2.05	.98	.72	.91	.005
UCLA-LS 3	1.64	.88	.63	.91	.004
UCLA-LS 4	1.66	.87	.54	.91	.004
UCLA-LS 5	1.62	.80	.61	.91	.003
UCLA-LS 6	1.66	.95	.68	.91	.005
UCLA-LS 7	2.25	.95	.55	.91	.006
UCLA-LS 8	1.66	.84	.44	.92	.005
UCLA-LS 9	1.30	.62	.58	.91	.002
UCLA-LS 10	1.86	.85	.68	.91	.003
UCLA-LS 11	2.20	.99	.61	.91	.006
UCLA-LS 12	2.16	.99	.69	.91	.005
UCLA-LS 13	1.75	.89	.75	.91	.003
UCLA-LS 14	1.42	.72	.60	.91	.003
UCLA-LS 15	1.55	.75	.66	.91	.003
UCLA-LS 16	1.64	.85	.69	.91	.003
UCLA-LS 17	2.16	.98	.71	.91	.005
UCLA-LS 18	1.30	.59	.67	.91	.001
UCLA-LS 19	1.36	.64	.79	.91	.001

Step 4: Interscale Comparisons. The interscale comparisons of the total scores from the LSNS, MOS–SSS, and the UCLA–LS suggest that they are measuring somewhat different constructs. Pearson's correlations of total scale scores from each instrument indicate moderate correlations ranging from .58 to .67, supporting their relative distinction from each other. More specifically, the shared variance ranges from only 34 percent between the two scales with the lowest correlation (LSNS and UCLA–LS) to 45 percent between the two scales with the highest correlation (MOS–SSS and UCLA–LS). Higher social networks and social supports (LSNS and MOS–SSS scores, respectively) generally meant less loneliness.

More specifically, the LSNS was negatively correlated at about the same level with both UCLA–LS subscales: emotional loneliness (−.52) and social loneliness(−.57). The MOS–SSS scale was also negatively correlated with both the

UCLA–LS subscales at about the same level, but at somewhat higher levels than those observed for the LSNS. The MOS–SSS was correlated with the UCLA–LS emotional loneliness subscale at −.61 and the UCLA–LS social loneliness subscale at −.65. Thus, the LSNS and MOS–SSS correlations with the UCLA–LS were relatively stable, even when considering the UCLA–LS subscales.

Higher social networks as measured by LSNS scores were associated with higher social support as measured by the MOS–SSS. The LSNS correlation with the various MOS–SSS subscales were quite stable, ranging from .58 to .62. However, some differences were noted when examining the correlation of the MOS–SSS with the LSNS subscales. The MOS–SSS was much more highly correlated with the LSNS family and confidant subscales (.59 and .62, respectively) than with the LSNS friends subscale (.20). Accordingly, family relations and confidant relations are more predictive of social support as measured by the MOS–SSS than are friendships.

Additional interesting differences emerge when examining correlations among the various LSNS and MOS–SSS subscales. The LSNS family subscale was more highly correlated with the MOS–SSS tangible support subscale (.65) than it was with the MOS–SSS affectional support (.55) and emotional support (.47) subscales. However, the LSNS confidant subscale was more highly correlated with the MOS–SSS emotional support (.65) subscale than it was with the other two MOS–SSS subscales: affectional (.55) and tangible (.47). The LSNS friends subscale had relatively low correlations with all of the MOS–SSS subscales.

These interscale and subscale correlational data suggest the relative distinction of the three constructs measured by each scale as well as which component of each construct (social networks, social support, and loneliness) might be most predictive of the other scales as well as subscales. A factor analysis (varimax rotation) using all 47 items from the three scales is another means to identify any overlapping constructs measured by the three scales.

Step 5: Combined Factor Analysis. The combined factor analysis identified seven factors, as shown in Table 8.2. Of the LSNS items, 60 percent loaded on two factors: family networks and friendship networks. Three of the remaining four LSNS items were spread among two social support factors (emotional and instrumental). The remaining LSNS item ("is a confidant") loaded negatively on the introversion factor.

Table 8.2 also shows that an overwhelming proportion of the MOS–SSS (15 of 18) items loaded on the emotional support factor. The remaining three MOS–SSS items loaded on the instrumental support factor. Almost all (14 of 19) of the UCLA–LS items loaded on two factors (loneliness and alienation), which were exclusively comprised of UCLA–LS items. Three of the remaining five UCLA–LS items loaded on emotional support, and the last two UCLA–LS items loaded on the last factor (introversion).

Table 8.2: Factor Analysis of Three Social Integration Scales

Factor	Scale Item	Statement	Factor Loading
Factor 1	MOS-SSS 7	Someone to give you information	.83
	MOS-SSS 8	Someone to confide in	.83
Emotional	MOS-SSS 12	Someone to give advice you want	.82
Support	MOS-SSS 15	Someone to turn to for suggestions	.82
	MOS-SSS 17	Someone to understand your problems	.80
	MOS-SSS 14	Someone to share worries	.79
	MOS-SSS 2	Someone to listen	.77
	MOS-SSS 3	Someone to advise regarding a crisis	.77
	LSNS 7	Someone to turn to regarding decisions	.74
	MOS-SSS 16	Someone to do enjoyable things with	.68
	MOS-SSS 6	Someone to have a good time with	.68
	MOS-SSS 9	Someone who hugs you	.66
	MOS-SSS 18	Someone to love	.65
	MOS-SSS 5	Someone who shows love and affection	.65
	MOS-SSS 10	Someone to relax with	.64
	MOS-SSS 4	Someone to take you to the doctor if you need it	.59
	UCLA-LS 19	There are people I can turn to	.55
	UCLA-LS 3	There is no one I can turn to	.52
	UCLA-LS 6	I am no longer close to anyone	.44
Factor 2	UCLA-LS 10	I feel left out	.77
	UCLA-LS 13	I feel isolated from others	.75
Loneliness	UCLA-LS 16	I am unhapy being so withdrawn	.71
	UCLA-LS 17	People are around me but not with me	.68
	UCLA-LS 12	No one really knows me well	.63
	UCLA-LS 12	My social relationships are superficial	.62
	UCLA-LS 2	I lack companionship	.56
	UCLA-LS 7	My interests and ideas are not shared by others	.51

Table 8.2 (*continued*)

Factor	Scale Item	Statement	Factor Loading
Factor 3	LSNS 10	Do you live alone or with others	.79
	MOS-SSS 11	Someone to prepare meals if you were unable to	.71
Instrumental Support	LSNS 9	Does anyone rely on you or do you help others	.71
	MOS-SSS 13	Someone to help you with daily chores if you were sick	.67
	MOS-SSS 1	Someone to help you if you were confined to bed	.63
Factor 4	UCLA-LS 4	I feel part of a group of friends	.67
	UCLA-LS 5	I have a lot in common with others	.65
Alienation	UCLA-LS 9	There are people I feel close to	.62
	UCLA-LS 14	I can find companionship when I want it	.62
	UCLA-LS 18	There are people I can talk to	.61
	UCLA-LS 15	There are people who really understand me	.58
Factor 5	LSNS 5	How many friends do you hear from or see once a month	.88
Friendship	LSNS 4	How many close friends do you have	.86
Network	LSNS 6	How often do you see/hear from friend with most contact	.47
Factor 6	LSNS 1	How many relatives do you hear from or see once a month	.77
Family	LSNS 3	How many relatives do you feel close to	.73
Network	LSNS 2	How often do you see/hear from relative with most contact	.59
Factor 7	UCLA-LS 8	I am an outgoing person	.72
Introversion	UCLA-LS 1	I feel in tune with people around me	.58

Validity of the LSNS as a Screening Tool
for Social Isolation

At the time of the clinical interview, the MSHPT social worker rendered a judgement of the participant's level of social isolation based upon a 20-minute interview. To provide a possible clinical focus for that interview, the social worker had access to the participant's self-administered questionnaire regarding various aspects of social interaction. However, the worker did not have access to any scale scores. Social workers offered three judgements: confirmed isolation, possible isolation, and isolation ruled out. Examination of a subsample of 45 participants demonstrated relatively high interrater reliability (phi = .85) among the social workers. These data, together with those collected from the self-administered questionnaire, are used to evaluate the LSNS as a screening tool to detect social isolates.

According to Lubben (1988) and supported in the present analyses, three distinct structural dimensions of social networks are measured: family, friends, and mutual support relationships. He has also suggested a scale score of 20 as a clinical cut-point for social isolation. For the present analyses, scores were grouped into four categories: isolated (LSNS scores less than or equal to 20), high risk (LSNS scores of 21–25), moderate risk (LSNS scores of 26–30), and low risk (LSNS scores greater than 30).

A large majority (66 percent) of the well elderly were deemed to be at low risk for social isolation, having scored 31 or above on the LSNS. Another 16 percent were rated at moderate risk, 10 percent at high risk, and only 8 percent were rated isolated using the LSNS scores. There was strong consensus between the LSNS classification and social worker judgement of social isolation. Among those classified as isolated by the LSNS, social workers either confirmed or considered isolation possible in more than 80 percent of the cases. At the other extreme, very few of the elderly rated at a low risk for isolation on the LSNS were found to be isolated following the clinical interview with the social worker.

Social workers were asked to identify the most likely cause of isolation among those elderly they deemed to be either isolated or at high risk. The most common causes of isolation reported were bereavement or losses, an elder's own health, and caretaking responsibilities. A significant minority were judged to be life-long isolates.

DISCUSSION

This study of elderly people in California demonstrates that social networks, social support, and loneliness among respondents are relatively distinct constructs. The need for separate measures of each construct is suggested. For example, four of the seven factors in the combined factor analysis are made up of items exclusively from either the Lubben Social Networks Scale or the

UCLA–Loneliness Scale. Furthermore, a fifth factor was overwhelmingly consti-
tuted by items from the Medical Outcome Study–Social Support Survey. Only
two of the factors in the combined factor analysis showed much overlap of the
three scales.

There are important practice ramifications suggested by these data. An elder
with a strong social network is more likely to have a strong social support system
and is less likely to be lonely. However, there are some details that should be
examined by the practitioner. For example, family ties are more predictive than
friendship ties of an elder's social support. Although there is a correlation between social networks, social supports, and loneliness, the three constructs are
relatively distinct and should be measured separately in practice settings.

Some overlapping of constructs is also evident in this analysis with regard to
social support. The instrumental support factor (Factor 3) demonstrated considerable overlapping of scales. This factor was constructed from three MOS–SSS
items and two LSNS items. Conceptually, this was not unexpected because the
MOS–SSS is, by definition, a support scale, and the LSNS was originally reported to have "mutual support" as one of its three factors.

The other area with notable overlap was the emotional factor (Factor 1). Although emotional support was predominately made up of MOS–SSS items, three
of the UCLA–LS items also loaded onto this factor. Again, this is not conceptually inconsistent, because one could conceive of some facets of loneliness being
attributed to limited emotional support.

From an applied gerontological research perspective, there is growing pressure
to develop short and efficient scales (e.g., Rubinstein et al., 1994). As discussed
by Kohout and colleagues (1993), elderly populations with specific physical or
cognitive limitations may not do well with long questionnaires. Furthermore,
constraints in most clinical practice settings necessitate efficient and effective
assessment instruments. Shorter scales require less time and energy for both ad-
ministrator and respondent. Therefore, parsimonious and effective screening
tools will be more acceptable to both elders and health-care providers.

The Lubben Social Network Scale, with roughly half as many items as the
MOS–SSS and UCLA–LS, is clearly the most parsimonious of the three scales.
However, this parsimony necessarily restricts the internal consistency of the
LSNS, as shown by a lower Cronbach alpha than the other two scales. As indi-
cated by the semipartial coefficients, the unique contribution of each LSNS item
to the scale score is relatively strong. Accordingly, these analyses suggest that the
LSNS cannot be further abbreviated.

Conversely, our findings suggest that the MOS–SSS can be readily shortened.
The large number of items that make up the MOS–SSS compared to the relatively small number of factors are strong evidence of redundancy of scale items.
Furthermore, a Cronbach alpha of .97 also indicates redundancy of scale items,
as do the very low semipartial coefficients. It is suggested that a scale should
have an alpha above 0.70 but no higher than 0.90 (Streiner and Norman, 1995).

We also found that the MOS–SSS may represent a more limited scope of domains than the developers of the scale claim. Whereas the original description of the MOS–SSS purports measuring four domains of support, the present analyses only demonstrated three domains in the individual scale factor analysis and two domains when all three social integration scales were factor analyzed together.

MOS–SSS items designed to measure affectional and positive social interaction all loaded on the emotional support factor in our analysis. Also, the item "have someone to take you to the doctor" loaded on emotional support rather than tangible support (what we call instrumental support). A possible explanation for finding fewer dimensions in our analyses than the four originally reported may be due to differences between our sample and that upon which the MOS–SSS was developed. More specifically, the MOS–SSS was designed for use on adults from the age of 18 upwards, and our study included only adults over the age of 65.

It has been suggested previously that the UCLA–LS could be abbreviated without sacrificing its internal consistency (Hays and Dimatteo, 1987). The present analysis supports this position. However, given that the sample upon which the UCLA–LS was developed consisted of young adults, the present analysis may suggest a different set of UCLA–LS items to be included in a shortened version for use among an elderly population. For example, issues of being withdrawn and left out of activities may be less salient for older persons than for college students with a mean age of 21.

We also examined the use of one of the scales—the LSNS—as a tool to detect elderly at high risk of social isolation. It proved to be highly correlated with clinical judgement, suggesting its potential to detect those at high risk of social isolation more efficiently. However, these analyses also suggested that more than one type of intervention will be needed to address the diversity of social isolates and to strengthen social support networks.

Respite programs might be one type of intervention. Some spouses become so burdened with caretaking responsibilities that they no longer see their own friends. Cognizant of the importance of friendship to mental health, it is clear that spouses and other overburdened elder caretakers need a break. Counseling programs would be most appropriate for those elders whose social support networks may be diminished because of the elder's own despondency. Ecological and social systems clinical paradigms are especially appropriate for this form of counseling.

One of the most successful efforts in the United States both to strengthen existing social support networks and to fabricate new ones are the senior peer support and other self-help programs. In such programs, elders learn successful coping techniques for particular problems faced in aging as well as ways to maximize prevention of many problems. Furthermore, because the elders are themselves the counselors, they are engaged in a social activity that brings increased social contact and often increased self-esteem.

In summary, scale validation is a cumulative, ongoing process that requires testing and retesting of instruments on diverse populations in various settings and sociodemographic contexts. Far too often, the generalizability of social integration measures on various populations has been assumed rather than empirically tested. Social integration scales must be tested on a variety of levels, using both psychometric and practical standards to assess their actual clinical usefulness. Future analysis of the scales should include an assessment of their sensitivity to various differences within and between elderly groups—for example, cultural and sociodemographic differences or levels of health and functional status that might affect response patterns. Furthermore, the ever-changing social circumstances of the elderly may result in varying responses on measures of social integration status over time.

This study should be viewed as a step in the ongoing pursuit of well-constructed social integration scales that can be used in various settings on diverse populations. We examined the properties of two scales that were not originally designed for use with elderly respondents. We also retested the LSNS, which was originally designed for use among the elderly population. Each of the three scales examined in these analyses shows some limitations; further examination of measures of social integration provides a necessary avenue for future research. Improved measures of social networks, social support, and loneliness are essential for a better understanding of the reported link between social integration and health. Such improved knowledge will enhance future gerontological research and geriatric care.

NOTE

1. This study is part of a larger project funded by the U.S. Health Care Financing Administration (HCFA) under Cooperative Agreement No. 95–C–99161. Interpretations of the data are the authors' own and do not necessarily represent the official opinion of the U.S. Health Care Financing Authority. The authors wish to acknowledge Kathryn Atchison, Ruth Matthias, and Stuart O. Schweitzer for their extensive and helpful comments on earlier versions of this manuscript.

9

The Personal Network of Dutch Older Adults: A Source of Social Contact and Instrumental Support

Marjolein Broese van Groenou
and Theo van Tilburg

Compared to several other countries in Western Europe, the percentage of older adults in the Netherlands is still relatively low. In 1990, for example, the percentage of people age 65 and above was approximately 12.8 percent, as opposed to 14.0 percent in France, 14.7 percent in Belgium, 15.3 percent in Germany, and 15.6 percent in the United Kingdom (Walker, Alber, and Guillemard, 1993). However, like elsewhere in Europe, the effects of the "baby boom" of the 1950s will significantly alter the age distribution after the year 2000. The percentage of people above the age of 60 in the Netherlands is, thus, expected to rise to 33 percent in the year 2030 (Van der Wijst and Van Poppel, 1994a).

The elderly in the Netherlands, like those in most other Western European countries, are in a reasonably privileged position. They live in a welfare state, have a guaranteed minimum income after the age of 65, and have access to an ample supply of care and care facilities. Given the continuing rise in average life expectancy and the concomitant increase in health problems over a longer part of the life span, however, Dutch authorities are currently concerned by the rising expenses of health care for the elderly. In this regard, authorities are appealing increasingly to the "caring society," in particular for support from the informal networks of the elderly.

For example, admission to a nursing home is not granted until it is no longer feasible for relatives and others in the vicinity to care for the elderly person. As more elderly people now live alone for longer periods, it is not an easy task for adult children to provide the required care, especially if they do not live close by.

It is consequently important for the elderly to have people in the vicinity who are willing to help them out, if necessary.

It must be recognized, nevertheless, that the rising numbers of older adults does not portend only negative effects for society. In the first place, only a small percentage of elderly people need a great extent of care; approximately 4 percent of the people above the age of 55 have severe problems with one or more of the general daily needs (SCP, 1990). Many elderly people are socially active in various facets of society, particularly those under the age of 75. Political parties, volunteer work associations, and hobby clubs of all kinds benefit from the role the elderly play. Moreover, older adults have sufficient resources to constitute a target group for the world of trade and commerce. Finally, many elders actively contribute within their personal network in supporting the other members, as, for example, with minding the grandchildren and giving financial aid to adult children.

Rising life expectancy, the growing need for care on the part of some elderly people, and having greater financial resources are all factors that variously affect the social networks of the aged. In order to study the specific effects of growing older on personal networks, two network dimensions must be distinguished (Antonucci, 1990). First is the structure of the network. With how many people does a person associate? With how many different types of relationships does he or she maintain contact? How active or how latent are these relationships? These structural features of the network indicate how socially active the older adult is. In this sense, the network is seen as a source of social contact and as an indication of the elderly person's extent of social integration.

The second network dimension is functional in nature. In this regard, interaction with others is seen as a means for coping with day-to-day problems and fundamental life events. It is not the contact itself that is important but, rather, the exchange of support that takes place as a result. Such support from network members may help one to deal with negative events and to cope with large and small problems. By support we mean both instrumental support, which includes performing services and giving practical help, and emotional support, which entails giving personal attention and a sense of security. For older adults, having instrumental support is a particularly important prerequisite for being able to live and function independently. From this point of view, the network is viewed as a collection of potential and actual support-givers.

In this chapter, we describe the networks of Dutch older adults on the basis of these two dimensions: the network as a collection of social contacts and the network as a collection of support-givers. Neither of these dimensions can be fully examined without taking the other into consideration. Interactions take place within the structure of the network, but only some of these are supportive. The next section thus presents both of these dimensions in greater detail and elaborates upon the specific research questions addressed in this inquiry.

As classification of network features depends, to a great degree, on the method used to delineate the network, extensive attention is devoted in a following section to the method we used for identification of network members. Through this method we distinguish between the "total" personal network—that is, all individuals who meet with our network criteria—and the "contact" network, or the network members with whom the most frequent contact is maintained and who, thus, can be viewed as potential support-givers. The features of the total network indicate how socially integrated older adults are; the contact network indicates the extent to which the network functions as supplier of support. Both aspects are explored in subsequent sections in the chapter. Given the unique importance of instrumental support for the functioning of elderly people, we focus the analysis upon this particular type of support. In the final section, attention is devoted to the research and policy implications of these findings on the personal networks of Dutch older adults.

NETWORK DIMENSIONS AND RESEARCH QUESTIONS

The Network as Source of Social Contact

A prevalent myth is that elderly people are lonely and socially isolated. Actually, numerous recent studies demonstrate that the large majority of older adults maintain various social ties and that they are satisfied with the number and the quality of these relationships (Antonucci and Akiyama, 1987b; Cantor, 1979; Dykstra, 1990a; Kendig, 1986; Knipscheer, 1980; Wenger, 1993). In general, the social networks of older adults contain family members as well as non-kin with whom they have regular contact.

Nonetheless, elderly people constitute a heterogeneous population, and this also holds true of their social contacts. Some older adults have a small network consisting mainly of relatives and others living in the immediate vicinity, whereas other older people have contact with a larger network of non-kin (Wenger, 1993). Differences in size and composition can be attributed in part to the fact that the network in existence at any given moment is the result of the life history of the individual. Throughout a lifetime, the network changes under the influence of voluntary and involuntary choices (e.g., to enter into a friendship), critical life-events (e.g., changes in employment status, the death of network members), and social structural factors (e.g., opportunities that accompany being at a certain age stage). As a result of these developments in the course of a lifetime, we can expect to find differences between the networks of the following subgroups: elderly men and women, different old-age cohorts, older adults with and without partners, and older adults with and without children.

Differences between men and women stem largely from different social structural circumstances over the life course. Thanks to their occupational career, older men usually have a larger pool of social contacts. Women's work in and around the home, on the other hand, tends to keep them within the circles of their relatives and neighbors (Dykstra, 1990b; Fischer and Oliker, 1983).

It has been demonstrated in the literature, moreover, that the networks of people of different ages differ in size and composition. In general, as people age, their networks tend to become smaller, and the percentage of relatives within their networks becomes greater (Marsden, 1987; Morgan, 1988). Underlying reasons are the fact that peers such as siblings, friends, and other non-kin are no longer available due to death or reduced mobility, and the physical capacities needed on the part of the elder actively to maintain relationships continue to decrease.

The size and composition of the network also largely depend on whether or not there is a partner and/or children in the course of a person's lifetime. People who have or have had a partner have access to a larger circle of social contacts than people who do not have or have not had a partner (Milardo, Johnson, and Huston, 1983). It is equally well known that children constitute an important source of contact and support for the elderly (Connidis, 1989; Shanas, 1979). The never-married and the childless consequently have less access to possibilities for contact and support. The question remains whether they have found replacements for these relationships and maintain closer contact with other relatives and non-kin than do older adults who do have a partner and/or children.

In this chapter, we address the extent to which the Dutch elderly are integrated in relationships with kin and non-kin. As indices for the extent of social integration, we use the size of the network, the number of types of relationships in the network, and the frequency of the contact maintained with the network members. The differences are described between males and females, and between older adults of different ages and those with or without partners and/or children.

The Network as Source of Support

Following the work of Kahn and Antonucci (1980), we draw a distinction between network structure and supportive interaction within the network. More specifically, we draw further attention to the distinction between interacting with network members and getting support. After all, support is not given within all relationships. Some ties are based upon sharing a common context, such as a work site, neighborhood, or tennis club, or upon something else that people have in common without any exchange of support necessarily taking place. By examining with whom the elderly frequently associate and from whom they get support, we have an indication of the various functions network relationships serve. (Is it a question of just "being there," or of actually being supportive?)

The correlation between contact frequency and the quantity of support received should be high. This is true for two reasons: (1) people will (want to) maintain more contact with someone who responds positively than with someone who is not supportive, and (2) contact is a necessary prerequisite for receiving support. It is true, however, that not all frequent contacts are necessarily supportive, and that some infrequent contacts can, nevertheless, be very supportive.

The people with whom older adults maintain regular contact and exchange support has been the subject of research for quite some time. Based upon findings of high contact frequency and high intensity of support, partner and children are widely considered the most important persons in the network (Cantor, 1979; Cantor and Little, 1985; Connidis, 1989; Dykstra, 1990a, 1993; Litwak and Szelenyi, 1969; Stoller and Earl, 1983; Wellman and Wortley, 1989). This presumes a preference on the part of the elder for certain kinds of ties to give support, regardless of the task involved. High in this hierarchy we find the partner and children, followed to a lesser degree by neighbors, friends, and relatives. Low in the hierarchy are acquaintances and fellow members of organizations. A dynamic seems to exist, however, according to which ties lower in the support hierarchy are invoked if a type of relationship higher in the hierarchy is not available. Older adults who have no partner and/or children consequently receive more support from their other relatives (Kendig, 1986; Lee, 1985), neighbors, and friends (Adams and Blieszner, 1989; Cantor, 1979; Peters and Kaiser, 1985).

Whether the older adult receives support and to what extent also depends on his or her need for it. A need for instrumental support is precipitated by a person's reduced capacities for performing certain tasks. The process of growing older is generally accompanied by reduced physical capacities and a greater chance of losing one's loved ones. Consequently, there is an increase in old age in the support that is both desired and received from the network (Chappell, 1989; Miller and McFall, 1991; Stoller and Pugliesi, 1988).

The size and nature of the care-related chores also influence who is able to give support to the elderly person (Litwak and Szelenyi, 1969). If an older adult is confronted with severe physical problems and requires complex personal care (washing, getting dressed, eating), professional caregivers are usually indispensable. These formal providers mainly supplement the help given by the members of the network rather than replace it. The less available informal support-givers are, however, the more important the role of professional support-givers is likely to be.

To summarize, we focus in this chapter on the extent to which the elderly receive support from their network members. These data are presented for male and female elderly people of different ages, with and without partners and/or children. We consider from whom the elderly receive instrumental support and whether there is a certain hierarchy in the types of support-givers. Then we examine whether the people who give the most support are also the people with whom the most frequent contact is maintained. Lastly, we explore whether the extent of support received within different types of relationships depends on the state of older adults' health and, in the case of people with health problems, on the presence of professional caregivers.

DESIGN OF THE STUDY

Sample and Data Collection

In 1992, face-to-face interviews were conducted with 4,494 respondents who participated in the research program "Living Arrangements and Social Networks of Older Adults"[1] (Knipscheer, de Jong Gierveld, van Tilburg, and Dykstra, 1995). They constitute a stratified random sample of men and women born in the years 1903 to 1937. The oldest respondents—and the oldest men in particular—are overrepresented. The random sample was taken from the Registers of 11 municipalities in three regions of the Netherlands: the city of Amsterdam (population 714,000, density 4,400 inhabitants per square kilometre) and two rural communities in the west (population 18,000 and 14,000, density 300 and 400, both consisting of a number of small villages), one city (population 52,000, density 1700) and two rural communities (population 36,000 and 9,000, density 600 and 300) in the south, and one city (population 97,000, density 1,000) and four rural communities (populations between 4,000 and 18,000, density between 100 and 400) in the east. The three regions can be viewed as representing differences in culture, religion, urbanization, and aging in the Netherlands. The response rate was 61.7 percent. Data were collected by 88 interviewers, trained in a four-day session and supervised during the collection period.

In this chapter, we confine the analysis to 4,033 respondents. Excluded are 345 respondents with very serious health problems who consequently filled in a short version of the questionnaire, and another 116 respondents due to missing values. After weighting the data in accordance with differential stratum size, the entire sample is representative of the Dutch in the 55–89 age group.

Of the sample, 44 percent are males, and 56 percent are females. The average age of respondents is 67.7 ($SD = 8.8$). The majority are married (66 percent); 6 percent are unmarried, 6 percent are divorced, and 22 percent are widowed. Currently, 70 percent of the older adults are in a partner relationship (either married or not). Half of the elderly live with a partner or spouse (66 percent); 27 percent live alone, 5 percent live in another kind of multiperson household, and the rest (3 percent) live in an institution of some sort, such as a nursing home, a home for the aged, a psychiatric hospital, a monastery, or a shelter for the homeless. About 13 percent of the sample never had children. Almost all the respondents were born in the Netherlands (94 percent) or have Dutch nationality (99 percent). The mean number of years of education is 8.8 ($SD = 3.3$). With respect to employment status, 16 percent are employed, 51 percent are retired, 17 percent have left the work force, 6 percent never had a job, 9 percent are disabled, and less than 1 percent are unemployed. With respect to religion, 30 percent are Protestant, 28 percent are Roman Catholic, 2 percent belong to some other religious group, and 40 percent are not affiliated with a church.

Network Methodology

The main objective was to identify networks that reflect the socially active relationships of the elderly respondents. The identification method is derived from the one used in the study by Cochran et al. (1990). Two criteria govern who is included in the network. First, network composition must allow for variation, guaranteeing that every type of relationship has an equal chance to be included. This criterion led us to use a domain-specific approach with seven types of ties as initial probes: (1) household members (including the spouse/partner), (2) children and their partners, (3) other relatives, (4) neighbors, (5) colleagues from work or informal activity settings, (6) members of organizations (e.g., sport clubs, church congregations, political parties), and (7) others (e.g., friends and acquaintances).

A second objective was to include all the network members with whom the elderly respondents have regular contact, thus identifying their socially active relationships. However, in order to avoid including people with whom regular contact is understood (such as all the members of the bridge club), the importance of the relationship was added as a discriminating criterion. Respondents were directed to mention only network members above the age of 18 with whom they have regular contact and who are important to them. Moreover, respondents were told to "name the persons (e.g., in your neighborhood) you have frequent contact with and who are important to you," with respect to each of the seven domains. Limits were set on the number of names mentioned in each of the domains, but very few respondents actually reached the maximum. The total possible limit was 80.

Information was gathered on all identified network members with regard to type of relationship, gender, and frequency of contact. The network members with the highest contact frequency (maximum = 12) were then selected for further inquiry. For these 12 (or fewer) network members, data were gathered with respect to age, travel distance, duration of the relationship, employment status, marital status, and the exchange of instrumental and emotional support between the network member and the respondent.

The size of the total network is the number of persons mentioned, and 29 different relationship types were distinguished in the process. For the present analysis, the types are condensed into nine, based on Dykstra (1995): (1) the spouse or partner (regardless of whether he or she lives in the respondent's household), (2) children (including children of the partner/spouse who are not the children of the respondent), (3) partners of the children (married or not married), (4) siblings, (5) siblings-in-law, (6) other kin, (7) neighbors (including people living in the same neighborhood), (8) friends, and (9) other non-kin. The size of the partial networks of the nine relationship types are also calculated.

Frequency of contact was measured by means of one question: "How often are you in touch with . . .?" Answers were reported on an 8-point ordinal scale (never, yearly or less often, a few times a year, monthly, once every two weeks, weekly, a few times a week, daily). For the present analysis, the answers are recoded to the number of days a year. The mean frequency of contact with the older adult is calculated for each of the nine types of relationships.

As noted earlier, information was collected on received instrumental support with respect to the network members selected in the top 12. One question was posed: "How often did it occur in the past year that X helped you with daily chores in and around the home, such as preparing meals, cleaning house, transportation, small repairs, or filling in forms?" Response categories were: never, seldom, sometimes, and often, with values from 0 to 3, respectively. The mean score of received instrumental support was then calculated for each of the nine types of relationships.

As indicator of the physical health status of the elderly, we used the capacity to perform four Activities of Daily Living (ADL). The questions were:

Can you walk up and down stairs?

Can you walk for five minutes outdoors without resting?

Can you get up from and sit down in a chair?

Can you get dressed and undressed (including putting on shoes, doing up zippers, fastening buttons)?

Response categories were: not at all, only with help, with a great deal of difficulty, with some difficulty, and without difficulty. The scale score, ranging from 4 (numerous problems) to 20 (no problems) was homogeneous (Loevingers $H = .68$) and reliable ($\rho = .87$).

All the respondents who reported having problems with at least one of the four ADL items ($n = 2,259$) were asked how often they are assisted with the performance of ADL activities. Persons who receive at least some assistance ($n = 877$) were asked to indicate the type of assistant. Distinctions were drawn between informal assistants (partner, household members, children, other relatives, friends, acquaintances, and neighbors) and professional assistants (community nurse, service flat personnel, social services).

Analytic Procedure

First, the characteristics of the total network are described—that is, all the network members mentioned in the identification procedure. Means are provided of the number of persons mentioned and the mean frequency of contact with respect to the total network and for each of the nine relationship types. ANOVAs are used to test the statistical significance between the means by gender, five-year birth cohorts (from 55–59 to 85–89), partner status, and parental status, controlling for the influence of each.

With respect to the contact network, or the maximum of 12 selected network members, we describe the composition of the network, the mean contact frequency, and the mean received instrumental support for each of the nine types of relationships. ANOVAs are conducted to test differences between subsamples by gender, five-year birth cohorts, partner status, and parental status in the manner just described. For each of the nine types of relationships, Pearson correlations are calculated to measure the relation between contact frequency and support. Next, the mean received instrumental support is calculated for respondents with no ADL problems (a score of 20), slight ADL problems (a score of 13–19), and severe ADL problems (a score of 4–12). For all respondents reporting ADL problems (score < 20) and receipt of at least some assistance with ADL tasks ($n = 877$), mean received instrumental support is calculated for each of the nine types of relationships, distinguishing between those who receive assistance from at least one of the professionals ($n = 226$) and those who do not receive professional help ($n = 651$). ANOVAs are performed in order to test the difference in the means adjusted for differences in gender, age, partner status, and parental status.

It should be noted that not all older adults have relationships reflecting all the tie-types, and not all the tie-types are represented within the top 12. The number of respondents for whom the mean contact frequency and the mean received instrumental support are calculated thus differ by type of relationship. Reported mean differences are statistically significant at the $p < .01$ level, unless stated otherwise.

THE NETWORK AS A SOURCE OF SOCIAL CONTACTS

The size, network composition, and contact frequency with each of the nine types of relationships indicate the extent to which the older adult is integrated in relationships with kin and non-kin. The means of the total sample are presented in Table 9.1. Differences between several subsamples are described in the text.

Size

The 4,033 older adults mention an average of 11.9 network members. Network size differs widely, however, with 10 percent of the respondents identifying three network members or fewer and 10 percent mentioning 22 or more network members; 15 older adults mention no network members at all.

Interestingly, there is no difference between the average network size of men and women. On the other hand, the general finding that network size shows a linear decrease with age is replicated in this study. Network size decreases from an average of 12.6 for the youngest (55–59 years of age) to 8.3 for the oldest (85–89 years; $F = 19.9$). Being in a partner relationship adds to one's network size. Older adults with a partner have an average network of 12.5, and those without a partner have an average of 10.7 network members ($F = 36.1$). Children also add to the size of the network: parents have an average network of 12.3, whereas the childless have an average network size of 9.2 ($F = 69.2$). Thus differences in network size are, in part, the result of the availability of a partner and children.

Table 9.1: Characteristics of the Total Network

	Composition[a] (N = 4,003)			Contact Frequency[b]			
	M	SD	Range	M	SD	Range	N
Total	11.9	8.0	0-68	132.8	74.1	0-365	4,033
Partner	0.7	0.5	0-01	364.8	13.8	52-365	2,698
Child	2.3	1.7	0-11	167.1	111.6	12-365	3,361
Child-in-law	1.3	1.5	0-11	100.0	88.9	12-365	2,441
Sibling	0.9	1.4	0-11	72.8	89.1	12-365	1,903
Sibling-in-law	1.1	2.0	0-16	55.6	68.3	12-365	1,670
Other kin	0.9	1.6	0-25	78.9	95.1	12-365	1,615
Neighbor	1.6	2.2	0-22	165.6	123.6	12-365	2,269
Friend	1.2	2.4	0-35	67.9	76.8	12-365	1,543
Other non-kin	1.9	3.3	0-33	75.6	81.1	12-365	1,999

[a] absolute number.   [b] days per year.

Composition

With respect to the composition of the network, Table 9.1 shows that children are most often mentioned as network members, followed by other non-kin, neighbors, children-in-law, friends, siblings-in-law, other kin, and siblings. As follows from our guidelines, partners are always included as network members.

Several gender differences are apparent in the composition of the networks. Women mention, on the average, a larger number of siblings (1.0, vs. 0.8 mentioned by men, $F = 32.2$), other kin (1.0, vs. 0.8 for men, $F = 24.4$), and friends (1.3, vs. 0.9 for men, $F = 24.1$). The networks of men, on the other hand, more frequently include a partner (0.8, vs. 0.6 for women, $F = 302.9$), and other non-kin (2.1, vs. 1.7 mentioned by women, $F = 14.7$). No gender differences emerge regarding the number of children, children-in-law, siblings-in-law, and neighbors in the networks.

The decrease in network size with age draws attention to the types of network members who may be lost during aging. While we are as yet unable to draw conclusions regarding the actual loss of relationships over the years, as findings are based on cross-sectional data, the cohort differences can, nevertheless, provide an indication of possible changes within the network. As expected, inclusion of a partner in the network decreases sharply with age ($F = 79.0$). About 80 percent of the youngest cohort (age group 55–59) has a partner in the network, as compared with 28 percent of the oldest (age group 85–89). A decrease with age is also found with respect to the number of siblings ($F = 18.1$), siblings-in-law ($F = 14.3$), friends ($F = 11.5$), and other non-kin ($F = 20.6$) in the network. The number of children-in-law shows a different pattern among the cohorts, however ($F = 9.5$). Both the youngest (55–59) and the oldest (85–89) cohorts in the sample have the smallest number of children-in-law in their network (1.0 and 1.2, respectively), and the elderly between 75 and 79 years of age have the largest number of children-in-law (1.5). With respect to the number of other kin, we also find a more curvilinear relationship with age, but the other way around. In this case, the youngest as well as the oldest have the largest number of other kin in their network (both 1.0) and the middle cohorts have the smallest numbers (about 0.8; $F = 5.4$). No differences between cohorts are found, on the other hand, with respect to the number of children and neighbors mentioned in the network.

Older adults who are in a partner relationship have networks of a somewhat different constellation when compared to older adults who do not have a partner. The main differences are with respect to relationships with close kin: the elderly with a partner mention more children ($F = 75.8$), children-in-law ($F = 80.9$), and siblings-in-law ($F = 28.5$), but fewer siblings ($F = 6.8$) in their networks. As some of the elderly without a partner were never married and are also childless, the differences with respect to children and children-in-law are not surprising. Siblings-in-law are also more likely to enter a network if one has a partner. The finding that the elderly without a partner are more involved with their siblings, on the other hand, suggests that this type of close kin may compensate for the lack of a partner.

Differences in network composition between older adults who are childless and those who are parents reveal that the childless are less likely to include a partner in their network ($F = 233.6$), and that they mention fewer siblings-in-law ($F = 11.8$), but more other kin ($F = 112.0$), in their network. This suggests that the absence of ties with children is compensated to some degree by a larger involvement with selected other relatives.

Network Interaction

Table 9.1 also shows the mean frequency of contact with the total network and with each of the nine types of relationships. The findings indicate that, on the average, older adults interact on a weekly basis with their network members (about 132 days a year). It is also clear that they interact very often with some network members and less often with others. Obviously most of the respondents contact their partner on a daily basis. Only partners who do not share a household are contacted less frequently. Children and neighbors are contacted very often— on the average, between a few times a week and daily. Children-in-law are also contacted very often, but about 67 days less a year than the children, on the average. The other types of relationships are contacted less frequently. In decreasing order, they include other kin, other non-kin, friends, siblings, and siblings-in-law.

It appears that frequent interaction with network members is facilitated by either emotional closeness (partner, children, children-in-law) or geographical proximity (neighbors). These types of relationships are the most socially active. The less frequently maintained ties with other relatives suggest that, by itself, the blood connection is an insufficient basis for relationship. Ties with friends and other non-kin may be more socially arranged ones, such as the weekly meetings of a political organization or a bridge club.

THE NETWORK AS A SOURCE OF SUPPORTERS

As noted earlier, the supportiveness of network ties was studied for the top 12 (or fewer) network members of the older adults. Table 9.2 contains the mean size, mean received instrumental support, and mean contact frequency for the total contact network, and for each of the nine types of relationships.

Size, Composition, and Interaction

Respondents report an average of 8.9 network members in their contact network. For about 60 percent of the adults, this is also their entire network, because their total network size is 12 or fewer. For the other 40 percent, we selected the

Table 9.2: Characteristics of the Contact Network

	Composition[a] (N = 4,003)			Contact Frequency[b]			Received Instrumental Support[c]		
	M	SD	Range	M	SD	N	M	SD	Range
Total	8.9	3.5	0-12	148.6	77.6	4,033	0.9	0.7	4,033
Partner	0.7	0.5	0-01	364.4	13.9	2,616	2.6	0.9	2,616
Child	2.1	1.5	0-10	172.2	112.2	3,315	1.2	1.0	3,315
Child-in-law	1.1	1.2	0-06	108.8	92.8	2,320	0.9	1.0	2,320
Sibling	0.6	1.0	0-06	91.2	99.6	1,538	0.5	0.9	1,538
Sibling-in-law	0.6	1.0	0-8	72.8	81.6	1,337	0.4	0.8	1,337
Other kin	0.6	1.1	0-08	95.6	103.2	1,358	0.4	0.8	1,358
Neighbor	1.4	1.7	0-12	176.9	124.4	2,198	0.6	0.9	2,198
Friend	0.7	1.3	0-10	82.8	83.6	1,319	0.5	0.9	1,319
Other non-kin	1.2	1.9	0-11	91.3	91.0	1,796	0.4	0.7	1,796

[a] N = absolute number   [b] days per year   [c] 0 = never, 3 = often.

12 with the highest contact frequency from among the 13–68 reported network members. As Table 9.2 shows, children are most often cited as network members, followed by neighbors, other non-kin, children-in-law, friends, siblings, other kin, and siblings-in-law. As children and neighbors constitute the most frequent contacts in the total network, it is not surprising that these types of relationships dominate the contact network.

Table 9.2 also shows the mean contact frequency of the type of network members in the contact network. In decreasing order, contact is most often maintained with the partner, neighbors, children, children-in-law, other kin, other non-kin, siblings, friends, and siblings-in-law. On the average, contact with neighbors and children takes place between a few times a week and daily; contact with the other types of network members takes place between once a week and a few times a week. This is even the case for siblings-in-law, who are ranked the lowest in contact frequency.

Receipt of Instrumental Support

On the whole, older adults receive little instrumental support from their contact network. Average support is 0.9 on a scale of 0 to 3, which falls between never and seldom receiving assistance. Some differences are evident, however, with respect to respondents' gender, age, partner status, and parental status. It appears that, on the average, men receive more instrumental support than do women (1.0 vs. 0.8, $F = 37.7$). Next, there is a positive, linear relation with age: older respondents receive more support than do younger ones ($F = 4.9$). The differences between the cohorts are small, however, the oldest (85–89) receiving on average a score of 1.1, and the youngest (55–59), one of 0.9. Having a partner and/or children adds to the degree of support received from the contact network. The elderly with a partner receive more support than do those without a partner (0.9 vs. 0.8, $F = 12.5$). Older parents receive more support than do the childless elderly (0.9 vs. 0.8, $F = 11.7$). It can be concluded, therefore, that men, the oldest respondents and those with a partner and children receive the most instrumental support from their network.

Table 9.2 also shows sizeable differences between instrumental support received from various types of network members. Such support is most often received from the partner, who provides, on the average, nearly the maximum extent. Next, children and children-in law provide support relatively more often, but even so the average rate is between seldom and sometimes. Then there is a gap with the other types of network members. In decreasing order, the elderly receive instrumental support only occasionally from neighbors, friends, siblings, other kin, siblings in-law, and other non-kin. While this relative ranking is consistent with our expectations, the small intergroup differences do not allow more definitive conclusions.

The network members with the highest contact frequency were also expected to be the main providers of instrumental support. The findings only partly confirm this. First, the correlations between mean contact frequency and mean instrumental support are positive for every type of relationship (with the exception of the partner, for whom a statistically significant relationship was not evident), but they are not very high. Correlations are strongest for the children ($r = .28$) and weakest for the other non-kin ($r = .12$). These findings suggest that some infrequent contacts can be very supportive and that frequent contacts can sometimes be very low in support.

A second indication of the correlation between contact frequency and support is the similarity in the ranking of the relationship types in contact frequency and received support. However, the rankings do differ in some aspects. One important exception concerns neighbors who maintain very frequent contact with the older adults but seldom provide instrumental support. A higher rank on contact frequency than support intensity is also reported for other kin and non-kin. Siblings and friends, on the other hand, are ranked lower in contact frequency than support intensity. Contact with them may be limited but is, nevertheless, supportive.

Availability of Partner and Children

As partner and children are generally considered the most important informal supporters, we examine the identity of most important supporters for older adults who are lacking these relationships. It appears that, as compared with older adults with a partner, older adults without a partner receive instrumental support more often from children (1.3 vs. 1.1, $F = 24.5$), children-in-law (1.1 vs. 0.9, $F = 22.6$), siblings (0.6 vs. 0.4, $F = 23.0$), siblings-in-law (0.6 vs. 0.4, $F = 12.5$), other kin (0.5 vs. 0.4, $F = 7.5$), and other non-kin (0.4 vs. 0.3, $F = 8.5$). No such differences were found with respect to the support received from neighbors and friends.

As compared with older parents, childless older adults receive instrumental support more often from siblings (0.7 vs. 0.4, $F = 27.3$), siblings-in-law (0.6 vs. 0.4, $F = 6.8$), and other kin (0.6 vs. 0.4, $F = 15.4$). We also found an interaction effect between partner status and parental status, indicating that being partnerless and childless increases the likelihood of receipt of instrumental support from siblings ($F = 16.4$).

Received Support, ADL Capacity, and Professional Helpers

A separate category of respondents addressed here are the elderly who experience problems with their physical health and are thus likely to have an increased need for instrumental support. The network members of these older adults may be under greater pressure to assist with instrumental tasks. Depending on the severity of the physical problems and the availability of network members, moreover, formal helpers may be called upon to assist.

We examine first the degree of instrumental support received in relation to the severity of physical problems, as indicated by the capacity to perform ADL tasks. The findings suggest that older adults with severe ADL problems receive significantly more instrumental support from their contact network. On the average, older adults with severe problems receive the most support (1.2), those with slight problems receive somewhat less (1.0), and those with no problems receive the least instrumental support ($0.8; F = 39.9$).

The same trend appears for some types of relationships. Elderly people with severe problems receive instrumental support relatively more often from children ($F = 28.7$), children-in-law ($F = 11.8$), other kin ($F = 12.1$), neighbors ($F = 18.6$), friends ($F = 6.5$), and other non-kin ($F = 9.7$). No such differences were found, on the other hand, with respect to support received from partner, siblings, and siblings-in-law.

Of the 1,525 elderly respondents who experience at least some problems with ADL, 877 indicate that they are assisted by others to some degree in performing these activities. Among them, 226 (26 percent) are assisted by formal organizations. In comparison with respondents who do receive help but not from formal organizations, a larger proportion of the formal aid recipients are female (18 vs. 30 percent, $\chi^2 = 13.2$) and not in a partner relationship (15 vs. 38 percent, $\chi^2 = 58.8$). In addition, the recipients of formal assistance are, on the average, older than are the nonrecipients (76.9 vs. 70.8, $t = 8.9$). Thus it is older women without a partner who are most likely to be assisted by formal caregivers in the performance of ADL tasks.

Regarding support received from the network, we found one significant difference at the $p < .01$ level between recipients and nonrecipients of formal aid. Those who receive formal assistance also receive more support from their children-in-law ($F = 9.0$). Differences (significant at the $p < .05$ level) were also observed with respect to other types of relationships, in particular with children, siblings-in-law, other kin, and non-kin. Lastly, we found that the recipients of formal assistance report less instrumental support from their partner, when a partner is available.

SUMMARY AND SOCIAL POLICY IMPLICATIONS

The first point of note is the extent to which Dutch older adults between the ages of 55 and 89 are integrated in relationships with kin and non-kin. The findings on the size and composition of their total networks and their interaction with network members indicate that most of the elderly respondents do, indeed, maintain contact with relatives and with other people who live in the neighborhood, friends, members of organizations, and agencies for volunteer work of all kinds.

On the average, the Dutch elderly maintain contact with almost 12 network members, but there are some who mention fewer than 4 network members and others whose network is comprised of more than 20 members. With the majority of the network members, contact is maintained anywhere from once a week to daily. Outside the partner relationship, the most frequent contact is maintained with neighbors and children. The contact within other types of relationships, on the other hand, is less frequent.

These findings should be viewed in relation to the method used to delineate the networks. As opposed to other delineating methods, such as the affective approach (Antonucci and Akiyama, 1987b; Morgan, Schuster, and Butler, 1991; Wellman, 1979) or the exchange approach (Kendig, 1986; McCallister and Fischer, 1978), our method produces a network of average size with relatively numerous non-kin relationships (Broese van Groenou and van Tilburg, 1996; Milardo, 1992). Moreover, it poses specific questions about network members with whom the respondents maintain regular contact, which accounts for the relatively high average contact frequency in the networks.

In view of our point of departure—that is, to describe the social integration of Dutch older adults—we believe that this delineating method accurately depicts the social life of older adults. Unlike a method that poses questions about "significant others" in identifying network members (affective approach) or about persons with whom significant interactions occur (exchange approach), we are primarily interested in the existence of contact with the other person. However, our method differs from the traditional interaction approach, which focuses on daily social contact (Milardo, 1989), in that the criterion of importance is added here. The specific contents of the contact do not play a role, but the contact itself must be of some importance. Our findings show that Dutch older adults maintain a large number of contacts of this kind, indicating that they are, indeed, socially integrated.

More subtle details can be added to this general conclusion by examining the networks of different categories of elderly people. Gender differences are found mainly in the composition of the networks. The findings suggest that men and women partly socialize in different social circles. Women participate more in ties with kin and friends. Men are involved more often in formal organizations, which they apparently use as recruitment grounds for social contacts. Women were expected to be more involved in neighborhood contacts than men, but this is not the case. It could be that men increase their involvement in the neighborhood after they leave the work force and have more time to socialize closer to home.

The oldest respondents have smaller networks than do younger ones, and the networks of the oldest respondents also contain a higher percentage of relatives. These networks are relatively small because older respondents have fewer age peers (siblings, siblings-in-law, friends, and other non-kin). The aspect that gives rise to concern is that the oldest respondents have fewer network members who can be classified as major support-givers, such as partner, children, and children-in-law. Why relatively fewer children and children-in-law are mentioned in the networks of the oldest respondents is not completely clear. On the basis of the cross-sectional data employed here, however, we are unable to determine whether long-distance moves or the death of children, for example, are the reasons for this. Longitudinal data will hopefully be more conclusive.

In keeping with earlier research, we, too, find that the availability of a partner and/or children has major consequences for the composition of the kin network. Relationships associated with a partner, such as those with children, children-in-law, and siblings-in-law, occur much more frequently in the networks of respondents with a partner. Older adults who have no children mention more other kin in their networks. Having a partner and/or children, however, does not have much effect on contact with non-kin. Our data tend to confirm, moreover, that kin relationships, particularly relationships with siblings, are important for older adults without children and partners.

The second major issue addressed in this chapter is the extent to which the networks of older adults serve as a reservoir for actual and potential support-givers. Our findings on receipt of instrumental support pertain to the 12 most frequent contacts in the network (or fewer than 12, if fewer are available). In general, older adults rarely receive help with practical matters from the network. Those who do receive instrumental support relatively often are the oldest respondents, the men, and those with a partner and/or children. Most of the help is received from the partner, and to lesser degrees from children, children-in-law, neighbors, friends, siblings, other kin, siblings-in-law, and other non-kin.

There appears to be a large difference, moreover, between people with whom respondents maintain frequent contact and people from whom they receive support. There does appear to be a positive correlation between contact frequency and support received, but as there are also many frequent contacts that barely provide any support, this correlation is rather weak. A clear example of this are the neighbors, with whom there is extremely frequent contact but from whom relatively little support is received. In addition, there are network members with whom not much contact is maintained, but with whom the contact nonetheless provides a reasonable amount of support. This holds true, for example, for friends and siblings. The results thus show that there is not a consistent overlap between the contact network and the instrumental support network.

The extent of support received also depends largely on the availability of a partner and/or children. In most cases, they are the most important support-givers. Older adults lacking these relationship types tend to receive relatively more support from their other relatives, in particular from their siblings. In general, neighbors and friends appear to be much less important support-givers for older adults without partners and/or children than is commonly assumed.

Yet we have seen that these types of network members do play an active role after all, if and when there is a great need for instrumental support on the part of the elderly, as in the case of limited capacity for performing ADL tasks. Older adults with severe or slight capacity problems receive more instrumental support from virtually all the relationship types than do older adults with no ADL difficulties. In this regard, siblings, siblings-in-law, neighbors, friends, and other non-kin seem primarily to constitute potential support-givers. But it is not until there is an emergency that these network members become actual support-givers.

We have also observed that the presence of professional help does not seem to contribute to the informal network becoming more-or-less supportive. At the same time, we found that older adults who receive professional help are the very ones whose partner is less available or not at all. Conversely, they are also the ones whose family (children, children-in-law, other kin) also give relatively large amounts of support. It may be tentatively concluded, therefore, that formal professional help mainly constitutes a replacement for the help of the partner and a supplement to the help of children and close relatives.

Our findings thus indicate the importance of the personal network for the social life and functioning of the elderly. Many older adults have a partner and/or children, who generally serve as major actual support-givers. Other types of network members tend to play an active role if the primary support-givers are unavailable, or if an emergency situation arises in which the older adult has greater need for help.

The findings also confirm the importance of family relationships for elderly people (Blieszner and Hilkevitch Bedford, 1995). It is mainly the siblings, siblings-in-law, and other kin with whom contact is maintained and from whom support is received if partner and/or children are not present. Given the future demographic trends in which older adults are expected to have fewer children and siblings and more elderly people to have been single throughout their lives (Van der Wijst and Van Poppel, 1994b), the demonstrated importance of family relationships gives rise to serious concern in terms of the evolving policies of social care. If fewer older adults will have support-givers of this kind, and if they run an increased risk of physical ailment due to greater longevity, they will be less able to rely on informal networks in the future. The professional care that now serves merely as a supplement to the support provided by the personal network will most probably have to take over many of the network's caregiving tasks.

It is also conceivable that social policies will have to focus more on mobilizing other parts of the network, such as neighbors and friends. Our data show that the greater the need for care on the part of the elderly person, the more neighbors, friends, and other non-kin are likely to help. However, the question remains as to whether these second-line helpers will ever serve the same function as the members of the immediate family.

Today's older adults without partners and/or children demonstrate that, in general, non-kin relationships are not as supportive as the relationships with partners and children. It is equally obvious that the oldest people who need the most support are the very ones who have the least number of non-kin relationships of this kind. It is particularly the oldest–old without a partner, without children, and with only a few non-kin relationships who will require the most professional care. In developing future scenarios for social and home health care, therefore, Dutch authorities will have to take into account an ever greater number of older adults who have increasingly smaller family networks and who will not always be able to rely on neighbors, friends, and other non-kin, who are themselves growing older.

NOTE

1. The study is conducted at the Departments of Sociology and Social Gerontology and Social Research Methodology of the Vrije Universiteit in Amsterdam, and the Netherlands Interdisciplinary Demographic Institute in The Hague. The research is supported by a program grant from the Netherlands Program for Research on Aging (NESTOR), which is funded by the Ministry of Education, Culture and Sciences and the Ministry of Health, Welfare and Sports.

10

The Interpersonal Milieu
of Elderly People in Jerusalem

Gail Auslander

The population of Israel is diverse, characterized by a range of cultures, races, and languages. While intergroup differences are fading among the country's youth, however, among its older residents they are still quite pronounced. This diversity and the circumstances leading to it, make Israel an especially interesting laboratory for the study of the social networks of its elders.

The age distribution of Israel as a whole is changing. During the period between 1950 and 1990, the proportion of people aged 65 and over has tripled, rising from 3 percent to 9 percent of the population. Among them, the proportion of old–old persons is also increasing, with 40 percent of the elderly cohort aged 75 and over in 1990. Moreover, the number of persons over age 85 has increased by almost 100 percent in the last decade (Habib and Factor, 1994). The pace at which this shift in the age structure has occurred places a severe strain on the existing health and social services. These services, in turn, voice expectations and make demands on the informal social networks of older persons to share or bear the burden of care (Ben-Zvi, 1993). The ability of these networks to meet such demands led to the study that forms the basis of this chapter.

There are several explanations for the rapid pace of growth of the older segment of the population in Israel. In part it is due to increasing life expectancy, particularly among men. More important, however, is the asymmetrical age structure of the population, which resulted from the mass immigration of Jews from Europe, Asia, and North Africa immediately following the establishment of the State (Habib, 1988). Although migration is generally not considered a major factor in determining the age structure of countries, in Israel it has played a central role.

Thus, while in most countries the principal determinant of age distribution is the size of their birth cohorts, in Israel about 80 percent of the population currently aged 45 and over was born abroad. During the four-year period subsequent to the establishment of the State in 1948, nearly 700,000 immigrants arrived, doubling the Jewish population. At that time, both the immigrant population and the receiving population were disproportionately young. Consequently, the aging of both the young adults of the 1950s and their offspring has affected cohort flows, causing "shock waves" in the growth rates of ensuing elderly populations (Eisenbach and Sabatello, 1991).

Due to its diversity and size, it is probably more appropriate to speak of the aging populations of Israel. The discussion here is based on a sample of these populations—the elderly Jewish residents of Jerusalem. While the sample is similar in diversity and character to the elderly Jewish population of Israel as a whole, a number of differences should be noted. According to the Central Bureau of Statistics (1994), most elderly Jewish Israelis are female (56 percent). In terms of ethnic origin, 72 percent of Israelis aged 65 and over are of Western (European and American) origin, 26 percent are of Eastern (Asian and African) origin, and about 2 percent are native Israeli. As we will see later, women and persons of Western origin were somewhat underrepresented in the sample examined here.

More important than the sample's representativeness of the population at the time of data collection in 1985–65 is its relative reflection of the current aged cohort. While still reasonably representative of the majority of elderly Israelis, the sample excludes three emerging groups of older people in Israeli society—new immigrants from the former Soviet Union and from Ethiopia, and Israeli Arabs. We look briefly at the demography and social network characteristics of these groups before entering into an in-depth discussion of our focal population.

Since these data were collected, Israel has experienced two major waves of immigration. During the two-year period from 1990 to 1991, for example, over 330,000 Jews immigrated to Israel from the former Soviet Union, and they continue to arrive today, albeit at a slower rate. This compares to only 30,000 who immigrated during the ten years between 1980 and 1989. Among these immigrants, 13.5 percent were already aged 65 and over when they arrived (Central Bureau of Statistics, 1994). It is expected that further aging of this immigration will increase the total number of elderly persons by five times more than had been expected (Habib and Factor, 1994).

As in previous migrations, most of the older immigrants are women (62 percent). On other dimensions, however, the current Soviet immigrants differ from their predecessors. For example, they are more highly educated, with over half having completed 13 years of school or more. With regard to social networks, a recent analysis shows that immigration has led to an overall reduction in the size of their networks. Correspondingly, most of their social support derives from the nuclear family, with whom they often share accommodation in multigenerational households (Litwin, 1995a).

Another immigrant group of note are those from Ethiopia. While they are fewer in number, their arrival was equally dramatic and has placed an additional strain on the society's service resources. Between 1990 and 1994, close to 30,000 Ethiopian Jews immigrated to Israel, some 14,000 of them during the 24-hour Operation Solomon airlift. The Ethiopian immigrants differ demographically from the native population and from their fellow immigrants from the former Soviet Union. They tend to be much younger, with 60 percent under the age of 20, as opposed to only 4.8 percent aged 65 and over. Another important difference is that within the elderly cohort, men predominate, comprising 61 percent (Central Bureau of Statistics, 1994). Most are married (88 percent of men; 56 percent of women) or widowed (3 percent of men; 38 percent of women).

There are a number of reasons for these sociodemographic differences. As in most less developed countries, mortality rates were high and life expectancy was low in Ethiopia. Hence, the aged population was smaller initially. High maternal mortality rates prevented many women from reaching old age. Moreover, the long trek from rural villages to the embarkation point in Addis Ababa led some older people to remain in Ethiopia, while others succumbed en route (Friedman, 1992).

A third emerging elderly group not addressed in the study sample is the Arab sector of the Israeli population. This is a relatively small group—only 7 percent of older Israelis are non-Jewish (Moslem, Christian, and Druze). The Arab population tends to be very young, with older persons representing only 3.4 percent among them. This age distribution stems from both higher birth rates and lower life expectancy.

The sex distribution of older Israeli Arabs is similar to that of the Jewish sector, with 50 percent to 55 percent females among those aged 65 or over in both groups. Likewise, about 80 percent of older men are married in both sectors. Among elderly Arab women in Israel, however, only 31 percent are married as opposed to 44 percent of Western Jews and 35 percent of Eastern Jews—the gap largely being due to age differences between spouses at marriage (Habib and Factor, 1994). In addition, non-Jewish elderly tend to be poorly educated, with 69 percent having no formal education, as compared to 50 percent of Jewish elderly of Eastern origin and 6 percent of Western origin (Habib and Factor, 1994).

The social networks of older Israeli Arabs tend to be largely family-based. Only 22 percent live alone, as compared to nearly 30 percent of Jews. They have an average of 5.5 children, as compared to 3.1 among Jews. Like the Russian immigrants, the majority of elderly Arabs (67 percent) live in the same household or building as at least one of their children, as opposed to 11 percent of Western Jews and 37 percent of Eastern Jews.

STUDY SAMPLE

As noted earlier, the current analysis focuses on the majority population—older Jewish residents of Jerusalem, most of whom arrived during earlier waves of immigration. The study sample is comprised of 200 older persons, in two groups. The first group included 100 recent applicants to the Social Welfare Bureaux of the Municipality. These bureaux are the main providers of statutory social services for the elderly in Israel, including personal social services, referral to residential care, personal care services, and various assistance schemes. (Since these data were collected, responsibility for domiciliary care of severely functionally impaired elderly people has been assumed by the National Insurance Institute.) New applicants for services at the three welfare bureaux that serve the predominantly Jewish quarters of the city were referred to the research project until a quota of 100 subjects was attained.

A second group of respondents was selected from the membership rosters of the Sick Fund of the General Federation of Labor in Israel, drawn from the same neighborhoods as respondents from the first sample. At the time the data were collected, 95 percent of older Jewish Israelis were members of this Sick Fund. Older members were selected randomly from the lists, in proportion to the geographic distribution of members of the first group.

Overall response rate for both groups was 70 percent. In most of the analyses carried out here, both groups are considered as a single sample for the purposes of this discussion. In multivariate analyses, however, applicant status is included as a control variable.

Members of the study sample range in age from 60 to 95 (mean = 74.1, SD = 6.7). The majority (66 percent) are female. Most are either married (57 percent) or widowed (40 percent). Education levels range from 0 to 22 years, with an average of 7.5 years of school completed (SD = 5.1). The sample includes persons born in 25 different countries, ranging from Russia and Afghanistan to Argentina and the United States. For the purposes of the study, ethnicity is collapsed into three categories: 57 percent of the respondents are of Western (European and American) origin, 37 percent are of Eastern (Asian or African) origin, and only 6 percent were born in Israel.

METHODOLOGY

The central data collection instrument used in this study is the Norbeck Social Support Questionnaire (NSSQ), translated and adapted for use in Israel (Norbeck, Lindsey, & Carrieri, 1981). This instrument combines four different approaches to the study of social support networks, enabling us to address networks from a number of directions and to draw comparisons among them in terms of their relationship with other indicators of interest (van der Poel, 1993).

The *affective approach* limits network membership to persons who are especially important to the anchor individual. This is a subjective determination, with each respondent utilizing his or her personal criteria. In the NSSQ, respondents are asked to list the persons to whom they feel close, up to a maximum of 25. It also takes into account the loss of important network members in the recent past.

The *role relation approach* assumes that individuals are primarily influenced by the people with whom they have a culturally defined role relation. In the NSSQ, respondents are asked to indicate their role relationship with each network member listed. These include spouse, children, other family members, friends, school or work associates, neighbors, and professionals (health care, mental health, and clergy). In a divergence from the original NSSQ, children and spouse in this study are distinguished from other family members, due to the expected importance of differences in role functioning vis-à-vis an older family member.

The *interaction approach* focuses on actual contacts between network members over a given period of time. It excludes from the network persons with whom there is no contact. The NSSQ varies from this approach somewhat. It includes data on frequency of contact with all members, ranging from once a year or less to daily, and duration of contact, ranging from less than six months to more than five years. Both of these ordinal scales are treated as continuous variables in the analyses. In addition, we include frequency of attendance at religious services, which has been shown in other studies to be a significant element of the social support networks of older people (Lubben, 1988).

The *exchange approach* is based on social exchange theory and assumes that people's importance in interpersonal relationships is based on rewarding or supportive interactions. The NSSQ addresses three different dimensions of social support—affirmational, affective, and instrumental—following the theoretical scheme of Kahn and Antonucci (1980). It measures perceived, rather than actually received support. For each support dimension, respondents are asked to rate each of their network members on two items, as follows:

a. *affective support:* the degree to which the individual makes the respondent feel liked or loved, respected or admired;

b. *affirmative support:* the degree to which the respondent can confide in this person; the degree to which the individual supports the respondent's actions or thoughts;

c. *instrumental aid:* the degree to which the respondent can expect the individual to provide immediate assistance (i.e., a small loan or a ride), or to help if the respondent were confined to bed.

Because data are compiled from individual members' scores, the NSSQ support scores are confounded by network size; persons with larger networks have more support. To overcome this limitation, average "supportiveness" scores are calculated, whereby each element of support as well as the total score is divided by network size (House and Kahn, 1985). In addition, an ordinal measure is used to obtain a subjective assessment of the amount of support that was previously provided by people who are no longer in the network, due to death, moving away, and so on.

Four measures of health status are included in the study as determinants of personal well-being, as follows.

Functional disability is measured by a scale developed in the Yale Health and Aging Project and used in a national U.S. collaborative study of disability in aged persons (Cornoni-Huntley et al., 1985). It is a 10-item scale that assesses whether or not respondents require help to perform instrumental activities such as walking across a small room, bathing, and eating. Scores ranges from 0 to 10, with low scores indicating poor health; $\alpha = 0.81$ in this sample.

Physical capacity, also adapted from the Yale Health and Aging Project, is a 5-item scale on which respondents are requested to assess the degree of difficulty with which they undertake such activities as lifting, stooping, and reaching. Each item is rated from 1 ("no difficulty at all") to 5 ("impossible"). Scores range from 5 to 25, with low scores indicating good health; $\alpha = 0.86$ in this sample.

Self-rated health status is adapted from a scale introduced in the U.S. National Survey of Personal Health Practices and Consequences (Foley, 1984; Wilson and Elinson, 1981). Most studies utilize the single item "Would you say your health is excellent, good, fair, or poor?" Here, four additional items are added (satisfaction with physical condition, comparison with past health, health worries, and comparison with age peers). Scores on the 5-item scale range from 5 to 20, with a reliability of $\alpha = 0.81$ in this sample.

Psychological state is measured by the 4-item How Are You Scale (HAYS), also adapted from the National Survey of Personal Health Practices and Consequences. It represents general feelings of malaise and outlook on life, asking respondents how often they felt cheerful and light-hearted, loved and wanted, down-hearted and blue and lonely. Scores range from 4 to 16, with $\alpha = 0.82$ in this sample.

SOCIAL NETWORK STRUCTURE

The size of the social networks of elderly Israelis in the sample range from 0 to 21, with a mean of 6.2 ($SD = 3.9$). Six individuals reported having no close ties whatsoever. Frequency of contact with network members ranges from once a year or less to daily contact, with most people in touch with someone in their social network on a weekly basis. Moreover, most of the network contacts are of long standing, ranging from six to twelve months to more than five years. Most people have known their network members for more than five years.

Other than the spouse, networks include four main elements: children, other family, friends, and neighbors. Respondents average 2.7 children ($SD = 2.2$), with a maximum of 11; on the other hand, 34 respondents did not include any children in their networks. Other family members range from zero to five, with an average of 1.8 ($SD = 2.4$); 81 persons did not include extended family members in their networks. Similarly, most of the respondents did not include any friends or neighbors in their social networks (*n* = 142 and 133, respectively). For each category, the mean is less than one.

The study sample varies widely with regard to attendance at religious services. Most respondents (61 percent) attend synagogue once a year or less; on the other hand, 32 percent attend religious services on a weekly basis, or even more frequently.

While our analyses focused on the *informal* social networks of the elderly, the NSSQ allows for the inclusion of members of the formal social network. Accordingly, it was found that 17 respondents include professional helpgivers in their social networks, 9 of whom mention physicians and nurses; 5 people include mental health professionals; and 4 people cite rabbis as members of their social network.

Finally, the NSSQ also relates to a reduction of network ties by asking respondents whether they have lost any important relationships during the past year. A total of 54 persons (27 percent) did, indeed, report the loss of a significant person. Among them the loss of a family member is most common (13 percent), followed by loss of friends (10 percent) and loss of spouse (5 percent). As for the scope of network reduction, most common is one loss over the course of the year (11 percent of the sample).

Structural Variation

There are several aspects of social networks that tend to vary among different groups of elderly Israelis, along demographic and psychosocial lines. Data regarding these relationships are summarized in Table 10.1. Looking at selected sectors of the population, several differences become clear.

Age. Some network elements seem to diminish with increasing age. For example, the older members of the sample are less likely to have a spouse. They are also less likely than young–old respondents to include neighbors in their networks. In addition, age is negatively correlated with frequency of contact with the social network. The latter two elements may well reflect diminished functional levels with age, particularly mobility.

Gender. Although there is no difference by gender in network size, differences do emerge in regard to composition. Men are more likely to include a spouse and other family as members of their network. Women, on the other hand, are more likely to be widowed and to have suffered a personal loss during the past year. Moreover, women's networks have twice as many friends as men's networks and almost three times as many neighbors. Synagogue attendance, however, proves to be a much more important source of network contact for men than for women.

Table 10.1: Network Structure and Support by Background and Health State Variables

Network Elements	Gender[a]			Ethnic Origin[a]				Marital Status				
	Male	Female	Sig.	East	West	Israeli	Sig.	Mar.	Wid.	Div.	Unmar.	Sig.
Structure												
Size	---	---		---	---	---		7.0	=	5.1	---	***
Spouse	76%	42%	***	---	---	---		=	=	=	=	=
Children	---	---		3.7	2.0	2.9	***	2.9	---	2.3	---	
Family	---	---		---	---	---		---	---	---	---	
Friends	0.33	0.69	+	0.32	0.75	0.25	+	---	---	---	---	
Neighbors	0.24	0.70	***	---	---	---		---	---	---	---	
Losses	18%	33%	*	20%	31%	50%	*	---	---	---	---	
Contact	---	---		---	---	---		---	---	---	---	
Synagogue	62%	26%	***	54%	29%	---	**	22%	---	7%	---	*
Support												
Total	23.7	22.3	+	---	---	---		23.3	22.3	15.4	26.6	*
Affective	---	---	+	---	---	---		8.8	8.5	6.2	9.6	*
Affirmational	7.7	7.1	+	---	---	---		---	---	---	---	
Instrumental	7.3	6.6	*	---	---	---		7.0	6.7	4.1	9.0	+
Loss	2.7	3.6	+	---	---	---		2.9	---	3.9	---	*

Table 10.1 (*continued*)

Network Elements	Education[b]	Age[b]	Self Rated Health[b]	Mental State[b]	Functional Disability[b]	Physical Capacity[b]
Structure						
Size	.18**	---	.14*	.17**	---	---
Spouse	.13*	-.16*	.22***	.30***	.10+	-.19**
Children	-.19**	---	---	.12+	-.11+	---
Family	-.17**	---	.12*	.12*	---	---
Friends	.15*	---	.13*	---	---	-.09+
Neighbors	---	-.11+	---	---	---	---
Losses	---	---	---	---	---	---
Contact	---	-.19**	---	.17**	---	-.13*
Synagogue	---	---	.13*	.14*	.13*	-.11*
Support						
Total	.22***	---	.28***	.47***	.16**	-.29***
Affective	.17**	---	.36***	.50***	.18**	-.28***
Affirmational	.17**	---	.18**	.38***	---	-.17**
Instrumental	.20**	---	.19**	.32***	.16*	-.27***
Loss	---	-.15**	---	.10+	---	---

\\ = not calculated   [a] percentage or means   [b] correlation coefficient.
Significance levels: + $p < .10$ * $p < .05$ ** $p < .01$ *** $p < .001$.

Ethnicity. Some differences also appear according to ethnicity. There is no difference in network size, but people of Eastern origin are somewhat more likely to be married. The networks of elderly Eastern Jews also included a substantially larger number of children. This finding is consistent with past research in Israel (Shuval, Fleishman, and Shmueli, 1982) and stems from a combination of sources—the death of many close ties among European Jews in the Holocaust as well as higher birth rates among persons of Eastern origin.

The relative lack of family members in the networks of Western Jews is balanced by the predominance of friends in their networks. It may be that friends serve as compensation for family members lost through immigration and the Holocaust. Persons of Western origin are also more likely to have suffered a personal loss during the past year. Synagogue attendance, on the other hand, is higher among persons of Eastern origin.

Marital Status. Due to the inclusion of the spouse in the social network measure, marital status is strongly related to network size, with married people having larger networks than nonmarried people. Married persons also cite more children in their networks and are more likely to attend synagogue services on a regular basis.

Education. Education level is associated in various ways with social network structure. While the highly educated are more likely to be married, they tend to have fewer children. Extended family members and friends are also important elements in the networks of the more highly educated.

Functional Health Status. Several measures of health status are related to the structure of social networks. However, as will be discussed in greater detail later on, the direction of the relationship is not unequivocal. For example, persons with higher levels of functioning are also more likely to be married. They also have higher levels of synagogue attendance and are in more frequent contact with their networks. The latter relationships may reflect the importance of mobility among older persons, as a necessary condition for active participation in social relationships.

Self-Rated Health Status. Persons with larger networks tend to rate their overall health status higher. In addition, those with better health are more likely to be married and to cite more family members and friends in their networks. They also attend synagogue services more frequently.

Psychological State. Persons with larger networks tend to have a more positive outlook on life, with less general malaise ($R = .17, p < .01$). In particular, the presence of a spouse and children is positively related to the HAYS score. Psychological state is also related to frequency of contact, with persons having more contact having a more positive outlook on life.

SOCIAL SUPPORT

Looking at the three types of support addressed by the NSSQ, we find that affective support is the type of aid most frequently cited (8.6), followed by affirmation support (7.3) and instrumental aid (6.9). This finding is consistent with that of Antonucci and Depner (1982), who claim that social networks are best at providing emotional sustenance. The specific supportive nature of the social network varies somewhat with certain characteristics of the anchor person.

Men in the sample perceive their networks as offering significantly more instrumental aid and affirmational support than do women. Education is also strongly positively related to perceived availability of all types of support. On the other hand, divorced and widowed individuals perceive their networks providing significantly less support of all kinds than do either married or never-married respondents.

Combining the three aspects of social support, men perceive their networks as more supportive than do women. There are a number of potential explanations for this. Most likely is that many more women in the sample are widowed, and they have lost the most important source of social support, a spouse. Indeed, in viewing the relationship between marital status and overall support, we see that widowed and divorced persons have less available support than do the married and the never-married. Thus it seems that losing a spouse is extremely damaging to perceptions of assistance. On the other hand, there is no relationship between having suffered a *recent* loss and the perceived level of support available. Rather, it seems that the loss of an intimate or confidant damages perceptions of support that persist over time.

Finally, educational level is strongly related to all three measures of support. If we interpret the education variable as a proxy for socioeconomic status, the findings point to the importance of personal resources for the development and maintenance of a strong social support network (Auslander and Litwin, 1988). On the other hand, age is not related to any of the support measures. While the age range of the population studied here is limited, we might nevertheless expect the old–old to suffer from reduced levels of support and from increasing levels of social isolation. This does not appear to be the case.

The key most probably lies in the nature of the measure utilized in this analysis: the *supportiveness* of the social network, as opposed to the quantity of support available. While network size may diminish with increasing age of the anchor person, the quality of the support available appears to remain stable. Alternatively, it may be argued that expectations of support change over the life course—that is, the old–old have diminished expectations of support from their networks, in comparison to younger old people.

Health Status. The relationship between social support and health status was found to be very strong on all dimensions, with people in better health reporting more supportive social networks. The relationship with affective support is particularly strong. Among the four health measures, supportiveness is most strongly related to psychological state.

However, neither the direction of the relationship between health status and social support nor the biological processes at work between them is entirely clear (House et al., 1988; Schwarzer and Leppin, 1991). Do the elderly who are in good health enjoy more support by virtue of their ability to establish and maintain social relationships? Do the limited demands for assistance made on their networks allow them to maintain some degree of reciprocity? Or, alternatively, does social support serve as a buffer against a series of life events and stresses that might otherwise detrimentally affect the health of older persons?

It was hoped to address this issue through analysis of recent losses recorded on the NSSQ. As noted earlier, 54 persons reported a significant loss during the year preceding the interview. The corresponding amount of support lost ranged from a little (21 percent) to a great deal (31 percent). Surprisingly, however, no relationship was found between either the existence of a loss or the amount of support lost with any of the health status or other support measures.

It is possible that the effects of the loss of network support on physical health are only discernible over a longer period of time. The lack of some relationship with mental state, on the other hand, is puzzling. One explanation may lie in the age of the respondents. It is conceivable that loss is an integral fact of life in old age, with less deleterious effects than one might expect. In fact, some losses may come as a relief—for instance, in the case of elderly women caring for a chronically ill spouse.

As for the absence of a relationship between the amount of support lost during the year and the supportiveness of the network, the most likely explanation lies in the subjective nature of the support construct. It could well be that people who perceive their networks as most supportive are more attuned to their losses. If this is the case, we would expect persons reporting a significant amount of loss to have had higher levels of preloss support than those who did not report any loss of support. After experiencing the loss, the supportiveness of their networks would then become similar to that of people who were less affected by a loss.

NETWORK TYPES

Several researchers have attempted to uncover patterns of covariation between different social network elements, condensing them into a number of network types. Frequently, such analysis is based on the structural components of the network. The approach taken here combines van der Poel's (1993) four approaches to the study of social support networks—interaction, role relation, affective, and exchange—as detailed earlier. This allows for the characterization of and differentiation between various network configurations on the one hand, while on the other hand examining concurrently both the structure and content of the network.

Factor analysis is the means employed to identify meaningful network types among the study respondents. Thirteen variables are entered into the analysis: the three social support measures (affective, affirmational, and instrumental supportiveness); average frequency and duration of contact; six components of network membership (spouse, children, other family, friends, and neighbors); attendance at religious services; and two indicators of network reduction—loss during the past year and amount of support lost. Three factors were extracted using principal components analysis; these were rotated through the varimax procedure to refine the factor solution. Together, they account for 45 percent of the variance in network dimensions.

The three factors reflect distinct network types, which may be termed: (1) the *supportive* network, (2) the *replacement* network, and (3) the *traditional* network. Table 10:2 summarizes their characteristics, as well as their relationships with key sociodemographic and health status variables included in the study. A number of tests are employed to ascertain the significance of relationships: for continuous variables, Pearson's product–moment correlation is used; for gender, student's T-test. For ethnicity, Scheffé's multiple comparison test is used to test for intergroup differences.

1. The *Supportive* Network. Composed of four items—(1) affirmational, (2) affective and (3) instrumental supportiveness and (4) average frequency of contact—this factor explains 20 percent of the variance in the network elements. The convergence of the three supportiveness items plus the strength of the factor reinforces the importance of distinguishing between the structure and content of networks in general and, specifically, the uniqueness of the supportive content of network interactions (Thoits, 1982). On the other hand, the inclusion of average frequency of contact in this factor would indicate that perceived support is also available support—that is to say, network contacts that are perceived as supportive seem to be highly accessible. Whether this is because an effort is made to maintain contact with ties that are perceived as supportive or vice versa is yet to be determined.

This network factor is strongly related to age, education, mental state, self-rated health status, and functional state. Old people with strongly supportive networks are relatively younger and more highly educated. Their physical health is relatively good overall and in terms of both physical capacity and psychological state.

2. *The Replacement Network.* This factor is composed of three items—loss of a network member during the last year, amount of support lost during the past year, and number of friends in the network. Together, they account for 15 percent of the variance in all the network elements. As noted earlier, most of the losses cited by respondents are of family members and friends. The combination of elements found here indicates that the number of friends in the network increases

Table 10.2: Network Types: Factor Loadings and Relationship to Background Characteristics

Factor Derivation[a]	Support Network	Replacement Network	Traditional Network
Variables:			
Affirmational support	0.84		
Instrumental support	0.76		
Affective support	0.74		
Frequency of contact	0.62		
Loss during past year		0.91	
Amount of support lost		0.89	
Number of friends		0.43	
Presence of spouse			0.66
Number of children			0.63
Synagogue attendance			0.63
Relationship with other variables: (correlations)			
Age	-.14*	-.17*	-.12
Education	.24***	.06	-.03
Mental State	.20**	-.03	.16*
Self-rated health	.17	.04	.01
Functional state	-.27***	.01	-.19*
(Means)			
Ethnicity:			
Asia/Africa	-.09	-.14[+]	.58***
Europe/America	.03	.06	-.23***
Israeli	.40	.58[+]	-.01
Gender			
Male	.11	-.23*	.56***
Female	-.07	.14*	-.23***

[a] Only factors with eigenvalues greater than or equal to 1.0 are retained.
$^{+}p < .10$ $*p < 0.05$ $**p < .01$ $***p < .001$.

with the loss of network members and support—that is, although family members cannot be regenerated, it seems that their place in the network structure is taken over by friends. What is not known is whether these friends fulfill roles previously filled by family members. Of particular interest is whether they replace the support—both in quality and quantity—provided by those persons who were lost to the network (Litwak, 1985).

This network factor is related to age, sex, and ethnicity, so that persons with a strong replacement factor tend to be younger, of native Israeli origin, and female. It most probably reflects, on the one hand, the longer life expectancy among women common to all developed countries and, on the other, the role of women as "social secretaries" within the family. It has been noted in other studies that men who are widowed tend to become isolated due to a pattern of learned dependency. Their wives traditionally managed the family's social life (Lynch, 1977). Following the loss of a close network member, it seems that women are much more likely to establish new ties.

3. *The Traditional Network.* This factor is composed of three variables— presence of a spouse, number of children, and synagogue attendance. That is to say, it is primarily based on intimate relationships, at both the interpersonal and spiritual level.

This network factor is strongly associated with mental and functional state, as well as ethnicity and gender. It is particularly strong for men, persons of Eastern origin, with good physical capacity and a positive mental state. The presence of a spouse is much more common among men because of differences in life expectancy noted earlier. The importance of ethnicity is probably related to high childbearing rates among persons of Eastern origin in Israel. This may reflect traditional as well as religious norms, as well as adherence to manifest government policy at the height of immigration of Asian and African Jewry to Israel in the early 1950s.

The importance of traditional behavior is also reflected in the higher rates of synagogue attendance by both Sephardic Jews and men. In orthodox Judaism, only men are mandated to engage in communal prayer. While women may attend services, their presence in the synagogue is neither required nor encouraged, with physically separated seating areas distancing men and women. Thus, formally organized religious activities do not seem to be an important source of network strength for older Jewish women in Israel.

There has been no small amount of debate in the literature as to the order in which the above sets of variables are related (Schwarzer and Leppin, 1991). Of particular interest is the relationship between social network support and health. With a large body of evidence pointing to the relationship between these two areas, the direction of the relationship has yet to be pinpointed. On the one hand, traditional theories of network relationships point to the social support network as promoting positive health, either by buffering the deleterious effects of stress on health or by positively promoting normal human development. On the other hand, good health may be a necessary precondition for the existence of some network ties—that is, marriage and childbearing. Furthermore, poor health may make demands on the network, alter patterns of reciprocity and exchange, and thus lead to its weakening.

Some of the confusion lies in the multitude of health status measures that are in use. It may well be that social support network characteristics and strengths relate differentially to a variety of health status elements. An attempt to examine the ordering of these variables is illustrated by the path analysis shown in Figure 10.1.

The variety of health status variables employed in this study allows us to separate them into models that take advantage of several possible paths of causality simultaneously. It is assumed here that functional limitations lead to less opportunity for contact and hence to lower perceived support. On the other hand, based on both the buffering and developmental arguments, it is assumed that psychological state and self-perceptions of health are, at least in part, the result of network support. Thus they are placed after the support network measures in the model. Because of the presumed correlated error between self-perceptions of health and mental state, no assumption of directionality between them is made.

The model indicates, first of all, relatively strong first-order correlations between most of the background variables. Of particular note is the strong negative relationship between education and Eastern origin among the Israeli elderly; among the older generations ethnicity still proves to be a strong proxy for socioeconomic status.

Four variables are strongly related to physical capacity. Increasing age and lower education levels are associated with reduced physical capacity. Females are likely to be limited in physical capacity, as are applicants for formal assistance.

Physical capacity is then associated with the supportive type of network, so that persons who are less limited enjoy higher levels of support. Note that all of the relevant sociodemographic variables are related to the supportive network type *through* their relationship with physical capacity.

Physical capacity is not related to either of the other two network types—replacement or traditional—taking into consideration background variables. Rather, the background variables are related directly, with female gender positively associated with replacement networks and strongly negatively associated with traditional networks. Other factors relating to traditional networks are Eastern origin and nonapplicant status.

Finally, psychological health is arrived at via three different paths. It is, first of all, directly related to physical capacity, so that people who are functionally limited tend to have worse psychological health. However, the presence of a supportive network intervenes to some extent in this relationship—that is, persons

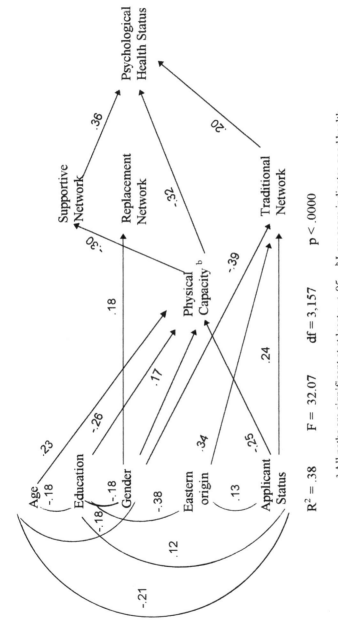

Figure 10.1: Path Analysis of Background, Functional Health Status, and Network Types on Psychological Health Status

who have good functional health also tend to have supportive networks; and the presence of a supportive network is positively associated with psychological health.

In addition, having a traditional network—spouse, children, synagogue attendance—seems to contribute to positive psychological health. This relationship is independent of physical capacity. Rather, for men of Eastern origin who are not applicants for assistance, the presence of a traditional network contributes positively to psychological health.

All things being equal, strong supportive and traditional networks seem to promote positive health. Less intimate or nonsupportive networks do not. While not examined here, it is certainly plausible that networks that are nonsupportive in the extreme may even damage health, particularly among vulnerable populations like the elderly.

THE INTERFACE BETWEEN FORMAL AND INFORMAL NETWORKS

The study of the interface between formal and informal networks was a main goal of the project described here, focusing on one aspect of the formal network—the municipal social services. The nature of this interface, with its implications, has been presented in detail elsewhere and is summarized here. Several aspects of the interface were investigated, including: (1) identifying factors that distinguish between applicants for social services and nonapplicants (Auslander and Litwin, 1990); (2) the nature of the involvement of the informal networks with the formal social services (Litwin and Auslander, 1993); and (3) determinants of the extent of social worker contact with the informal network (Litwin and Auslander, 1994). All these questions were examined within the help-seeking framework posited by Andersen, Kravits, and Anderson (1975), delineating three groups of predictors: (1) predisposing characteristics, chiefly, sociodemographic; (2) enabling characteristics, which promote the ability to reach care; and (3) perceived need. Social networks and support can be considered part of the second and third groups, to the extent that they provide information on sources of care and legitimize the need for care.

The elderly applicants for social services were found to be similar to nonapplicants on all of the predisposing characteristics, with the exception of age and marital status. Applicants are older and are less likely to be married. As far as perceived need is concerned, the applicants are more limited functionally than the nonapplicants, as measured by both functional disability and physical capacity. Finally, the applicants have fewer network resources than do the nonapplicants; their social networks are smaller, due primarily to the absence of a spouse; and they perceive their networks as less supportive in affective terms. Thus, they are more needy, on the one hand, and have fewer resources to meet those needs, on the other.

Follow-up interviews were conducted with the social workers of 90 of the 100 applicants. In an attempt to describe the nature of the involvement of the informal network, we looked first at the initiation of contact with the social services, distinguishing between contacts that were initiated by a member of the network ($n = 53$) and those initiated by the older person ($n = 37$). Interestingly, no differences were found between the two groups on any of the social network (enabling) characteristics or on predisposing characteristics, other than the age of the applicant. Those whose networks initiated contact are significantly older ($X = 76.6$) than those whose networks did not initiate contact with the social worker ($X = 73.0, T = 2.13, p < .05$). Major differences are evident, on the other hand, in terms of perceived need; persons whose networks initiated contact are much more limited in their functional state, both in terms of physical capacity ($T = -2.72, p < .01$) and functional disability ($T = -2.10, p < .01$).

In general, network involvement is more pronounced for persons seeking residential placement than for those requesting other kinds of assistance ($\chi^2 = 4.79$, $p < .05$). However, for three-quarters of the involved network members, such involvement was limited to making the application instead of the client or on his/her behalf. Thus in most cases, the network's main role was to facilitate the request for residential care rather than to prevent it.

As for social workers' contacts with the social networks of their older clients, the number of contacts per problem was examined. No relationship was found between any of the enabling (network) or predisposing variables and social worker's contacts. Rather, measures of need were most strongly related, with higher contact for clients with low functional capability ($R = -.30, p < .01$) and for three types of problems: (1) residential placement ($R = .30, p < .001$), (2) daily functioning ($R = .29, p < .01$), and (3) network relations ($R = .26, p < .01$). The most important predictor of social workers' contact with the informal network, however, is the number of presenting problems. Network contact is the most intensive among applicants with multiple problem situations.

IMPLICATIONS FOR SOCIAL POLICY

Several findings from this study have implications for social welfare policy and service delivery. As has been found in other studies, the social networks of elderly people in Jerusalem are most effective in the provision of emotional support. The provision of practical support, on the other hand, is what older people and their social networks seem to be seeking from the formal social services system.

Moreover, social networks and the support they offer vary to a large degree according to the sociodemographic characteristics of the older population. The findings of this study suggest that one can differentiate between the networks of the young–old and those of the old–old, those of women and those of men, and those persons of Eastern origin and those of Western or native Israeli origin. The findings here regarding ethnic differences are particularly important in light of the recent waves of immigration to Israel that were cited at the beginning of the chapter.

Given the differences between the social networks of varying ethnic groups, policymakers should proceed with care when trying to formulate service provisions for newcomers based on our knowledge of previous groups. In particular, social policy aimed at interweaving formal services and informal networks cannot be based on the assumption that informal networks are a uniform entity. The extent to which they vary and the characteristics associated with that variation make it clear that social networks must be evaluated on an individual basis to determine their strengths, their weaknesse, and their potential for cooperative endeavor.

Of particular importance is the degree of supportiveness of social networks, which, as we found, is not distributed equally among the population. As it turns out, the supportive network is most common among the stronger elements in the elderly population—among the young–old, the better educated, and the relatively healthy. Attempts to build social policy on the basis of informal support, therefore, need to be cognizant of the fact that elderly people most in need of assistance may lack network support.

Finally, this study allows us to examine in greater depth the network-related behavior of those people who are of central interest in developing and implementing social policy—that is, elderly applicants for formal assistance. In earlier writings, it was suggested that the interweaving of formal and informal care would be most appropriate under two conditions: the availability of a network that provides social support, and the amenability of the client's problems to network care (Auslander and Litwin, 1987). To a large extent, however, this was not the pattern observed in this study.

The availability of the informal network and affective support are, indeed, important predictors in distinguishing between applicants and nonapplicants to formal social services. Paradoxically, however, application for formal support is higher among those who *lack* network support. Among those who apply to the formal network, moreover, network involvement is higher for those with problems that are less amenable to shared responsibility—for example, when the older client's physical or mental state is such that residential care is needed (or perceived to be so). This pattern is mirrored in the social workers' interactions with the informal network, with contact being highest in cases of severely limited older persons requesting residential care.

Recommendations for Future Research

The findings of this study and their place in the growing body of literature on the social supports of elderly people highlight several areas of research that require further development, on both a theoretical and a practical level.

In spite of numerous studies, the way or ways in which social support affects health has yet to be determined. This gap can only be closed by long-term panel studies, which follow people with various network types over a long period of time. Such research needs to take into account changes in social network structure and in the types and amount of social support provided by the network, side-by-side with changes in health status. While the experimental manipulation necessary to determine causality is clearly out of the question, rigorous quasi-experimental designs based on a long-term investment should go a long way in clarifying this critical area.

This analysis also underscores the important role of ethnicity in distinguishing between network types. What is particularly interesting is the clarity of differences within a limited segment of one society—elderly Jewish Israelis. One would expect to find even greater differences in a cross-section of that society that would include new immigrants and elderly Arabs, and even greater variety in cross-national and cross-cultural analyses. This volume provides a basis for such study. However, further systematic analyses are needed to examine the extent to which cultural expectations and norms regarding social roles and relationships vary over the life cycle. Do the health implications of the lack of informal social support vary between cultures? And are there relationships that are stable across cultures, which may enable us to identify "truths" about the essence of social network support and its importance for elderly persons?

Finally, as we noted earlier, in Israel as well as in other countries, social policymakers tend to see the informal social network as a resource for the provision of care for elderly persons. This analysis suggests that these resources are of limited potential. It does not, however, rule out the possibilities of *changing* the nature of the network interaction with the society's formal caregiving institutions. Based on the findings of this and other studies, difficulties in those interactions should be identified and serve as the basis for interventions aimed at their resolution. Such intervention strategies could then be tested experimentally. The results of studies of this type would help to integrate the theoretical knowledge developing in this area with the practical possibilities for its application for the benefit of both elderly people and the milieus in which they live.

11

A Cross-National
Social Network Analysis

Howard Litwin

This concluding chapter consolidates the main themes that emerge from each of the country reports and views them in a comparative perspective. The salient findings on the social networks of older people in each country are examined in the same order in which the study topics were presented in the introductory chapter: (1) methodology, (2) study sample, (3) social network structure and interaction, (4) variations in the social networks of older people, (5) social support, (6) network typologies, (7) the interface between informal networks and the formal sector, (8) implications for policy and practice, and (9) needed future research. As will become evident in the ensuing paragraphs, despite the several differences in design and execution of the country analyses, a coherent and cohesive picture does emerge of the social networks of elderly people.

METHODOLOGY

Beyond the methodological differences already alluded to in the introductory chapter, perusal of the respective approaches to network analysis in this collection reveals a range of procedures and techniques. Stated more simply, the social networks of older people are addressed in different ways in the participating countries. These differences are evident in three principal areas: the varying sources of data on the social network, the differing conceptual bases for delineation of social network, and the divergent methods of data analysis.

In terms of data source, three primary directions seem to emerge. First is the use of preexistent general social survey data. The Swedish, Canadian, and Finnish studies are all drawn from such data sets. The network analyses performed on these data bases are, in effect, subsequent applications that were not planned in the original data collection design.

The second source may be termed network-related research data. Both the French and the Spanish studies exemplify this utilization. The study of intergenerational exchange in France parallels selected aspects of network research, allowing application of the data to network-related analysis. Similarly, the epidemiological study in Leganés allows consideration of the networks of the Spanish elderly irrespective of the public health concerns that guided that study.

The third source reflects direct network-focused inquiry. The British, U.S., Dutch, and Israeli studies were all conducted with the predetermined intent of measuring the social networks of older adults. As such, these sources represent the closest empirical convergence in this collection between data source and network measurement outcome.

Social networks tend to be conceptualized in terms of three main factors: structural or morphological criteria, interactional characteristics, and exchange relationships—particularly in the area of social support. All the studies in this book address both the structural and interactional aspects of the network phenomenon, though not all utilize the same structural criteria. Thus, all include the components of adult children and/or other family members as determinants of network boundaries. The spouse is included in most cases either directly or indirectly in terms of living arrangements. However, the assessment instrument developed in England and Wales does not have specific reference to a spouse.

Friends of the older person are an integral network delineator in most country reports. Neighbors are also addressed in a majority of the network analyses, excluding those in Canada, France, and Sweden. Confidants as a network determining criterion, on the other hand, are specifically addressed in four of the studies: Spain, Finland, the United States, and Israel.

Religious facility attendance as a network marker is cited in the Spanish, British, and Israeli studies directly, and indirectly in the Dutch case (whether members of a church congregation are included in the respondent's network). Other organizational ties are seldom invoked in the network measurement efforts, however, with the exception of England and the Netherlands. Finally, a unique network measure applied in the Spanish study only is "going to the *plaza*," reflecting a culturally relevant network criterion in that society.

Interactional features of the network are measured almost universally in terms of frequency of contact with network members. Among the chapters in this book, the actual measures indicate some diversity across nations in the meaning of "contact," ranging from face-to-face contact to monthly telephone calls.

The receipt of support as an exchange criterion in network determination, on the other hand, is utilized in five countries: Finland, France, the Netherlands, the United States, and Israel. In the first three, the provision of instrumental support is incorporated as the relevant measure. In the U.S. study, the Lubben Social Networks Scale tends more toward support of an affirmative nature, whereas in Israel instrumental and emotional aid are addressed as network determinants.

The third and final methodological divergence apparent in the network studies is the range of methods of data analysis. The Swedish report presents a descriptive secondary analysis. The French describe frequency and associational aspects of the network, particularly in the realm of intergenerational exchange. The Spanish study utilizes logistic regression to identify the strength of various factors as network predictors. Both the Canadian and Finnish analyses employ a quick clustering procedure for the identification of network types.

The British and U.S. studies use their unique network inventories to characterize respondents' networks. The former uses its inventory to discover significant correlates of network types; the latter's use of the network inventory is to examine the relationship of networks to other measures of social integration.

The Dutch inquiry also seeks network correlates, but it does so by means of analysis of variance. Finally, the Israeli research applies factor analysis to the data set in its attempt to characterize networks and implements path analysis as the means to trace the networks' effects on personal well-being.

THE STUDY SAMPLE

The studies in this collection represent a divergence from the usual scope of network analysis of elderly populations. As recalled from the introduction, most research reported in the literature is based upon small samples. Only one in five generally reflect study samples of 1,000 subjects or more.

In contrast, all but two of the country reports considered here have samples of the elderly of more than 1,000 respondents. The largest are those of the United Kingdom and the Netherlands, with over 4,000 each, followed by the Canadian study with over 3,000 respondents. The smaller study populations in this comparative analysis belong to the U.S. study, with a focused sample of 429 subjects, and the Israeli study, which mapped the networks of 200 elderly persons.

A second comparative feature of the samples worth noting is the relative scope of coverage and the resulting representativeness of each. Three country reports—Sweden, Canada, and Finland—reflect national probability sampling. Two others—France and Holland—used regional sampling of areas reflective of each country's general population. As such, these studies achieve a high degree of representativeness.

The British, Spanish, U.S., and Israeli studies, on the other hand, each take place in a single locality, Liverpool, Leganés, Los Angeles, and Jerusalem, respectively. Their samples are shown to be reflective, to varying degrees, of the aged population at large.

SOCIAL NETWORK STRUCTURE AND INTERACTION

Despite the methodological and sampling differences just cited, it is still possible to characterize the social networks of older people on the basis of the comparative data in this collection. The construction of an "average" network comes, of course, at the expense of the variation and diversity that exist in the networks of many older individuals. Nevertheless, consideration of the networks' major common features underscores the current state of the informal milieu of the elderly population.

Accordingly, this section presents the common themes of network structure and interaction that occur across countries. The specific factors addressed in this regard include network size, composition, contact frequency, church attendance, network loss, the presence of a confidant, living arrangements, and trends in network development. The following section in the comparative analysis considers variations that appear in the networks of older persons.

Network Size. This variable is the one most commonly considered among all the network features. The findings suggest, moreover, that the networks of the elderly are generally small. The British and Israeli studies, for example, cite modal network ranges of 5–7 members. The Dutch figures are slightly larger, ranging from 9 to 12 members, depending upon the definition of network employed. Based on an index ranking rather than an exact count, the Finnish data note a modal size of 8, while the Canadian statistics suggest that up to 60 percent of the networks of the elderly range between 4 and 10 members.

The opposite trend is cited in but a minority of countries. The Spanish data reflect a large average network size of 18 members, most of whom are family members. The French analysis cites a multigenerational family-based network of 22 members on the average. Both of these studies, it should be recalled, reflect inferred network size as opposed to an ego-generated measurement of the phenomenon.

Network Composition. The most immediate network tie available to older adults—that of spouse—is reported in a majority of cases. Both the Swedish and Spanish studies indicate a 60 percent marital rate among their study populations. The Finns note that three-quarters of older men are married, but only one-third of older women. The Canadians reflect a similar situation by noting simply that most elderly men are married. The British, on the other hand, report a marital rate, undifferentiated by gender, of 43 percent.

Beyond spousal relations, the networks of older people are overwhelmingly family-oriented. Children and other kin dominate the networks of the elderly in Israel, Spain, France, and Sweden. In Finland, ties with children and siblings are the most important, but ties with friends are more prevalent. In England, the locally integrated network that is characterized by a large number of family members as well as some friends and neighbors is the most common of the network types. In the Netherlands, adult children most frequently comprise the elder's social network, followed in frequency by neighbors.

Contact Frequency. Either through direct measurement or by inference, most of the participating countries report a relatively frequent rate of contact between older people and their social networks. Contact is generally more frequent with family members, particularly with children, than with friends. Nonetheless, it seems that in no country does a week go by without some sort of interpersonal contact between elderly persons and their interpersonal milieu.

Church Attendance. In contrast to the previous network feature, it is possible to cite the average rate of religious attendance in only a minority of countries. The Leganés results indicate that as many as half of the Spanish elderly, most usually women, regularly attend church. Roughly one-quarter of the Liverpool sample report regular church attendance. One-third of the Jerusalem elderly, mostly men, indicate weekly synagogue attendance. The lack of such information in the remaining countries may reflect their more limited degree of religious participation, as is the case in Sweden, Finland, and the Netherlands, or the simple lack of its measurement, as in France and the United States. Thus, our knowledge of the importance of church attendance as a network resource for older people is uneven and limited, on the whole.

Network Loss. Data on network reduction due to the death or moving away of network members is available in even fewer of the country reports. In Israel about one-fourth of the respondents cited a network loss in the past year. In the Spanish case, one-half of the sample reported suffering a loss over the previous two years. While a fairly similar rate of loss is evident in these figures, it may not be assumed, necessarily, that these rates also prevail in the networks of older adults in other countries.

The Presence of a Confidant. The same may be said concerning the presence of confidant relationships in the network. Only two countries present sample-wide descriptive statistics on this subject. In the Spanish sample, three-quarters of respondents report having a confidant, most usually a spouse or daughter. In Finland, the corresponding figure is similar—70 percent of respondents. Thus, once again, these data may reflect the reality in other countries, but this assumption remains tentative. The relatively widespread availability of confidants may be indirectly reinforced, on the other hand, by the data on loneliness in Sweden. Only 1 percent of the Swedish elderly are considered truly lonely.

Living Arrangements. Residential patterns provide an additional measure of social network, in that for many older people the household is the primary network. Specific summary data on this subject is available from four of the countries in the collection: Finland, Sweden, Britain, and Spain. The first three show very similar trends—about 40 percent of older people residing alone and between 40 and 50 percent residing with spouse only. The proportion of those who report co-residency with children varies from a low of 2–3 percent in Sweden to some 15 percent in Liverpool, England.

The same may not be said of the Spanish sample. In Leganés, only 10 percent of the elderly reside alone, while over 40 percent reside jointly with children, occasionally as a couple that is not considered the head of household. In France, the rate is somewhat smaller but nevertheless noteworthy—20 percent share a residence with a child. Thus, the general cross-national trend is one of independent living on the part of older adults, with familial co-residency occurring in but a minority of cases.

Trends in Network Development. Characteristic trends in the evolution of older people's social networks are specifically reported in four countries. The Swedes report that while households are becoming smaller, the networks of the elderly are becoming somewhat more differentiated with a move from close-knit family-based networks to more extended family-based ones. In Spain, the networks are said to shrink over time; in the Netherlands, they are seen to decrease with age. The common trends observed among the elderly in the United Kingdom are moves from more independent types of social network to less independent types. Thus, while the social networks of older people seem, on average, to be quite resilient, the dominant developmental trend among them is a move towards a less resilient and more dependent state.

VARIATIONS IN THE SOCIAL NETWORKS OF OLDER PEOPLE

While there are many common themes in the social networks of older people, there are also discernible differences according to gender, age, and marital status of the person in question. Additional variation by functional status and rural/urban residence is also evident, but to a lesser degree. Several of these differentiating factors are interrelated.

Gender differences are the most salient of features in network variation, and the data suggest that women have more limited network resources than do men. The greater prevalence of women living alone is cited in Sweden, Canada, and Finland. In Israel and France, the higher likelihood of widowhood is noted. Women are widely reported to have more friends in their networks, and more confidants, but they have fewer long-term caregiving resources. The greater frequency of women in small child-focused networks, for example, is noted specifically in Canada and Finland. An exception to this trend is the lack of gender differences on network scores in Los Angeles, and in network size reported in Jerusalem.

The social networks of the old–old are similarly less endowed in terms of network availability. Living alone rises with age in Sweden, while in Finland lower interaction intensity and fewer intimates are reported among the eldest cohorts. Octogenarians in the U.S. sample had lower social network scores. Neighbors are less likely to be included in the networks of older–old people in Israel, even though they may be less mobile and more inclined to remain at home.

Age also covaries with marital status. The higher the respondent age, the greater the likelihood of having lost a spouse. In Spain, co-residency with children is reported to be higher among the widowed. On the other hand, younger married people in the elderly cohort have relatively larger social networks, as reported in Finland, Israel, Canada, and the Netherlands.

A similar pattern of variation is suggested regarding older people with functional impairment. Those with poor health tend to have smaller networks. They also have a greater likelihood of co-residing with someone other than a spouse.

Rural–urban differences, on the other hand, are reported in but a few country reports. In both Finland and the United Kingdom, the data suggest that rural networks of the old are larger than those of their urban counterparts. The French data indicate, however, that rural networks are less endowed in terms of available resources.

Finally, it seems that external network sources are utilized by those with more internal resources as well. In Spain, for example, elders with higher socioeconomic status, good health, and more siblings and friends also frequent church and the *plaza* more often. In Israel, men attend the synagogue more frequently than do women. In France, people from higher occupational ranks make greater use of privately purchased support services.

SOCIAL SUPPORT

The relationship between social network and social support was examined in all the country reports in one way or another. Virtually all the reports focus on the provision of instrumental assistance in the tasks of daily living as the support measure of interest, although the Israeli study found affective support to be the type of aid that is relatively most available from the informal network. The comparative data suggest, moreover, that most elderly people are not in receipt of informal instrumental supports emanating from outside the household.

Nevertheless, practical assistance is not equally available. The Swedish, Spanish, Israeli, Dutch, French, and British data all suggest that men receive instrumental support primarily from their spouse, but the reverse is not always the case. Rather, women receive more help from outside the household and are more likely to be in receipt of formal assistance.

The U.S. study found the family factor in its social network scale to be the one most highly correlated with tangible assistance. The confidant factor was most highly correlated, on the other hand, with emotional support. The friends factor of the network scale was also correlated, to some degree, with all the kinds of support. However, these correlations were very low, indicating that friends are a less resourceful source of support than are family and intimates.

Wenger postulates a hierarchy of support, on the basis of her longitudinal data in England and Wales, in which spousal aid is followed by familial aid from outside the household and subsequently by aid from friends and neighbors. The last resort in this assistance hierarchy is paid professional help. Attias-Donfut and Rozenkier confirm that spouses are the primary source of assistance. However, as most of the dependent elderly in France are widows, it is their children who are the main caregivers.

Two additional and perhaps partially contradictory phenomena are evident in the data on support. First, there is a "levelling effect" in which different amounts of initial informal assistance provided by different groups is apparent, to varying degrees, in the Dutch and Spanish reports. In such a case, provided assistance levels off at a high rate of aid when the degree of need requires it, despite the differential initial levels of informal aid given. However, the Israeli and Finnish data suggest that those with better health also have more supportive social networks.

On the other hand, having more supportive networks does not necessarily mean getting more support—that is, the quality of support actually provided may be independent of the extent of available assistance. The Israeli chapter presents this explanation in light of its finding that age is not related to support, even though it is known that the networks of the oldest–old are smaller than those of the young–old.

NETWORK TYPOLOGIES

Perhaps the most innovative contribution of this collection is its treatment of network types among the eldest cohort of society. Wenger applies and further refines her network assessment instrument in the chapter prepared for this book. The authors from Canada, Finland, and Israel all report the results of new network typology conceptualization and examination. These efforts were implemented in response to the invitation to participate in this cross-national analysis. The common themes running across the resultant network types, as well as unique network manifestations uncovered in the process, are spelled out next.

It can be said, first, that in deriving the network types, each of the researchers relies most heavily upon morphological and interactional criteria. In Liverpool, Wenger repeats application of an assessment instrument based upon eight variables that reflect the availability of local close kin, level of involvement with family, friends, and neighbors, and level of interaction with community groups. Stone and Rosenthal choose five distinguishing factors in their typology development in Canada: network size, composition, having a spouse or partner, living arrangements, and frequency of contact (for example, with children, siblings, and friends). Melkas and Jylhä focus upon four variables of interest in their typology construction in Finland: the number of friends, having a confidant, frequency of contact with network members, and the exchange of practical help. However, number of friends and contact frequency were the most influential variables in producing the Finnish network clusters.

The Israeli study by Auslander presents the major exception to this trend in that it includes three measures of support and an additional one of support loss among the 13 variables selected to differentiate between the networks. These support indicators have a strong influence on the derivation of two of the three network factors uncovered in the Israeli analysis. The contribution of the support variables to network typologization is also reflected in the terms used to identify the respective network factors, the first of which is called the supportive network.

A second trend cutting across most of the typologies is their systematic association with demographic and other background characteristics of the elderly population. The derived network types are frequently differentiated by age, socioeconomic status, and gender of the respondent, as well as by his or her functional status. By comparing the network types and their correlates across countries, an interesting tendency is evident.

Considering both structural and interactional features, some network types are clearly more resilient, and hence more supportive over time, than are others. Similarly, the elderly people who are members of certain network types may be more functionally independent and/or more endowed with interpersonal resources than others. This creates a situation in which one can distinguish between structurally robust and weak social networks, on the one hand, and between resourceful and vulnerable elderly population groups, on the other.

In the British study the most common network type is a robust network consisting of resourceful elderly people: the locally integrated network. The second most common grouping is a robust network type, which supports a potentially vulnerable elderly population. Two less predominant weak network types are nevertheless characterized by having resourceful elderly populations, thus making their weak network structure less of a risk for them. The fifth and final network type, on the other hand, reflects a vulnerable elderly population in a weak network setting.

This last case represents about 12 percent of the elderly population in Liverpool. However, if we also take into account the robust network type comprised of vulnerable elderly groups, many of whom may eventually need additional support, the proportion of elderly people at risk in this respect is about one-third of the elderly British cohort.

The figures from Finland show a similar trend. Five network types were identified in that study. Three of the types reflect a rich social life according to the authors—that is, they are robust networks. The fourth derived network type is family-focused in structure and strongly reflective in its background characteristics of the average elderly Finnish population. It is not extraordinary in any particular sense. The fifth network type, however, is relatively weak, both in structure and in the nature of the population groups that comprise it. This last network type, and the risk situation it represents, accounts for 35 percent of the elderly Finnish cohort.

Combining network type and background correlates in Canada reveals that 36 percent of elderly men and 28 percent of elderly women are at similar risk. As recalled, the Canadian study derived network types independently by gender, producing six different classifications. Two of these types reflect particularly fragile network structures in which the elderly members have fewer interpersonal resources upon which they can call for support.

Thus, about one-third of the elderly in Britain, Finland, and Canada may be said to be in jeopardy due to their own frailty or that of their supportive networks. This comparative observation is not meant to overshadow the fact that in these same countries, between one-half and two-thirds of the elderly population is either engulfed in supportive social networks or so functionally independent that the lack of one is not an immediate danger. Nevertheless, it should raise concern as to the extent of informal support available to needy and frail elders in the community. This point is considered further in the subsequent sections of this comparative review.

A third trend evident in the typology analyses is the systematic relationship between network type and social support, both in terms of informal assistance and use of formal services. In Liverpool, for example, spousal and relative-provided aid is prevalent among the locally based network types when illness strikes an older person. The wider-community-focused type, on the other hand, reports a spouse and friends helping in combination, while elders in the private restricted type rely as much on neighbors as on spouse. With regard to formal domiciliary services, only cleaning services are significantly related to network type. However, the trend suggests that elderly people with more resourceful network types also make greater use of such paid services.

A similar finding is evident in the Finnish network typology. Elderly people in the most endowed network type also had received or knew someone who could provide a range of informal practical help. More than half of those in the least endowed network type, on the other hand, lacked at least one kind of informal help. Another variation is the greater tendency of one network type in Finland—the "agentic network"—to make use of municipal services.

In the Canadian case, living arrangements were utilized as a proxy measure of exchange, given the lack of specific intrahousehold exchange measures. Higher rates of help, particularly from children, are suggested in selected network types. When disaggregated by marital status, moreover, the small network types reflect the greatest likelihood of such help. The authors conclude that "general morphological and functional features of network clusters are pointers to actual and potential rates of involvement in the exchange of social supports."

These findings suggest the existence of some systematic variation in the exchange of supports by network types. However, the body of evidence is still very tentative, reflecting the preliminary stage of such inquiry. This important area is not yet sufficiently developed and will require significant additional attention if it is to inform policymaking effectively on social care.

THE INTERFACE BETWEEN INFORMAL NETWORKS
AND THE FORMAL SECTOR

A second innovative feature of this cross-national analysis is its treatment of the interface between the informal social networks of elderly people and the formal care sector. Two countries—Israel and Britain—specifically examine the dynamics and the outcomes of contacts between informal caregivers and formal service personnel. Most of the remaining countries address this issue by means of inference, associating service utilization rates with selected network factors. The results of this comparative inquiry center on three interlocking themes: the characteristics of older persons who make use of public services and their networks, the motivation of informal caregivers in seeking formal help, and the relationship between formal and informal care systems.

The composite profile of elders in receipt of public services reflects limited personal resources. In Canada, older people without offspring are seen as being at greater risk of entry into long-term care institutions. In Israel, applicants to services from the welfare bureau are older than elderly nonapplicants in the community, and they are more likely to be widowed. They are also more functionally limited. In Sweden, formal services are widely available but are used more frequently by elderly people who live alone.

Moreover, the social networks of older people using public services are characteristically less resourceful than the networks of elders not in receipt of formal care services. Formal service users among the Dutch elderly, for example, tend to be those whose partner is less available, if at all. Use of out-of-household services among the Spanish elderly is negatively related to the quality of interaction with family members.

In the British context, as confirmed in the earlier Welsh studies, the caseloads of social services are made up largely of people with private restricted networks, the weakest of the network types. Those with relatively stronger network types, such as the locally integrated and local-family-dependent types, are underrepresented on social service caseloads. However, in both France and the United Kingdom, privately purchased services are prevalent among the more affluent social networks.

Information on the actual motivation for seeking formal help is available from the Welsh studies and the Israeli analysis only. In the former case, the appeal to formal services is seen as a step of last resort for the informal network, due to the relative absence of informal helpers. In the latter case, the turn to the welfare system stems primarily from the desire of the informal network to seek residential placement for their elderly relative. In both cases, therefore, motivation for formal help is characterized by limited ability or willingness to continue the provision of informal care.

The relationship between formal and informal care sectors, or what occurs when one system encounters the other, is an especially important factor in the overall picture of caregiving in an aging society. The reports from the countries in this collection seem to suggest that, on the whole, there is little active collaboration between the two sectors. While most elderly people in Sweden favor public-sector care, for example, little care is shared. Rather, caregiving starts with the family, and then, as needs grow, the elderly person either goes over to exclusive public care or the family continues alone. In Spain, a high preference for formal help is countered by the very low availability of such assistance. Paid sources of help in the Spanish context are seen to act mainly as a substitute for the daughter's role as caregiver.

Formal help in the Netherlands is viewed as a replacement for spousal help, and as a supplement to help by adult children and other relatives. Nevertheless, the provision of formal help in that context is not seen to cause a lesser provision of informal help. In the United Kingdom, on the other hand, purposive network interventions on the part of formal care services improved informal care provision in some cases but clearly exacerbated the situation in others.

The French data seem to offer the only major deviation from the picture that has been presented thus far. The authors report that only a minority of older people in their sample rely exclusively on formal caregiving—between 5 and 10 percent, depending upon level of dependence. On the other hand, 40 to 60 percent of care is provided solely by informal caregivers from the elder's support network. Nevertheless, they claim that the ability to remain at home depends most frequently on the cumulative benefit of both sources of care—formal and informal. Moreover, the higher the level of need, the greater the proportion of older people in France who report getting both kinds of assistance.

In sum, there is relatively little evidence of the effective interweaving of care sectors, formal and informal, in the ongoing care of elderly people. The data do not suggest that collaborative intersectorial caregiving is impossible under current circumstances, but, rather, that it is not a prevalent occurrence in most of the countries studied in this comparative analysis. The policy implications of this caregiving reality are considered next.

IMPLICATIONS FOR POLICY AND PRACTICE

The findings on the social networks of older people in nine different countries suggest some common implications for the policy and practice of long-term care of the elderly cohort of society. Toward this end, selected points of interest from the respective country reports are grouped into three main themes: (1) the identification of particularly vulnerable groups among the elderly population, (2) a critique of the "back-to-the-family" focus of community-care-oriented social policy, and (3) an extrapolation of some guidelines for the practice of community care in light of social network developments. A brief consideration of the value base of social policy for the elderly concludes this particular section of the comparative analysis.

While the general findings on social networks confirm that certain sectors of the elderly cohort—particularly women, the frail, and the old–old—are at greater risk than others, specific vulnerable groups are identifiable in several countries. In Canada, for example, the childless elderly are cited as a high-risk group due to their more fragile social networks. This is especially the case among Canadian women.

In the Netherlands, older people with smaller family networks—particularly the unmarried—are marked as an at-risk group. Illiterate older people and former farm workers in Spain are found to constitute a unique subset of the elderly cohort requiring public attention. In the United Kingdom, retirees who migrate to new communities and leave their family behind are seen to comprise a vulnerable group of future importance. Thus, policymakers in each country should give attention to the unique demographic manifestations of vulnerability within their society, in addition to paying heed to the general implications that stem from cross-national social network research.

The current popularity of community-based long-term care, in which members of the informal social network are expected to provide the bulk of care, needs to be selectively re-examined in light of several findings presented in this collection. As recalled, the dominant trend in network development is one toward less intensive and more fragile informal support structures. The Dutch study mentions in this regard that while social policy must look to activating friends and neighbors of older people as future sources of support, there is little reason to believe that they will be as supportive as family-based networks are today.

This concern is underscored by data from Canada, where sibling help is currently described as more limited and less intensive than help from the children and spouse. Evidence from Spain citing lack of assistance in daily living tasks by friends of the elderly is yet another example of the limitations of nonfamilial aid. Thus, the unbridled enthusiasm currently expressed in most Western countries in favor of a "back-to-the-family" policy of long-term care must be reconciled with the demonstrated reduction in the resilience of family networks and the more limited support roles found to be fulfilled by the nonfamilial members of older people's social networks. The future development of community care of the elderly will most probably have to take into account both greater public support of informal caregiving networks and more thoughtful development of public alternatives to informal care by the social support networks of the elderly.

Several practice implications are also forthcoming from the findings from this comparative study—in particular, the need on the part of practitioners to differentiate between the social networks of older people and to discern varying levels of support potential. The British chapter recommends doing so in terms of network type, according to an evolving assessment instrument. The Israeli analysis hints at the need to individualize the evaluation of older people's social networks, and specifically their potential for cooperation with formal services. The U.S. researchers point to the relative distinction between social networks, social supports, and loneliness, and the need to measure these phenomena separately in practice settings.

A related practice implication is to examine systematically the association between different kinds of networks and the utilization of formal social services. Especially important in this regard is the need to identify the kinds of networks for which formal residential care of the older person is the only realistic alternative. Differential assessment of formal service utilization by elders and their support networks will provide clearer guidelines for the management of the interface between the two care systems.

Finally, determination will have to be made as to the optimal way in which to benefit from the informal aid of older people's support networks. Most of the studies in this collection relate to informal support as instrumental or tangible assistance that is provided to an elderly care recipient. However, Auslander makes the case that networks are best equipped to provide emotional aid and that practical assistance is the preferred realm of the formal service sector. It is important to clarify, therefore, the nature of the contribution of networks to their elderly members, by means of active experimentation in community-based long-term care service delivery.

The development and implementation of social policy in relation to the needs of elderly people must be viewed in light of the dominant values of each society. The same may be said regarding the view of social networks as a tool of social policy. Two characteristic value models stand out in this collection. On the one hand is the traditional value base reflected in the Spanish study, where both larger familial networks and greater reliance on familial support for the elderly is the dominant norm. The relative lack of formal public services available to the Spanish elderly underscores the familial orientation in that society. At the opposite extreme is the case presented in Sweden. In that setting, older people's social networks are small, and a great many elders reside alone. Correspondingly, perhaps, there is widespread availability of formal services, and the elderly are seen to be well integrated into the overall fabric of society. Andersson and Sundström posit a Scandinavian model of welfare in which informal networks actually play but a small part in the provision of needed supports.

Is there a North–South division in the formulation of social policy for the elderly and in the conceptualization of the role of social networks vis-à-vis elders in society? The findings in this comparative analysis seem to suggest that there may well be. Moreover, the growing preference in several countries for the traditional and familial-oriented value base of social care may stand in contradistinction to the dominant demographic developments in the social networks of older adults in these same countries, as uncovered here. Additional focused inquiry into this policy domain is, indeed, warranted.

NEEDED FUTURE RESEARCH

Just as the approach to network analysis differs across countries, so the views of needed future research endeavors in this field vary. Some of the suggestions are essentially a reaction to the limitations of current work, while others constitute a continuation, and particularly an extension, of recent efforts. Due to the range of opinions on this topic, the data are reviewed by country, rather than by theme.

The Swedish contributors call for more theoretically guided inquiry into the social networks of the elderly, citing the limitations of general review of large-scale survey data. As recalled, the Swedish chapter is based upon secondary analysis, given the lack, to date, of focused network research on Swedish elders. Interestingly, the Finnish authors who engaged in a theoretically guided derivation of network types from survey data come to a somewhat different conclusion. They raise the need for more qualitative studies, such as ethnographies and narratives, in order to uncover the unique meanings of social network relationships among different individuals. Thus the need for both more structured network research, on the one hand, and more flexible modes of interpretation of network-related data, on the other, are forthcoming from Scandinavia.

The Dutch and the Israeli chapters present the case for continued longitudinal investigation of older people's social networks, each in their own way. The Dutch are doing this in practice, in LSN, the "Living Arrangements and Social Networks of Older Adults" study, and in LASA, the "Longitudinal Aging Study Amsterdam." The Israeli analysis, on the other hand, suggests three important foci for future longitudinal network inquiries: (1) the ongoing relationship between informal support and elders' health status, (2) interaction patterns between formal services and informal social networks, and (3) cultural variations in relation to social network relationships.

Authors from two other countries, the United Kingdom and Canada, call for continued efforts at verifying the dynamics of network types. The British study is drawn, of course, from a series of efforts in which the posited network typology was tried and tested. Future and more focused application of the typology, as is done in the current chapter in relation to dementia screening in Liverpool, is expected to produce results that will reinforce its reliability.

The Canadian analysis, on the other hand, is an initial attempt at the classification of the networks of Canadian older people. The results from this first effort underscore the need for continued examination of significant network types. The authors call, in this regard, for further study of the exchange of support within different network types and particularly for more focused inquiry of the reciprocity of informal support.

Finally, the researchers from the United States cite the need for continued examination of measures of social integration. They maintain that improved measures of social networks, social support, and loneliness are necessary for a better understanding of the reported link between social integration and health.

They believe, moreover, that the results of such inquiry will enhance both future gerontological research and geriatric care.

A SUMMARY COMMENT

This book set out to examine the state of social network research of elderly cohorts in a range of countries, and to consider the prospects for the purposive use of the social network as a tool and as a resource in the social care policy of the future. The wealth of material assembled in the many country reports presented here attests to the importance of the network phenomenon and to the fact of its active consideration by social researchers in several settings. As originally suspected, however, the approaches to network analysis vary greatly in different countries in terms of their conceptualization, methodology, and means of measurement. Nevertheless, common trends are discernible in the social networks of older people across countries, despite the differing methodologies adopted to address them. These trends have important implications, moreover, for social policy development in the area of care for the elderly.

Perhaps the most striking commonality is the abundance of informal support available to the vast majority of older adults, whether from family or from other close ties. Paradoxically, those who are more endowed in terms of informal support tend to make better use of formal sources of assistance. Even more ironic is the fact that older persons having the greatest access to supports of all kinds are generally the people who, themselves, are least in need of aid.

An equally impressive finding, however, is the significant minority of older people—up to one-third of the elderly cohort—who are at risk of having little or no informal support. These individuals tend to be personally in greater jeopardy as well, due to widowhood or childlessness, lower socioeconomic status, greater age, and frailty. The combination of rising dependence on the one hand and diminishing informal support on the other makes this subgroup of the elderly population the prime candidates for increased provision of formal care.

Current social policy aspires to recapture the vitality of social networks and to take greater advantage of informal supports in the community. However, most elderly people in need are already in receipt of care from the informal sources available to them, to the extent that they exist. Moreover, the trend in network development is one of diminution rather than growth. It seems, therefore, that social policy grounded in a return to informal care would be counterproductive.

Formal and informal sources of support should be able to join forces and to maximize their mutual potential. However, there is only limited evidence to date of the successful "interweaving" of the two caregiving systems. Where there is evidence for such, moreover, it seems to stem from the initiative of the social network rather than from purposive efforts by the formal agents of social care. The interface of social networks and formal care systems requires more serious attention, therefore, from social researchers and social policy analysts alike.

The social networks of older adults constitute a significant factor in the calculus of care. However, social networks are a changing phenomenon, and the nature of their contribution to the care of the elderly will necessarily change as well. It is incumbent upon all who are concerned with the welfare of society's oldest members to continue to scrutinize the interpersonal environments of the old and to guarantee a social care policy that is well informed of the dynamics and the transitions that occur in the social networks of older people.

Bibliography

Abrams, P. 1980. "Social Change, Social Networks and Neighborhood Care." *Social Work Service* 22: 12–23.

Adams, B. 1968. *Kinship in an Urban Setting*. Chicago, IL: Markham.

Adams, R. G. 1986. "Secondary Friendship Networks and Psychological Well-Being among Elderly Women." *Activities, Adaptation and Aging* 8 (2): 59–72.

Adams, R. G., and R. Blieszner, eds. 1989. *Older Adult Friendship: Structure and Process*. Newbury Park, CA: Sage.

Ahola, A., K. Djerf, M. Heiskanen, and K. Vikki. 1995. "Elinolotutkimus. Aineiston Keruu" [Living Conditions Survey. Data Collection]. *Tilastokeskus, Muistio* 95: 2.

Allan, G. A. 1979. *A Sociology of Friendship and Kinship*. London: Allen and Unwin.

Allen, K. R., and R. S. Pickett. 1987. "Forgotten Streams in the Family Life Course: Utilization of Qualitative Retrospective Interview in the Analysis of Lifelong Single Women's Family Careers." *Journal of Marriage and the Family* 49 (3): 517–526.

Anderberg, M. R. 1973. *Cluster Analysis for Applications*. New York: Academic Press.

Andersen, R., J. Kravits, and O. Anderson. 1975. *Equity in Health Services*. New York: Columbia University Press.

Andersson, L. 1992. "Family Care of the Elderly in Sweden." In: J. I. Kosberg, ed., *Family Care of the Elderly*. Newbury Park, CA: Sage.

Andersson, L. 1993. "Äldre i Sverige och Europa" [Elderly in Sweden and Europe]. *Ädelutvärderingen* 93: 4, Socialstyrelsen [The National Board of Health and Welfare, Stockholm].

Andersson, L. 1994. "Äldre och Äldreomsorg i Norden och Europa" [Elderly and Elderly Care in Scandinavia and Europe]. *Ädelutvärderingen* 94: 2, Socialstyrelsen [The National Board of Health and Welfare, Stockholm].

Angel, J. L., and R. J. Angel. 1992. "Age at Migration, Social Connections and Well-Being among Elderly Hispanics." *Journal of Aging and Health* 4 (4): 480–499.

Antonucci, T. C. 1990. "Social Supports and Social Relationships." In: R. H. Binstock and L. K. George, eds., *The Handbook of Aging and the Social Sciences* (3rd ed., pp. 205–226). Orlando, FL: Academic Press.

Antonucci, T. C., and H. Akiyama. 1987a. "An Examination of Sex Differences in Social Support among Older Men and Women." *Sex Roles* 17 (11–12): 737–749.

Antonucci, T. C., and H. Akiyama. 1987b. "Social Networks in Adult Life and a Preliminary Examination of the Convoy Model." *Journal of Gerontology* 42 (5): 519–527.

Antonucci, T. C., and C. E. Depner. 1982. "Social Support and Informal Helping Relationships." In: T. A. Willis, ed., *Basic Processes in Helping Relationships*. New York: Academic Press.

Arwyn, J. 1995. "Welfare Benefits and the Network Typology." *CSPRD Newsletter*, Summer, 35–37.

Atchison, K. A., S. A. Mayer-Oakes, S. O. Schweitzer, F. J. Dejong, and R. E Matthias. 1993. "The Relationship between Dental Utilization and Preventive Participation among a Well-Elderly Sample." *Journal of Public Health Dentistry* 53 (2): 88–95.

Attias-Donfut, C. 1993. "Coéducation des Générations et Effets en Retour de la Mobilité Sociale" [Generational Coeducation and Return Effects of Social Mobility]. In: G. Pronovost, C. Attias-Donfut, and N. Samuel, eds., *Temps Libre et Modernité: Mélanges en l'Honneur de Joffre Dumazedier* [Leisure and Modernity: Collection in Honor of Joffre Dumazedier]. Quebec and Paris: Presses Universitaires du Quebec and L'Harmattan.

Attias-Donfut, C., ed. 1995. *Les Solidarités Entre Générations: Vieillesse, Familles, État* [Generational Solidarity: Old Age, Families and the State]. Paris: Nathan.

Attias-Donfut, C., and S. Renaut. 1994. "Vieillir avec ses Enfants: Corésidence de Toujours et Recohabitation" [To Age with One's Children: Permanent and Renewed Co-Residency]. *Communications* 59: 29–53.

Auslander, G. K., and H. Litwin. 1987. "The Parameters of Network Intervention: A Social Work Application." *Social Service Review* 61: 305–318.

Auslander, G. K., and H. Litwin. 1988. "Social Networks and the Poor: Toward Effective Policy and Practice." *Social Work* 33 (3): 234–238.

Auslander, G. K., and H. Litwin. 1990. "Social Support Networks and Formal Help Seeking: Differences between Applicants to Social Services and a Non-applicant Sample." *Journal of Gerontology: Social Sciences* 45 (3): S112–S119.

Baldassare, M., S. Rosenfield, and K. Rook. 1984. "The Types of Social Relations Predicting Elderly Well-Being." *Research on Aging* 6 (4): 549–559.

Baldwin, S. 1993. *The Myth of Community Care: An Alternative Neighborhood Model of Care*. London: Chapman and Hall.

Banks, D., and K. Carley. 1994. "Metric Inference for Social Networks." *Journal of Classification* 11: 121–149.

Barrera, M. 1986. "Distinctions between Social Support Concepts, Measures and Models." *American Journal of Community Psychology* 14 (4): 413–445.

Bass, D. M., and L. S. Noelker. 1987. "The Influence of Family Caregivers on Elders' Use of In-Home Services: An Expanded Conceptual Framework." *Journal of Health and Social Behavior* 28 (2): 184–196.

Bazo, M. T. 1991a. "La Familia como Elemento Fundamental en la Salud y Bienestar de las Personas Ancianas" [The Family as a Key Element in the Health and Welfare of the Elderly]. *Revista Española de Geriatría y Gerontología* 1: 47–52.

Bazo, M. T. 1991b. "Institucionalización de Personas Ancianas: Un Reto Sociológico" [Institutionalization of the Elderly: A Sociological Challenge]. *Revista Española de Investigaciones Sociológicas* 53: 149–164.

Bear, M. 1989. "Network Variables as Determinants of the Elderly Entering Adult Residential Care Facilities." *Ageing and Society* 9 (2): 149–163.

Bear, M. 1993. "Caregiver Networks, Elderly Health, and Use of Residential Care Homes." *Adult Residential Care Journal* 7 (1): 31–42.

Béland, F., and A. Lemay. 1995. "Quelques Dilemmes, Quelques Valeurs pour une Politique de Services de Longue Durée" [Challenges and Values in Long-Term Care Policies]. *Canadian Journal on Aging/ La Revue Canadienne du Vieillissement* 14 (2): 263–293.

Béland, F., and M.-V. Zunzunegui. 1995a. "Presentación del Estudio 'Envejecer en Leganés'" [Presentation of the Study: Growing Old in Leganés]. *Revista de Gerontología*, número monografico (Supplement no. 2): 5–12.

Béland, F., and M.-V. Zunzunegui. 1995b. "El Perfil de las Incapacidades Funcionales en las Personas Mayores" [The Profile of Functional Disability]. *Revista de Gerontología*, número monografico (Supplement no. 2): 30–42.

Belford, H., C. J. Gilleard, J. E. Whittick, and K. Gledhill. 1984. "Emotional Distress amongst the Supporters of the Elderly Mentally Infirm." *British Journal of Psychiatry* 145: 172–177.

Bensman, J., and R. Lilienfeld. 1979. *Between Public and Private: The Lost Boundaries of the Self*. New York: Free Press.

Ben-Zvi, B. 1993. "The Nursing Care Law—Achievements and Unexpected Consequences in Its Application." *Social Security* 39: 5–26 (Hebrew).

Berkman, L. F. 1984. "Assessing the Physical Health Effects of Social Networks and Social Support." *Annual Review of Public Health* 5: 413–432.

Berkman, L. F. 1985. "The Relationship of Social Networks and Social Supports to Morbidity and Mortality." In: S. Cohen and S. L. Syme, eds., *Social Support and Health* (pp. 241–262). Orlando, FL: Academic Press.

Berkman, L. F. 1986. "Social Networks, Support, and Health: Taking the Next Step Forward." *American Journal of Epidemiology* 123: 559–562.

Berkman, L. F., and S. L. Syme. 1979. "Social Networks, Host Resistance, and Mortality: A Nine Year Follow-up Study of Alameda County Residents." *American Journal of Epidemiology* 109: 186–204.

Bermejo, F., and C. Colmenarejo. 1993. "Prevalencia de Demencia y Déficit Cognitivo" [Prevalence of Dementia and Cognitive Deficit]. In: *Nivel de*

Salud y Deficit Cognitivo en los Ancianos (Chap. 5). Barcelona: Editorial S. G. Caja de Madrid.

Bernard, H. R., E. C. Johnsen, P. D. Killworth, C. McCarty, G. A. Shelley, and S. Robinson. 1990. "Comparing Four Different Methods for Measuring Personal Social Networks." *Social Networks* 12: 179–215.

Biegel, D. E., J. Magaziner, and M. Baum. 1991. "Social Support Networks of White and Black Elderly People at Risk for Institutionalization." *Health and Social Work* 19 (4): 245–257.

Blazer, D. G. 1982. "Social Support and Mortality in an Elderly Community Population." *American Journal of Epidemiology* 116: 684–694.

Blieszner, R., and V. Hilkevitch Bedford, eds. 1995. *Handbook of Aging and the Family*. Westport, CT: Greenwood Press.

Bloch, F., and M. Buisson. 1991. "Du Don à la Dette: La Construction du Lien Social Familial" [From Donation to Debt: The Construction of Familial Social Ties]. La Découverte. *La Revue du Mauss* 11: 54–71.

Bloom, J. R. 1990. "The Relationship of Social Support and Health." *Social Science and Medicine* 30: 635–637.

Bocquet, H., F. Berthier, and A. Grand. 1994. "L'Aide Apportée aux Personnes Âgées Dépendantes par les Épouses, les Filles et les Belles-Filles" [The Aid to Dependent Elderly Persons Provided by Spouse, Daughters and Daughters-in-Law]. *Santé Publique* [Public Health] 3: 235–248.

Bocquet, H., S. Briand, S. Clement, M. Drulhe, A. Grand, A. Grand-Filaire, and J. Pous. 1993. "Modes de Prise en Charge des Personnes Âgées Atteintes de Démences Sénile" [Modes of Care for Elderly People with Senile Dementia]. *Rapport de Recherche Auprès du Conseil Régional Midi-Pyré-nées*, Toulouse.

Bouget, H., and R. Tartarin. 1990. *Le Prix de la Dépendance* [The Price of Dependence]. Paris: CNAV, La Documentation Française.

Bourdieu, P. 1989. *La Noblesse d'État: Grandes Écoles et Ésprit de Corps* [The State Nobility: Great Schools and Team Spirit]. Paris: Éditions de Minuit.

Bowling, A. 1990. "Associations with Life Satisfaction among Very Elderly People Living in a Deprived Part of Inner London." *Social Science and Medicine* 31 (9): 1003–1011.

Bowling, A., M. Farquhar, and P. Browne. 1991. "Use of Services in Old Age: Data from Three Surveys of Elderly People." *Social Science and Medicine* 33 (6): 689–700.

Branch, L., and A. Jette. 1983. "Elders' Use of Informal Long-Term Assistance." *The Gerontologist* 23 (1): 51–56.

Brody, E. M., S. J. Litvin, J. M. Albert, and C. J. Hoffman. 1994. "Marital Status of Daughters and Patterns of Parent Care." *Journal of Gerontology: Social Sciences* 49: S95–S103.

Broese van Groenou, M. I., and T. G. van Tilburg. 1996. "Network Analysis." In: J. E. Birren, ed., *Encyclopedia of Gerontology: Age, Aging and the Aged*. San Diego, CA: Academic Press.

Bryant, S., and W. Rakowski. 1992. "Predictors of Mortality among Elderly African–Americans." *Research on Aging* 14 (1): 50–67.

Bulmer, M. 1987. "Privacy and Confidentiality as Obstacles to Interweaving Formal and Informal Social Care: The Boundaries of the Private Realm." *Journal of Voluntary Action Research* 16 (1–2): 112–125.

Burt, R. S. 1984. "Network Items and the General Social Survey." *Social Networks*, 6: 293–339.

Campbell, K. E., and B. A. Lee. 1992. "Sources of Personal Neighbor Networks: Social Integration, Need or Time?" *Social Forces* 70 (4): 1077–1100.

Campos-Egozare, B. 1993. "Le Développement de Services de Soins et d'Aide. L'enjeu de la Décentralisation" [Developing Social Services and Medical Care. The Issue of Decentralization]. *Gérontologie et Société* 67: 146–156.

Cantor, M. 1979. "Neighbors and Friends: An Overlooked Resource in the Informal Support System." *Research on Aging* 1: 434–463.

Cantor, M., and V. Little. 1985. "Aging and Social Care." In: Robert H. Binstock and Ethel Shanas, eds., *Handbook of Aging and the Social Sciences* (2nd ed.). New York: Van Nostrand Reinhold.

Carrière, Y., and J. Legaré. 1993. "Viellissement Démographique et Institutionnalisation des Personnes Agées: Des Projections Nuancées pour le Canada." *Cahiers Québécois de Démographie* 22 (1): 63–92.

Cassel, J. 1976. "The Contribution of the Social Environment to Host Resistance." *American Journal of Epidemiology*, 104: 107–123.

Castells, M., and L. P. Ortiz. 1992. *Análisis de las Políticas de Vejez en España en el Contexto Europeo* [Analysis of Spanish Policies for the Aged in the European Context]. Madrid: Instituto Nacional de Servicios Sociales.

Cauchi, M. N. 1990. "The Maltese Aged in Victoria—Research Note." *Journal of Intercultural Studies* 11 (2): 55–58.

Central Bureau of Statistics. 1994. *Statistics Yearbook*. Jerusalem.

Chappell, N. L. 1983. "Informal Support Networks among the Elderly." *Research on Aging* 5 (1): 77–99.

Chappell, N. L. 1989. "Health and Helping among the Elderly: Gender Differences." *Journal of Aging and Health* 1 (1): 102–120.

Chappell, N. L. 1991a. "Living Arrangements and Services of Caregiving." *Journal of Gerontology: Social Sciences* 46 (1): S1–S8.

Chappell, N. L. 1991b. "The Role of Family and Friends in Quality of Life." In: J. E. Birren, J. E. Lubben, J. C. Rowe, and D. E. Deutchman, eds., *The Concept and Measurement of Quality of Life in the Frail Elderly* (pp. 172–190). San Diego, CA: Academic Press.

Chappell, N. L., and M. Badger. 1989. "Social Isolation and Well-Being." *Journal of Gerontology: Social Sciences* 44: S169–S176.

Chappell, N. L., and M. J. Prince. 1994. *Social Support among Today's Seniors*. Victoria: University of Victoria Centre on Aging.

Chappell, N. L., A. Segall, and D. G. Lewis. 1990. "Gender and Helping Networks among Day Hospital and Senior Centre Participants." *Canadian Journal on Aging/ Revue Canadienne du Vieillissement* 9 (3): 220–233.

Cicirelli, V. G. 1983. "A Comparison of Helping Behavior to Elderly Parents of Adult Children with Intact and Disrupted Marriages." *Gerontologist* 23 (6): 619–625.

Cicirelli, V. G., T. C. Raymond, and J. W. Dwyer. 1992. "Siblings as Caregivers for Impaired Elders." *Research on Aging* 14: 331–350.

Cobb, S. 1976. "Social Support as a Moderator of Life Stress." *Psychosomatic Medicine* 38: 300–314.

Cochran, M. M. Larner, D. Riley, L. Gunnarsson, and C. Henderson Jr. 1990. *Extending Families: The Social Networks of Parents and Their Children.* Cambridge, U.K.: Cambridge University Press.

Coenen-Huther, J., J. Kellerhals, and M. von Allmen. 1994. *Les Réseaux de Solidarité dans la Famille* [Solidarity Networks in the Family]. Lausanne: Réalités Sociales.

Cohen, C. I., J. Sokolovsky, J. Teresi, and D. Holmes. 1988. "Gender, Networks, and Adaptation among an Inner-City Population." *Journal of Aging Studies* 2 (1): 45–56.

Cohen, D. 1994. *Les Infortunes de la Prospérité* [The Misfortunes of Prosperity]. Paris: Juillard.

Cohen, S., and S. L. Syme. 1985a. "Issues in the Study and Application of Social Support." In: S. Cohen and S. L. Syme, eds., *Social Support and Health.* New York: Academic Press.

Cohen, S., and S. L. Syme, eds. 1985b. *Social Support and Health.* New York: Academic Press.

Cohen, S., and T. A. Wills. 1985. "Stress, Social Support, and the Stress Buffering Hypothesis." *Psychological Bulletin* 98: 310–357.

Commission of the European Communities. 1993. *Age and Attitudes. Main Results from a Eurobarometer Survey.*

Connidis, I. A. 1983. "Living Arrangement Choices of Older Residents: Assessing Quantitative Results with Qualitative Data." *Canadian Journal of Sociology* 8 (4): 359–375.

Connidis, I. A. 1989. *Family Ties and Aging.* Toronto: Buttersworths.

Connidis, I. A. 1994. "Sibling Support in Older Age." *Journal of Gerontology: Social Sciences* 49: S309–S317.

Connidis, I. A., and J. A. McMullin. 1994. "Social Support in Older Age: Assessing the Impact of Marital and Parent Status." *Canadian Journal on Aging/ La Revue Canadienne du Vieillissement* 13 (4): 510–527.

Cornoni-Huntley, J. C., D. F. Roley, L. R. White, R. Suzman, L. F. Berkman, D. A. Evans, and R. B. Wallace. 1985. "Epidemiology of Disability in the Oldest Old: Methodological Issues and Preliminary Findings." *Milbank Memorial Fund Quarterly/ Health and Society* 63: 350–376.

Cornwell, J. 1984. *Hard-Earned Lives: Accounts of Health and Illness from East London.* London: Tavistock.

Coward, R. T., and J. W. Dwyer. 1990. "The Association of Gender, Sibling Network Composition, and Patterns of Parent Care by Adult Children." *Research on Aging* 12 (2): 158–181.

Crawford, G. 1987. "Support Networks and Health-Related Change in the Elderly: Theory-Based Nursing Strategies." *Family and Community Health* 10: 39–48.

Curtis, S., and D. Bucquet. 1990. *Contacts Sociaux et Soutien Social Instrumental Chez les Personnes Âgées dans Trois Régions de France* [Social Contacts and Instrumental Social Support among Elderly People in Three Regions of France]. Montpellier: INSERM.

Curtis, S., D. Bucquet, and A. Colvez. 1992. "Sources of Instrumental Support for Dependent Elderly People in Three Parts of France." *Ageing and Society* 12 (3): 329–354.

Cutrona, C., D. Russell, and J. Rose. 1986. "Social Support and Adaptation to Stress by the Elderly." *Psychology and Aging* 1: 47–54.

Daatland, S. O. 1992. "Ideals Lost? Current Trends in Scandinavian Welfare Policies on Ageing." *Journal of European Social Policy* 2 (1): 33–47.

Dalud-Vincent, M., M. Forsé, and J.-P. Auray. 1994. "An Algorithm for Finding the Structure of Social Groups." *Social Networks* 16: 137–162.

Dechaux, J. H. 1994. "Les Trois Composantes de l'Economie Cachée de la Parenté: l'Example Français" [The Three Components of the Hidden Economy of Kinship: The French Case]. *Recherches Sociologiques* 3: 37–52.

Desjardins, B. 1993. *Population Ageing and the Elderly*. Statistics Canada Catalogue 91–533E. Ottawa: Minister of Industry, Science and Technology.

Devellis, R. F. 1991. *Scale Development: Theory and Application*. Newbury Park, London: Sage.

Dickens, W., and D. Perlman. 1981. "Friendship over the Life Cycle." In: S. Duck and R. Gilmour, eds., *Personal Relationship 2: Developing Personal Relation-ships*. London: Academic Press.

Doreian, P., and K. L. Woodard. 1992. "Fixed List versus Snowball Selection of Social Networks." *Social Science Research* 21: 216–233.

Doreian, P., and K. L. Woodard. 1994. "Defining and Locating Cores and Boundaries of Social Networks." *Social Networks* 16: 267–293.

Dorfman, R. A, J. E. Lubben, S. A Mayer-Oakes, K. A. Atchison, S. O. Schweitzer, F. J. Dejong, and R. E. Matthias. 1995. "Screening for Depression among a Well Elderly Population." *Social Work* 40: 295–304.

Duran, M. A. 1986. *La Jornada Interminable* [The Endless Labor Day]. Barcelona: Icaria.

Dykstra, P. A. 1990a. *Next of (Non)Kin: The Importance of Primary Relationships for Older Adults' Well Being*. Amsterdam: Swets Zeitlinger BV.

Dykstra, P. A. 1990b. "Disentangling Direct and Indirect Gender Effects on the Supportive Network." In: C. P. M. Knipscheer and T. C. Antonucci, eds., *Social Network Research: Methodological Questions and Substantive Issues* (pp. 55–65). Amsterdam: Swets and Zeitlinger.

Dykstra, P. A. 1993. "The Differential Availability of Relationships and the Provision and Effectiveness of Support to Older Adults." *Journal of Social and Personal Relationships* 10 (3): 355–370.

Dykstra, P. A. 1995. "Network Composition." In: C. P. M. Knipscheer, J. de Jong Gierveld, T. G. van Tilburg, and P. A. Dykstra, eds., *Living Arrangements and Social Networks of Older Adults* (pp. 97–114). Amsterdam: Free University Press.

Eckert, J. K. 1983. "Dislocation and Relocation of the Urban Elderly: Social Networks as Mediators of Relocation Stress." *Human Organization* 42 (1): 39–45.

Eisenbach, Z., and E. Sabatello. 1991. *Demographic and Socio-Economic Aspects of Population Aging in Israel*. Malta: International Institute of Aging (United Nations).

Ell, K. 1984. "Social Networks, Social Support and Health Status." *Social Service Review* 58 (1): 133–149.

Ezell, M., and J. W. Gibson. 1989. "The Impact of Informal Social Networks on the Elderly's Need for Services." *Journal of Gerontological Social Work* 14 (3–4): 3–18.

Feld, S., and L. K. George. 1994. "Moderating Effects of Prior Social Resources on the Hospitalizations of Elders Who Became Widowed." *Journal of Aging and Health* 6: 275–295.

Felton, B. J., and C. Berry. 1992. "Groups as Social Network Members: Overlooked Sources of Social Support." *American Journal of Community Psychology* 20 (2): 253–261.

Fischer, C. S. 1982. *To Dwell among Friends: Personal Networks in Town and City.* Chicago, IL: Chicago University Press.

Fischer, C. S., and S. J. Oliker. 1983. "A Research Note on Friendship, Gender and the Life Cycle." *Social Forces* 62: 124–133.

Foley, S. 1984. *Social Networks and Self-Perceptions of Health.* Unpublished doctoral dissertation, Columbia University, New York.

Forbes, W. F., J. A. Jackson, and A. S. Kraus. 1987. *Institutionalization of the Elderly in Canada.* Toronto: Harcourt Brace.

Freidson, E. 1970. "The Social Constructions of Illness." In: E. Friedson, *Profession of Medicine* (Part III). New York: Harper & Row.

Friedman, Y. 1992. *Operation Solomon.* Mevessaret Zion: Amitai (Hebrew).

Gallo, F. 1984. "Social Support Networks and the Health of Elderly Persons." *Social Work Research and Abstracts* 20 (4): 13–19.

Gaunt, D. 1983. *Familjeliv i Norden* [Family life in the Nordic countries]. Malmö: Gidlunds.

Gee, E. M. 1995. "Families in Later Life." In: Statistics Canada Catalogue 91–543E, *Family Over the Life Course.* Ottawa: Minister of Industry.

General British Registrar. 1970. *Classification of Occupations.* London: HMSO.

Gordon, D. S., and S. C. Donald. 1993. *Community Social Work, Older People and Informal Care.* Aldershot, U.K.: Avebury.

Gottlieb, B., ed. 1981. *Social Networks and Social Support.* Beverly Hills, CA: Sage.

Goudie, F. 1995. "Using the Support Network Typology in Practice." *CSPRD Newsletter* 12 (Winter): 19–21.

Gubrium, J. 1993. *Speaking of Life.* New York: Aldine de Gryuter.

Gulbrandsen, O., and D. Ås. 1986. *Husholdninger i 80-årene* [Norwegian Households in the 1980s]. Prosjektrapport 18, Norges Byggforskningsinstitutt, Oslo.

Habib, J. 1988. "Population Aging and Israeli Society." *Journal of Aging and Judaism* 3: 7–28.

Habib, J., and H. Factor. 1994. "Services for the Elderly: Changing Circumstances and Strategies." In: *Aging in Israel.* Jerusalem: JDC–Brookdale.

Habib, J., G. Sundström, and K. Windmiller. 1993. "Understanding the Pattern of Support for the Elderly: A Comparison Between Israel and Sweden." *Journal of Aging and Social Policy* 5 (1/2): 187–206.

Hareven, T. K. 1994. "Aging and Generational Relations: A Historical and Life Course Perspective." *Annual Review of Sociology* 20: 437–461.

Hays, R. D., and M. R. Dimatteo. 1987. "A Short Form Measure of Loneliness." *Journal of Personality Assessment* 51 (1): 69–81.

Health and Welfare Canada. 1982. *Canadian Governmental Report on Aging.* Ottawa: Minister of Supply and Services.

Hirsch, S. H., S. A. Mayer-Oakes, S. O. Schweitzer, K. A. Atchison, J. E. Lubben, and F. J. Dejong. 1992. "Enrolling Community Physicians and Their Patients for a Study on Prevention in the Elderly." *Public Health Reports* 102 (2): 142–149.

Hoch, C., and G. C. Hemmens. 1987. "Linking Informal and Formal Help: Conflict along the Continuum of Care." *Social Service Review* 61 (3): 432–446.

Hooyman, N. 1983. "Social Support Networks in Services to the Elderly." In: J. K. Whittaker and J. Garbarino, eds., *Informal Helping in the Human Services.* New York: Aldine.

House, J., and R. Kahn. 1985. "Measures and Concepts of Social Support." In: S. Cohen and S. L. Syme, eds., 1985. *Social Support and Health.* New York: Academic Press.

House, J. S., K. R. Landis, and D. Umberson. 1988. "Social Relationships and Health." *Science* 241: 540–545.

House, J., D. Umberson, and K. R. Landis. 1988. "Structures and Processes of Social Support." *Annual Review of Sociology* 14: 293–318.

Hurwicz, M. L., and E. Berkanovic. 1993. "The Stress Process in Rheumatoid Arthritis." *The Journal of Rheumatology* 20: 1836–1844.

Imamoulu, E. O., R. Küller, V. Imamoulu, and M. Küller. 1993. "The Social Psychological Worlds of Swedes and Turks in and around Retirement." *Journal of Cross-Cultural Psychology* 24 (1): 26–41.

INSERSO. 1993. *Plan Gerontológico* [Gerontologic Plan]. Madrid: Instituto Nacional de Servicios Sociales.

Instituto Nacional de Estadística [National Institute of Statistics]. 1992. *Censos de Población y Vivienda. Muestra Avance. Principales Resultados* [Population and Housing Census. Preliminary Sample. Principal Results]. Madrid.

Jacobson, D. E. 1987. "The Cultural Context of Social Support and Support Networks." *Medical Anthropology Quarterly* 1 (1): 42–67.

Johnson, C. L., and B. M. Barer. 1992. "Patterns of Engagement and Disengagement among the Oldest–Old." *Journal of Aging Studies* 6 (4): 351–364.

Johnson, C. L., and D. J. Catalano. 1981a. "Childless Elderly and Their Family Supports." *Gerontologist* 21 (6): 610–618.

Johnson, C. L., and D. J. Catalano. 1981b. "Family, Kin, and Friend Networks in Psychiatric Help-Seeking." *Social Science and Medicine* 12: 297–304.

Johnson, D. P. and L. C. Mullins. 1987. "Growing Old and Lonely in Different Societies: Toward a Comparative Perspective." *Journal of Cross-Cultural Gerontology* 2: 257–275.

Jylhä, M., ed. 1993. "Vanhuusikä Muutoksessa." *Selvityksiä* 93: 6 [Old Age in Transition—A Cohort Comparison of Health and Life Situation of the Elderly in Tampere in 1979 and 1989]. Helsinki: Sosiaali–Ja Terveysministeriö.

Jylhä, M., and J. Jokela. 1990. "Individual Experiences as Cultural—A Cross-Cultural Study on Loneliness among the Elderly." *Ageing and Society* 10: 295–315.

Kahn, R. L., and T. C. Antonucci. 1980. "Convoys over the Life Course: Attachment, Roles and Social Support." In: P. Baltes and O. G. Brim, eds., *Life-Span Development and Behavior, Vol. 3* (pp. 253–286). Orlando, FL: Academic Press.

Kaplan, G. A., T. E. Seeman, R. D. Cohen, L. P. Knudsen, and J. Guralnic. 1987. "Mortality among the Elderly in the Alameda County Study: Behavioral and Demographic Risk Factors." *American Journal of Public Health* 77: 307–312.

Kaufman, A. V. 1990. "Social Network Assessment: A Critical Component in Case Management for Functionally Impaired Older Persons." *International Journal of Aging and Human Development* 30 (1): 63–75.

Kaye, L. W., and A. Monk. 1991. "Social Relations in Enriched Housing for the Aged: A Case Study." *Journal of Housing for the Elderly* 9 (1–2): 111–126.

Kempen, G. I. J. M., and Th. Suurmeijer. 1991. "Factors Influencing Professional Home Care Utilization among the Elderly." *Social Science and Medicine* 32 (1): 77–81.

Kendig, H., ed. 1986. *Ageing and Families: A Social Networks Perspective*. Sydney: Allen and Unwin.

Killworth, P. D., E. C. Johnsen, H. R. Bernard, G. A. Shelley, and C. McCarty. 1990. "Estimating the Size of Personal Networks." *Social Networks* 12: 289–312.

Knipscheer, C. P. M. 1980. *Oude Mensen en Hun Sociale Omgeving: Een Studie van het Primaire Sociale Netwerk* [Older Adults and Their Social Environment: A Study of the Primary Social Network]. The Hague: VUGA.

Knipscheer, C. P. M., J. de Jong Gierveld, T. G. van Tilburg, and P. A. Dykstra, eds. 1995. *Living Arrangements and Social Networks of Older Adults*. Amsterdam: Free University Press

Kohut, F. J., L. F. Berkman, D. A. Evans, and J. Cornoni-Huntley. 1993. "Two Shorter Forms of the CES-D Depression Symptoms Index." *Journal of Aging and Health* 5 (2): 179–193.

Krause, N., A. R. Herzog, and E. Baker. 1992. "Providing Support to Others and Well-Being in Later Life." Journal of Gerontology: Psychological Sciences, 47: P300–P311.

Krause, N., and G. Jay. 1991. "Stress, Social Support, and Negative Interaction in Later Life." *Research On Aging* 13: 333–363.

Krause, N., and V. Kieth. 1989. "Gender Differences in Social Support among Older Adults." *Sex Roles* 21 (9–10): 609–628.

LaGory, M., and K. Fitzpatrick. 1992. "The Effects of Environmental Context on Elderly Depression." *Journal of Aging and Health* 4 (4): 459–479.

Langan, M. 1990. "Community Care in the 1990's: The Community Care White Paper: 'Caring for People'." *Critical Social Policy* 10 (2): 58–70.

Laumann, E. O., P. V. Marsden, and D. Prensky. 1983. "The Boundary Specification Problem in Network Analysis." In: R. S. Burt and M. J. Minor, eds., *Applied Network Analysis*. Beverly Hills, CA: Sage.

Lee, G. R. 1985. "Kinship and Social Support of the Elderly: The Case of the United States." *Aging and Society* 5: 19–38.

Lee, G. R., and L. B. Whitebeck. 1987. "Residential Location and Social Relations among Older Persons." *Rural Sociology* 52 (1): 89–97.

Leon, V., M.-V. Zunzunegui, and F. Béland. 1995. "El Diseño y la Ejecución de la Encuesta 'Envejecer en Leganés.'" [The Design and Conduct of the Survey Growing Old in Leganés]. *Revista de Gerontología*, número monografico (Supplement no. 2), 13–29.

Levitt, M. J., T. C. Antonucci, C. M. Clark, J. Rotton, and G. E. Finley. 1985–86. "Social Support and Well-Being: Preliminary Indicators Based on Two Samples of the Elderly." *International Journal of Aging and Adult Human Development* 21 (1): 61–77.

Lieberg, M., and B. Pederson. 1983. "Care and Social Network in the Neighborhood Unit; Projektet: Narmiljo, Omsorg och Sociala Natverk." *Sociologisk Forskning* 20 (3–4): 74–78.

Listhaug, O. 1990. "Macrovalues: The Nordic Countries Compared." *Acta Sociologica* 33 (3): 219–234.

Litwak, E. 1985. *Helping the Elderly: The Complementary Roles of Informal Networks and Formal Systems*. New York: The Guilford Press.

Litwak, E., and I. Szelenyi. 1969. "Primary Group Structures and Their Functions: Kin, Neighbors and Friends." *American Sociological Review* 34: 465–481.

Litwin, H. 1995a. *Uprooted in Old Age: Soviet Jews and Their Social Networks in Israel*. Westport, CT: Greenwood Press.

Litwin, H. 1995b. "The Social Networks of Elderly Immigrants: An Analytic Typology." *Journal of Aging Studies* 9 (2): 155–174.

Litwin, H., and G. K. Auslander. 1988. "Between Social Networks and Formal Social Services." *Ageing and Society* 8 (3): 269–285.

Litwin, H., and G. K. Auslander. 1992. "Understanding the Interface Between Formal and Informal Support Systems." *European Journal of Gerontology* 1 (8): 464–470.

Litwin, H., and G. K. Auslander. 1993. "Involvement of Informal Elderly-Care Networks in Contacts with Public Social Services." *Journal of Social Work and Policy in Israel* 7–8: 7–20.

Lobo, A., P. Saz, J. L. Dia Sahun, G. Marcos, F. Morales, M. J. Perez, L. F. Pascual, T. Ventura, and E. Gracia. 1990. "The Epidemiological Study of Dementia in Zaragoza, Spain." In: C. N. Stefanis et al., eds., *Psychiatry: A World Perspective, Vol. 4* (pp. 133–137). Amsterdam: Elsevier Science Publishers B. V.

Logan, J. R., and G. Spitze. 1994. "Informal Support and the Use of Formal Services by Older Americans." *Journal of Gerontology: Social Sciences* 49: S25–S34.

Lubben, J. E. 1988. "Assessing Social Networks among Elderly Populations." *Journal of Family and Community Health* 8: 42–51.

Lubben, J. E., P. G. Weiler, and I. Chi. 1989. "Health Practices of the Elderly Poor." *American Journal of Public Health* 79: 731–734.

Luggen, A. S., and A. G. Rini. 1995. "Assessment of Social Networks and Isolation in Community-Based Elderly Men and Women." *Geriatric Nursing* 16: 179–181.

Lund, D. A., M. S. Caserta, J. van Pelt, and K. A. Gass. 1990. "Stability of Social Support Networks after Later-Life Spousal Bereavement." *Death Studies* 14 (1): 53–73.

Lundin, L. and G. Sundström. 1994. *Det Riskabla Åldrandet* [The Risky Aging]. *Välfärdsbulletinen* 2: 7–9.

Lynch, J. L. 1977. *The Broken Heart*. New York: Basic Books.

MacRae, H. 1992. "Fictive Kin as a Component of the Social Networks of Older People." *Research on Aging* 14 (2): 226–247.

Malonebeach, E. E., and S. H. Zarit. 1991. "Current Research Issues in Caregiving to the Elderly." *International Journal of Aging and Human Development* 32: 103–114.

Marsden, P. V. 1987. "Core Discussion Networks of Americans." *American Sociological Review* 52: 122–131.

Marshall, V. W. 1995. "Social Models of Aging." *Canadian Journal on Aging/ La Revue Canadienne du Vieillissement* 14: 12–34.

Martin-Matthews, A. F. 1991. *Widowhood in Later Life*. Markham, Ontario: Butterworths.

Matthews, S. H., J. Werkner, and P. J. Delaney. 1989. "Relative Contributions of Help by Employed and Non-Employed Sisters to Their Elderly Parents." *Journals of Gerontology: Social Sciences* 44 (1): S36–S44.

Mayer-Oakes, S. A., H. Hoenig, K. A. Atchison, J. E. Lubben, F. J. Dejong, and S. O. Schweitzer. 1992. "Patient Related Predictors of Rehabilitation Use for Community Dwelling Older Americans." *Journal of the American Geriatrics Society* 40: 336–342.

McCallister, L., and C. S. Fischer. 1978. "A Procedure for Surveying Personal Networks." *Sociological Methods and Research* 7 (2): 131–149.

McDaniel, S. A. 1994. *Family and Friends*. General Social Survey Analysis Series, Statistics Canada Catalogue 11–612E, No. 9. Ottawa: Minister of Industry, Science and Technology.

McDaniel, S. A., and A. McKinnon. 1993. "Gender Differences in Informal Support and Coping among Elders: Findings from Canada's 1985 and 1990 General Social Surveys." *Journal of Women and Aging* 5 (2).

McNeely, D. 1995. "Dementia Sufferers and the Network Assessment Instrument." *CSPRD Newsletter*, Summer, 33–34.

Meyer-Fehr, P. C., and C. Suter. 1992. "Auswirkungen der Organisierung Zwischenmenschlicher Hilfe auf Informelle Hilfe" [Effects of the Organization of Interpersonal Help on Informal Help]. *Schweizerische Zeitschrift fur Soziologie/ Revue Suisse de Sociologie* 18 (2): 413–437.

Milardo, R. M. 1988. "Families and Social Networks: An Overview of Theory and Methodology." In: R. M. Milardo, ed., *Families and Social Networks*. Beverly Hills, CA: Sage.

Milardo, R. M. 1989. "Theoretical and Methodological Issues in the Identification of the Social Networks of Spouses." *Journal of Marriage and the Family* 51: 165–174.

Milardo, R. M. 1992. "Comparative Methods for Delineating Social Networks." *Journal of Social and Personal Relationships* 9: 447–461.

Milardo, R. M., M. Johnson, and T. Huston. 1983. "Developing Close Relationships: Changing Patterns of Interaction between Pair Members and Social Networks." *Journal of Personality and Social Psychology* 44: 964–976.

Miller, B., and S. McFall. 1991. "Stability and Change in the Informal Task Support Network of Frail Older Persons." *Gerontologist* 31: 735–745.

Ministerio de Sanidad y Consumo. 1995. *Segunda Encuesta Nacional de Salud* [Second National Health Survey]. Madrid.

Minkler, M. A., W. A. Satariano, and C. Langhouser. 1983. "Supportive Exchange: An Exploration of the Relationship between Social Contacts and Perceived Health Status in the Elderly." *Archive of Gerontology and Geriatrics* 2: 211–220.

Minor, M. J. 1983. "Panel Data on Ego Networks: A Longitudinal Study of Former Heroin Addicts." In: R. S. Burt and M. J. Minor, eds., *Applied Network Analysis*. Beverly Hills, CA: Sage.

Mitchell, J. C. 1969. "The Concept and Use of Social Networks." In: J. C. Mitchell, ed., *Social Networks in Urban Situations*. London: Manchester University Press.

Mor-Barak, M., and L. S. Miller. 1991. "A Longitudinal Study of the Causal Relationship between Social Networks and Health of the Poor Frail Elderly." *Journal of Applied Gerontology* 10 (3): 293–310.

Mor-Barak, M., L. S. Miller, and S. L. Syme. 1991. "Social Networks, Life Events, and the Health of the Poor, Frail Elderly: A Longitudinal Study of the Buffering versus the Direct Effect." *Family and Community Health* 14 (2): 1–13.

Morgan, D. L. 1988. "Age Differences in Social Network Participation." *Journal of Gerontology* 43: 129–137.

Morgan, D. L., and S. J. March. 1992. "The Impact of Life Events on Networks of Personal Relationships: A Comparison of Widowhood and Caring for a Spouse with Alzheimer's Disease." *Journal of Social and Personal Relationships* 9 (4): 563–584.

Morgan, D. L., T. L. Schuster, and E. W. Butler. 1991. "Role Reversals in the Exchange of Social Support." *Journal of Gerontology: Social Sciences* 46: S278–S287.

Moscicki, E. K., B. Looke, D. S. Rae, and N. H. Boyd. 1989. "Depressive Symptoms among Mexican Americans: The Hispanic Health and Nutrition Examination Survey." *American Journal of Epidemiology* 130: 348–360.

Mugford, S., and H. Kendig. 1986. "Social Relations: Networks and Ties." In: H. Kendig, ed., *Ageing and Families: A Social Networks Perspective*. Sydney: Allen and Unwin.

Mullins, L. C., and M. Mushel. 1992. "The Existence and Emotional Closeness of Relationships with Children, Friends and Spouses: The Effect of Loneliness among Older Persons." *Research on Aging* 14 (4): 448–470.

Nagi, S. Z. 1965. "Some Conceptual Issues in Disability and Rehabilitation." In: M. B. Sussman, ed., *Sociology and Rehabilitation* (pp. 100–113). Washington, DC: American Sociological Association.

National Center for Health Statistics. 1985. *The National Interview Survey Design 1973–1984* (pp. 85–1320). Washington, DC: U.S. Government Printing Office, DLTHS publication.

Norbeck, J. S., A. M. Lindsey, and V. L. Carrieri. 1981. "The Development of an Instrument to Measure Social Support." *Nursing Research* 30: 264–269.

Norland, J. A. 1994. *Focus on Canada: Profile of Canada's Seniors*. Statistics Canada and Prentice Hall Canada Inc., Statistics Canada Catalogue 96–312E. Ottawa: Minister of Industry, Science and Technology.

Olsen, R-B., J. Olsen, F. Gunner-Svensson, and B. Waldstrom. 1991. "Social Networks and Longevity. A 14-Year Follow-up Study among Elderly in Denmark." *Social Science and Medicine* 33 (10): 1189–1195.

Omaisten Suhde Ikäihmisten Palveluihin. 1991 [Old Age Services: Relatives' Attitudes]. Helsinki: Suomen Gallup.

Palinkas, L. A., D. L. Wingard, and E. Barrett-Connor. 1990. "The Biocultural Context of Social Networks and Depression among the Elderly." *Social Science and Medicine* 30 (4): 441–447.

Payne, B. J., and L. A. Strain. 1990. "Family Social Support in Later Life: Ethnic Group Variations." *Canadian Ethnic Studies* 22: 99–110.

Pelletier, L. 1992. "Vieillir en Institution ou à Domicile? Les Facteurs Associés à l'Hébergement des Personnes Agées." *Espace, Populations, Sociétés* 1: 71–86.

Perlman, D. 1987. "Further Reflections on the Present State of Loneliness Research." *Journal of Social Behavior and Personality* 2 (2): 17–26.

Petchers, M. K., and S. Milligan. 1987. "Social Networks and Social Support among Black Urban Elderly: A Health Care Resource." *Social Work in Health Care* 12 (4): 103–117.

Peters, G. R., and M. A. Kaiser. 1985. "The Role of Friends and Neighbors in Providing Social Support." In: W. J. Sauer and R. T. Coward, eds., *Social Support Networks and the Care of the Elderly* (pp. 123–158). New York: Springer.

Pfeiffer, E. 1975. "A Short Portable Mental Status Questionnaire for the Assessment of Organic Brain Deficit in Elderly Patients." *Journal of the American Geriatrics Society* 23: 433.

Rawlins, W. K. 1992. *Friendship Matters: Communication, Dialectics and the Life Course*. New York: Aldine de Gruyter.

Regional Trends. 1989. Office of Population Surveys and Census. London: Her Majesty's Stationery Office.

Registrar General. 1991. *Mortality Statistics: Review of the Registrar General and Deaths in England and Wales, 1989*. London, Chapman and Hall.

Rodríguez, P., and M. T. Sancho Castiello. 1995. "Nuevos Retos de la Política Social de Atención a las Personas Mayores" [New Challenges in Social Policies towards the Elderly]. *Revista Española de Geriatría y Gerontología* 30: 141–152.

Rosenthal, C. J. 1986. "The Differentiation of Multigenerational Households." *Canadian Journal on Aging* 5 (1): 27–42.

Rosenthal, C. J. 1987. "Aging and Intergenerational Relations in Canada." In: V. W. Marshall, ed., *Aging in Canada: Social Perspectives* (second ed.). Markham, Ontario: Fitzhenry and Whiteside.

Rubinstein, R. L., J. E. Lubben, and J. E. Mintzer. 1994. "Social Isolation and Social Support: An Applied Perspective." *The Journal of Applied Gerontology* 13 (1): 58–72.

Russell, D., L. A. Peplau, and C. E. Cutrona. 1980. "The Revised UCLA Loneliness

Scale: Concurrent and Discriminant Validity Evidence." *Journal of Personality and Social Psychology* 39: 472–480.

Sauer, W. J., and R. T. Coward, eds. 1985. *Social Support Networks and the Care of the Elderly: Theory, Research and Practice.* New York: Springer.

Schilling, R. F. 1987. "Limitations of Social Support." *Social Service Review* 61 (1): 19–31.

Schreck, H. 1991. "The Urban Church: A Healing Community for the Older Person." *Journal of Religious Gerontology* 7 (3): 1126.

Schroots, J. J. F. 1995. "Psychological Models of Aging." *Canadian Journal on Aging/ La Revue Canadienne du Vieillissement* 14: 44–66.

Schwarzer, R., and A. Leppin. 1991. "Social Support and Health: A Theoretical and Empirical Overview." *Journal of Social and Personal Relationships* 8: 99–127.

Seeman, T. E., and L. F. Berkman. 1988. "Structural Characteristics of Social Networks and Their Relationship with Social Support in the Elderly: Who Provides Support." *Social Science and Medicine* 26 (7): 737–749.

Seeman, T. E., L. F. Berkman, D. Blazer, and J. W. Rowe. 1994. "Social Ties and Support and Neuroendocrine Functions: The MacArthur Studies of Successful Aging." *Annals of Behavioral Medicine* 16: 95–106.

Serrano, P. 1990. "La Visión de las Personas de Edad en España" [The Vision of the Spanish Elderly]. In: *Epidemiología del Envejecimiento* [Epidemiology of Aging]. (pp. 129–194). Madrid: Fondo de Investigaciones Sanitarias, Ministerio de Sanidad y Consumo.

Shanas, E. 1979. "The Family as a Social Support System in Old Age." *Gerontologist* 19 (2): 169–174.

Shapiro, E., and R. Tate. 1988. "Who Is Really at Risk of Institutionalization?" *Gerontologist* 28 (2): 237–245.

Sherbourne, C. D., and A. L. Stewart. 1991. "The MOS Social Support Survey." *Social Science and Medicine* 32: 705–714.

Shuval, J. T., R. Fleishman, and A. Shmueli. 1982. *Informal Support for the Elderly: Social Networks in a Jerusalem Neighborhood.* Jerusalem: Brookdale Institute of Gerontology and Adult Human Development in Israel.

Silverman, D. 1993. *Interpreting Qualitative Data.* London: Sage.

Sociaal Cultureel Planbureau (SCP). 1990. *Social and Cultural Report.* The Hague, The Netherlands: Staatsuitgeverij.

Speare, A., and R. Avery. 1993. "Who Helps Whom in Older Parent–Child Families?" *Journal of Gerontology: Social Sciences* 48: S64–S73.

Stacey-Konnert, C., and J. Pynoos. 1992. "Friendship and Social Networks in a Continuing Care Retirement Community." *Journal of Applied Gerontology* 11 (3): 298–313.

Starrett, R. A., A. M. Todd, J. T. Decker, and G. Walters. 1989. "The Use of Formal Helping Networks to Meet the Psychological Needs of the Hispanic Elderly." *Hispanic Journal of Behavioral Sciences* 11 (3): 259–273.

Statistics Sweden. 1980. *Ensamhet och Gemenskap* [Loneliness and Community]. Levnadsförhållanden. 1976. Rapport 18. Stockholm, Statistiska Centralbyrån.

Steinbach, U. 1992. "Social Networks, Institutionalization and Mortality among Elderly People in the United States." *Journal of Gerontology: Social Sciences* 47 (4): S183–S190.

Stoller, E. P., and L. L. Earl. 1983. "Help with Activities of Everyday Life: Sources of Support for the Noninstitutionalized Elderly." *Gerontologist* 23: 64–70.

Stoller, E. P., L. E. Forster, and T. S. Duniho. 1992. "Systems of Parent Care within Sibling Networks." *Research on Aging* 14 (1): 28–49.

Stoller, E. P., and K. L. Pugliesi. 1988. "Informal Networks of Community-Based Elderly: Changes in Composition over Time." *Research on Aging* 10 (4): 499–516.

Stone, L. O. 1988. *Family and Friendship Ties among Canada's Seniors: An Introduction Report of Findings from the General Social Survey.* Statistics Canada Catalogue 89–508. Ottawa: Minister of Supply and Services Canada.

Stone, L. O., and H. Frenken. 1988. *1986 Census of Canada: Canada's Seniors.* Statistics Canada Catalogue 98–121. Ottawa: Minister of Supply and Services Canada.

Stone, R., G. Cafferata, and J. Sangl. 1987. "Caregivers of the Frail Elderly: A National Profile." *Gerontologist* 27 (5): 616–626.

Strain, L. A. 1992. "Social Networks and Patterns of Social Interaction among Ever-Single and Separated/ Divorced Elderly Canadians." *Canadian Journal on Aging/ Revue Canadienne du Vieillissement* 11 (1): 31–53.

Streiner, D. L., and G. R. Norman. 1995. *Health Measurement Scales: A Practical Guide to Their Development and Use.* New York: Oxford University Press.

Sudman, S. 1985. "Experiments in the Measurement of the Size of Social Networks." *Social Networks* 7: 127–151.

Sundström, G. 1987. "A Haven in a Heartless World? Living with Parents in Sweden and the United States 1880–1982." *Continuity and Change* 2 (1): 145–187.

Sundström, G. 1994a. "Hemma på Äldre Da'r" [At Home in Old Age]. *Ädelutvärderingen* 94: 17, Socialstyrelsen [The National Board of Health and Welfare, Stockholm].

Sundström, G. 1994b. "Care by Families: An Overview of Trends." In: P. Hennessy, ed., *Social Policy Studies, No. 14.* Paris: OECD.

Swinford, M. 1995. "Using the Network Typology in a Social Services Team." *CSPRD Newsletter,* Summer, 31–32.

Taylor, R. J., and L. M. Chatters. 1986. "Patterns of Informal Support to Elderly Black Adults: Family, Friends, and Church Members." *Social Work* 31 (6): 432–438.

Tennstedt, S. L., S. Crawford, and J. B. McKinlay. 1993. "Determining the Pattern of Community Care: Is Coresiding More Important than Caregiver Relationship?" *Journal of Gerontology: Social Sciences* 48: S74–S83.

Thissen, F., G. C. Wenger, and T. Scharf. 1995. "Community Structure and Support Network Variation in Rural Areas: A United Kingdom–Netherlands Comparison." In: T. Scharf and G. C. Wenger, eds., *International Perspectives on Community Care for Older People* (pp. 59–94). Aldershot, U.K.: Avebury.

Thoits, P. A. 1982. "Conceptual, Methodological, and Theoretical Problems in Studying Social Support as a Buffer against Life Stress." *Journal of Health and Social Behavior* 23: 145–159.

Thornton, M. C., S. I. White-Means, and H-K. Choi. 1993. "Sociodemographic Correlates of the Size and Composition of Informal Caregiver Networks among Frail Ethnic Elderly." *Journal of Comparative Family Studies* 24 (2): 235–250.

Thouez, J.-P., Y. Bussiére, N. Chicoine, P. Laroche, and R. Pampalon. 1994. "L'Aide á Domicile aux Personnes Âgées Dépendantes de la Région de Montréal: Analyse Secondaire de l'Enquête ESLA, 1986–1987" [Homemaking Services in Montreal for Frail Elderly: Secondary Analysis of the CSHA. 1986–1987 Data Set]. *Canadian Journal on Aging/ La Revue Canadienne du Vieillissement* 13: 187–200.

Torres, C. C., W. A. McIntosh, and K. S. Kubena. 1992. "Social Network and Social Background Characteristics of Elderly Who Live and Eat Alone." *Journal of Aging and Health* 4: 564–578.

Townsend, A. L., and S. W. Poulshock. 1986. "Intergenerational Perspectives on Impaired Elders Support Networks." *Journal of Gerontology* 41 (1): 101–109.

Trost, J. 1993. *Familjen i Sverige* [The Family in Sweden]. Stockholm: Liber Utbildning.

Tunstall, J. 1971. *Old and Alone: A Sociological Study of Old People.* London: Routledge and Kegan Paul.

Turner, R. J. 1983. "Direct, Indirect, and Moderating Effects of Social Support on Psychological Distress and Associated Conditions." In: H. B. Kaplan, ed., *Psychological Stress: Trends in Theory and Research.* Orlando, FL: Academic Press.

Twigg, J. 1989. "How Do Social Care Agencies Conceptualize Their Relationship with Informal Carers." *Journal of Social Policy* 18 (1): 53–66.

Twigg, J. 1993. "Integrating Carers into the Service System: Six Strategic Responses." *Ageing and Society* 13: 141–170.

United States Bureau of the Census. 1992. *An Aging World II.* International Population Reports P25, 92–93. Washington, DC: U.S. Government Printing Office.

Urry, J. 1991. "Time and Space in Giddens' Social Theory." In: C. G. A. Bryant and D. Jary, eds., *Giddens' Theory of Structuration. A Critical Appreciation.* London and New York: Routledge.

Van der Poel, M. 1993. "Delineating Personal Support Networks." *Social Networks* 15 (1): 49–70.

Van der Wijst, T., and F. van Poppel. 1994a. "Economic and Social Implications of Aging in the Netherlands." In: G. J. Stolnitz, ed., *Social Aspects and Country Reviews of Population Aging* (pp. 171–196). New York: United Nations.

Van der Wijst, T., and F. van Poppel. 1994b. "Living Conditions of the Elderly in the Netherlands." In: G. J. Stolnitz, ed., *Social Aspects and Country Reviews of Population Aging* (pp. 130–150). New York: United Nations.

Vanhuusbarometri. 1994. [Old Age Barometer]. *Selvityksiä* 94: 6. Helsinki: Sosiaali–Ja Terveysministeriö.

Vaux, A. 1988. *Social Support: Theory, Research and Intervention.* New York: Praeger Publishers.

Walker, A., ed. 1982. *Community Care: The Family, the State and Social Policy.* Oxford: Basil Blackwell and Martin Robinson.

Walker, A., J. Alber, and A.-M. Guillemard. 1993. "Older People in Europe: Social and Economic Policies." *The 1993 Report of the European Observatory.* Brussels: Commission of the European Communities.

Warren, D. I. 1981. *Helping Networks: How People Cope with Problems in the Urban Community.* Notre Dame, IN: University of Notre Dame.

Weiss, R. S. 1973. *Loneliness: The Experience of Emotional and Social Isolation.* Cambridge, MA: MIT Press.

Wellman, B. 1979. "The Community Question: The Intimate Networks of East Yorkers." *American Journal of Sociology* 84: 1201–1231.

Wellman, B. 1988. "Structural Analysis: From Method and Metaphor to Theory and Substance." In: B. Wellman and S. Berkowitz, eds., *Social Structures: A Network Approach.* Cambridge, U.K.: Cambridge University Press.

Wellman, B., and A. Hall. 1986. "Social Networks and Social Support: Implications for Later Life." In: V. W. Marshall, ed., *Later Life: The Social Psychology of Aging* (pp. 191–231). Beverly Hills, CA: Sage.

Wellman, B., and S. Wortley. 1984. "Brothers' Keepers: Situating Kinship Relations in Broader Networks of Social Support." *Sociological Perspectives* 32: 273–306.

Wenger, G. C. 1984. *The Supportive Network: Coping with Old Age.* London: Allen and Unwin.

Wenger, G. C. 1986. "A Longitudinal Study of Changes and Adaptations in the Support Networks of Welsh Elderly over 75." *Journal of Cross-Cultural Gerontology* 1 (3): 277–304.

Wenger, G. C. 1989. "Support Networks in Old Age—Constructing a Typology." In: Margot Jeffreys, ed., *Ageing in the 20th Century.* London: Routledge.

Wenger, G. C. 1990. "Change and Adaptation in Informal Support Networks of Elderly People in Wales 1979–1987." *Journal of Aging Studies* 4 (4): 375–389.

Wenger, G. C. 1991. "A Network Typology: From Theory to Practice." *Journal of Aging Studies* 5 (1): 147–162.

Wenger, G. C. 1992. *Help in Old Age—A Longitudinal Network Perspective: Facing Up to Change.* Liverpool: Liverpool University Press.

Wenger, G. C. 1993. "The Formation of Social Networks: Self Help, Mutual Aid, and Old People in Contemporary Britain." *Journal of Aging Studies* 7 (1): 25–40.

Wenger, G. C. 1994a. *Understanding Support Networks and Community Care.* Aldershot, U.K.: Avebury.

Wenger, G. C. 1994b. "Measurement of Network Type: Testing a New Technique." *CSPRD Working Paper Series.* Bangor, Wales: Centre for Social Policy Research and Development.

Wenger, G. C. 1994c. "Support Networks and Dementia." *International Journal of Geriatric Psychiatry* 9: 181–194.

Wenger, G. C. 1994d. "Dementia Sufferers Living at Home." *International Journal of Geriatric Psychiatry* 9: 721–733.

Wenger, G. C. 1994e. *Support Networks of Older People: A Guide for Practitioners.* Bangor, Wales: Centre for Social Policy Research and Development.

Wenger, G. C. 1995a. "Social Network Research in Gerontology: How Did We Get Here and Where Do We Go Next?" Paper presented at the International Sociological Association Research on Ageing Intercongress Meeting, Melbourne, Australia.

Wenger, G. C. 1995b. "A Comparison of Urban with Rural Support Networks: Liverpool and North Wales." *Ageing and Society* 15: 59–81.

Wenger, G. C. 1995c. "Support Network Variation and Informal Participation in Community Care." In: T. Scharf and G. C Wenger, eds., *International Perspectives on Community Care for Older People* (pp. 41–58). Aldershot, U.K.: Avebury.

Wenger, G. C., and A. Scott. 1995. "Change and Stability in Support Network Type: Findings from a UK Longitudinal Study." In: S. Formosa, ed., *Age Vault: An INEA Collaborative Network Anthology* (pp. 105–117). Malta: International Institute on Ageing (United Nations).

Wenger, G. C. and S. Shahtahmasebi. 1990. "Variations in Support Networks: Some Policy Implications." In: J. Mogey, ed., *Aiding and Ageing: The Coming Crisis in Support for the Elderly by Kin and State* (pp. 255–277). Westport, CT: Greenwood.

Wenger, G. C., and F. St. Leger. 1992. "Community Structure and Support Network Variations." *Ageing and Society* 12 (2): 213–236.

Wethington, E., and R. C. Kessler. 1986. "Perceived Support, Received Support and Adjustment to Stressful Life Events." *Journal of Health and Social Behavior* 27 (1): 78–89.

Whittaker, J. 1986. "Integrating Formal and Informal Social Care: A Conceptual Framework." *British Journal of Social Work* 16 (Supplement): 39–62.

WHO. 1983. *The Elderly in Eleven Countries. Public Health in Europe* 21. Copenhagen: WHO Regional Office for Europe.

Williams, A. W., J. E. Ware, and C. A. Donald. 1981. "A Model of Mental Health, Life Events, and Social Supports Applicable to General Populations." *Journal of Health and Social Behavior* 22: 324–336.

Wilson, R. W., and J. Elinson. 1981. "National Survey of Personal Health Practices and Consequences: Background, Conceptual Issues and Selected Findings." *Public Health Reports* 96: 218–255.

Wright, E. O. 1985. *Classes.* London: Verso.

Yates, F. E., and L. A. Benton. 1995. "Biological Senescence: Loss of Integration and Resilience." *Canadian Journal on Aging/La Revue Canadienne du Vieillissement* 14: 106–120.

Yoder, J. A., R. A. B. Leaper, and J. M. L. Jonker, eds. 1985. *Support Networks in a Caring Community: Research and Policy, Fact and Fiction.* Dordrecht: Martinus Nijhoff.

Zarit, S. H., L. I. Pearlin, and K. W. Schaie, eds. 1993. *Caregiving Systems: Informal and Formal Helpers.* Hillsdale, NJ: Lawrence Erlbaum.

Zuckerman, D. M., S. V. Kasl, and A. M. Ostfeld. 1984. "Psychosocial Predictors of Mortality among the Elderly Poor: The Role of Religion, Well-Being and Social Contacts." *American Journal of Epidemiology* 119: 410–423.

Name Index

Subject Index

About the Contributors

HOWARD LITWIN is Associate Professor at the Paul Baerwald School of Social Work at the Hebrew University of Jerusalem, where he teaches and investigates aspects of social gerontology and social care. He has published widely on the social networks of the elderly and has recently authored *Uprooted in Old Age: Soviet Jews and Their Social Networks in Israel* (1995).

LARS ANDERSSON is Director of the Section of Social Gerontology at the Stockholm Gerontology Research Center. He is also Associate Professor of Gerontology at the Karolinska Institute. He has contributed chapters in *Daily Life in Later Life* (1988), *Loneliness* (1989), *Family Care of the Elderly* (1992), and *Encyclopedia of Human Development* (1993), and he has published extensively in scholarly journals.

CLAUDINE ATTIAS-DONFUT is Director of Aging Research at the Caisse Nationale d'Assurance Vieillesse [The National Fund for Old-Age Insurance] in Paris. She has published widely on age topics, particularly *Sociologie des Générations* (1988). The latest work under her direction is *Les Solidarités Entre Générations: Vieillesse, Familles, État* (1995).

GAIL AUSLANDER is Senior Lecturer and Deputy Director of the Paul Baerwald School of Social Work at the Hebrew University of Jerusalem. Her main interests center on the relationship between the social environment and the health and well-being of individuals and communities, and on evaluation research and quality assurance in health care social work.

FRANÇOIS BÉLAND is Professor of Health Administration at the Université de Montréal. He is a member of the Groupe de Recherche Interdisciplinaire en Santé (GRIS) and a Canadian National Health Scholar. His main areas of research include population health and formal and informal support for the elderly. He is currently Editor-in-Chief of the *Canadian Journal on Aging*.

MARJOLEIN BROESE VAN GROENOU is a researcher at the Department of Sociology and Social Gerontology at the Vrije Universiteit, Amsterdam. Her research focuses on social networks and support, particularly in relation to important life-events (divorce, widowhood). She has been with the "Living Arrangements and Social Networks of Older Adults" program of NESTOR for five years.

MELANIE GIRONDA is a Lecturer in the Department of Social Welfare in the School of Public Policy and Social Research at UCLA. Dr. Gironda is also Deputy Program Director of the California Geriatric Education Center Health and Aging Faculty Development Program. She has extensive social work practice experience in various geriatric settings.

MARJA JYLHÄ is Senior Research Fellow at the Finnish Centre for Interdisciplinary Gerontology, University of Jyväskylä, and Docent at the Tampere School of Public Health, University of Tampere. She has published on many topics in health and aging and is currently engaged in the narrative construction of dementia and biographical research of the oldest–old.

JAMES LUBBEN is Professor of Social Welfare in the School of Public Policy and Social Research at UCLA, and Chair of its Department of Social Welfare. He is also Codirector of the California Geriatric Education Center Health and Aging Faculty Development Program. Dr. Lubben is a member of the National Geriatrics and Gerontology Advisory Committee of the U.S. Department of Veteran Affairs.

TUULA MELKAS is a researcher at Statistics Finland in the Department of Social Statistics and a doctoral student in sociology at the University of Tampere. Her research interests include the study of social relationships and urban sociology. She has published on social networks and informal help.

CAROLYN ROSENTHAL is Professor of Gerontology and Sociology at McMaster University, in Hamilton, Ontario, Canada. Her research interests focus on family and intergenerational relationships, the impact of institutionalization on family members, and aging and ethnicity. She is coauthor of *The Remainder of Their Days: Domestic Policy and Older Families in Canada and the United States.*

ALAIN ROZENKIER is a senior researcher at the Caisse Nationale d'Assurance Vieillesse [The National Fund for Old-Age Insurance] in Paris. His writings appear in several journals and collections of aging studies. He is also a member of the editorial board of *Retraite et Société* and *Gérontologie et Société.*

LEROY STONE is Associate Director General of the Analytical Studies Branch at Statistics Canada and Research Fellow in the Office on Aging at the University of Manitoba. He is the author of several books dealing with Canada's older population and winner of the 1992 Gold Medal of the Professional Institute of the Public Service of Canada. His latest book is *Dimensions of Job–Family Tension* (1994).

GERDT SUNDSTRÖM is a senior researcher and Professor at the Institute of Gerontology in Jönköping, Sweden. He holds a doctorate in social work from the University of Stockholm, where he previously worked as lecturer. Dr. Sundström has published extensively in gerontology and has lectured in Sweden and abroad on old age care, family sociology, and related fields.

THEO VAN TILBURG is Assistant Professor at the Department of Social Research Methodology at the Vrije Universiteit in Amsterdam, where he is affiliated with two research programs, "Living Arrangements and Social Networks of Older Adults" (LSN) and the "Longitudinal Aging Study Amsterdam" (LASA). His interests focus on methodology and on the impact of social network characteristics.

G. CLARE WENGER is Professor and Codirector at the Centre for Social Policy Research and Development at the University of Wales in Bangor. She has pioneered the scientific inquiry into support network type and has studied its application in the context of community care. Her first major book was *The Supportive Network: Coping with Old Age* (1984), and her most recent one, coedited with Thomas Scharf, is *International Perspectives on Community Care of Older People* (1995).

MARIA-VICTORIA ZUNZUNEGUI is an epidemiologist working as a teacher and researcher at the Andalusian School of Public Health at Granada, Spain. Her research interests are aging and disability and epidemiologic surveillance of human rights. She has published in both areas and is presently involved in the longitudinal study "Envejecer en Leganes" [Aging at Leganés].

ISBN 0-275-95327-0

9 780275 953270

90000>

EAN

HARDCOVER BAR CODE